I0189860

imlo

Inspire My Little One

Letter Tracing Workbook Handwriting Practice: Fruits & Vegetables

A fun way to practice writing alphabets for kids ages 3 and up

This Book Belongs to

imlo

Inspire My Little One

Copyright © 2020 InspireMyLittleOne
All rights reserved

For any questions, suggestions regarding our books, please contact us at **hello@inspiremylittleone.com**. You can also visit us as **www.inspiremylittleone.com**

A fun way to inspire toddlers to practice letter writing while learning about fruits and vegetables

A for Apple

A a

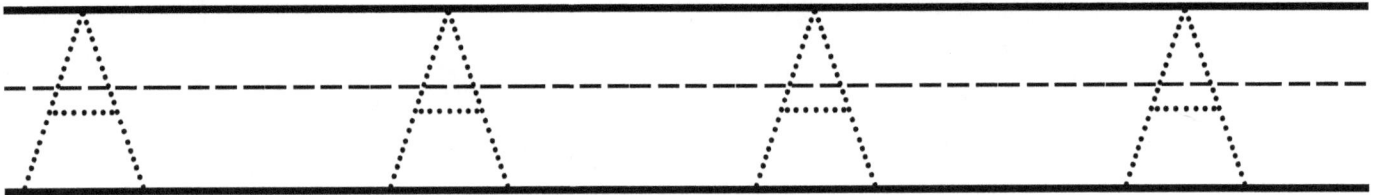

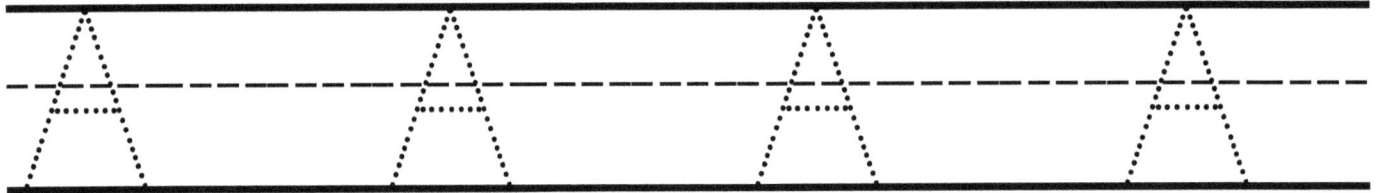

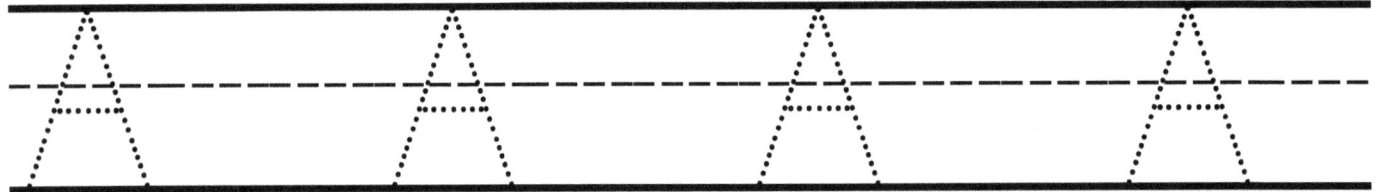

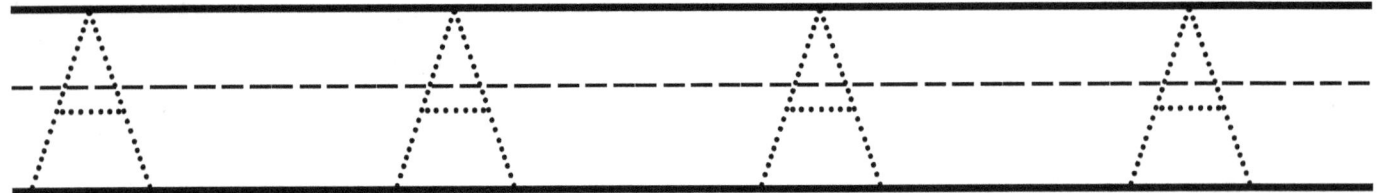

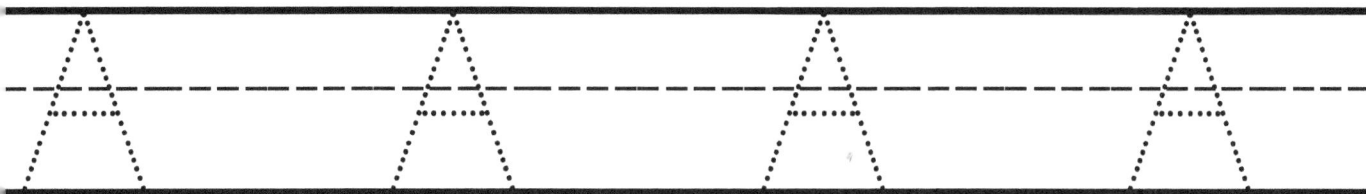

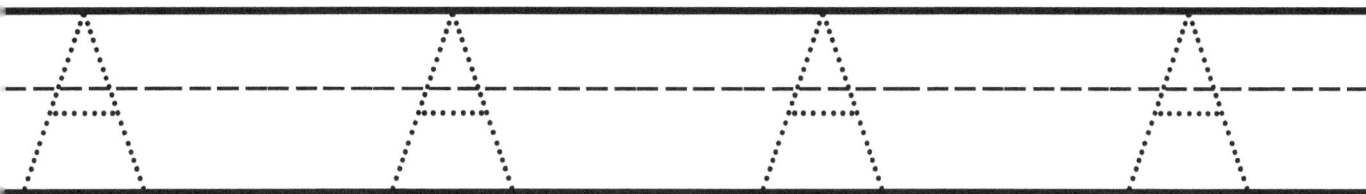

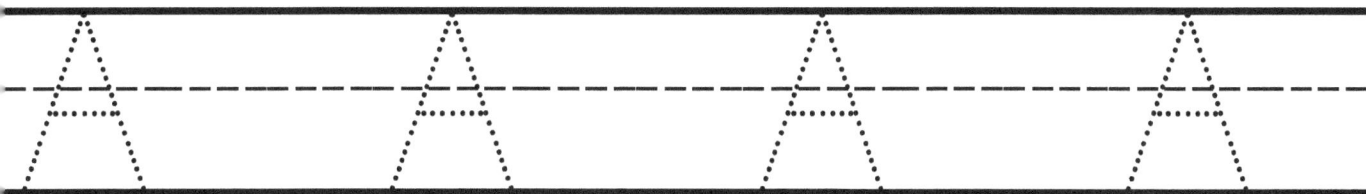

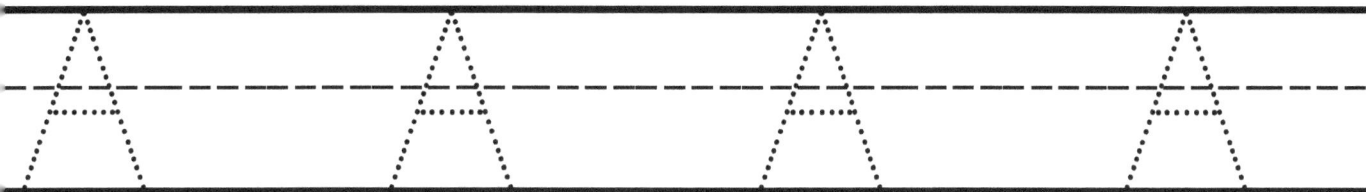

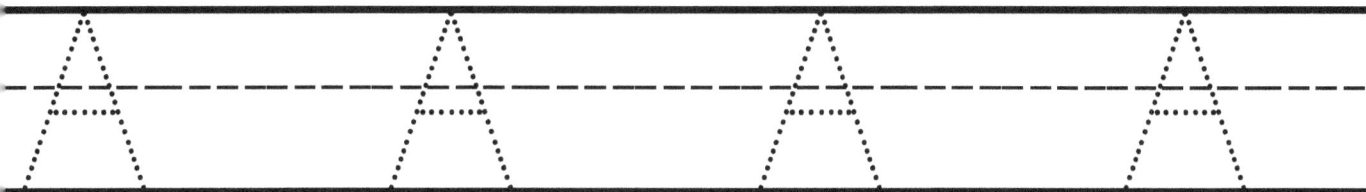

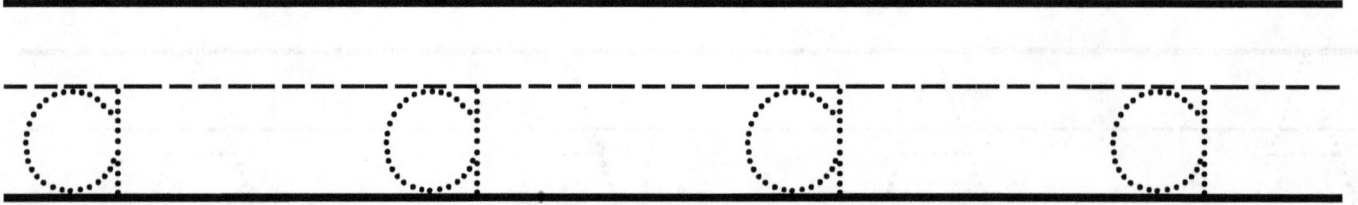

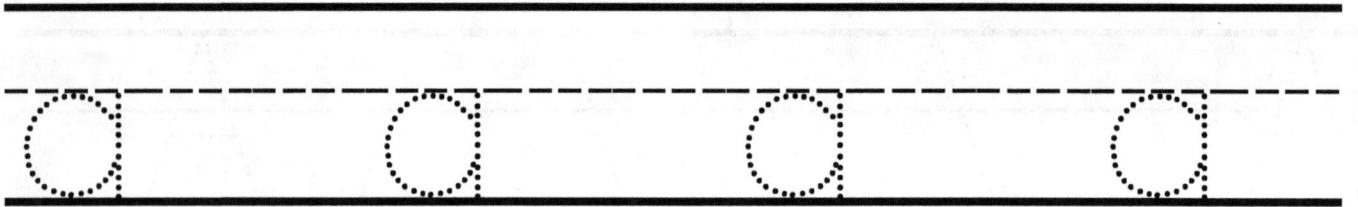

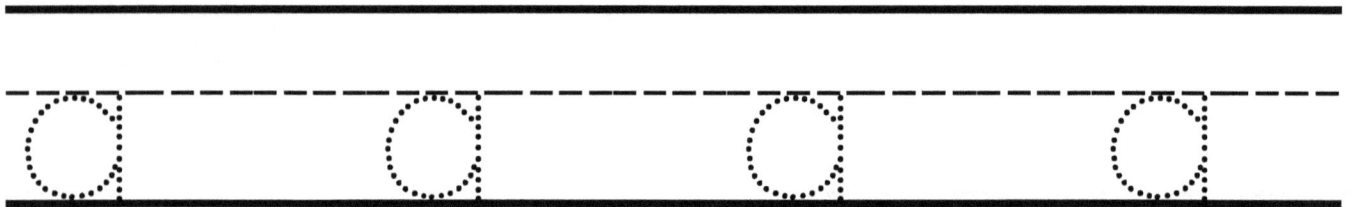

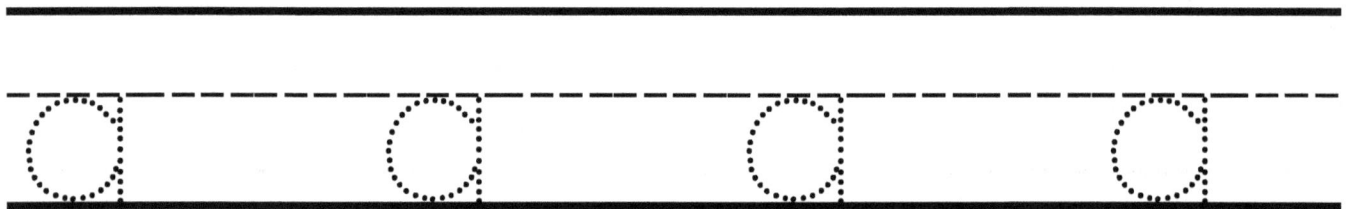

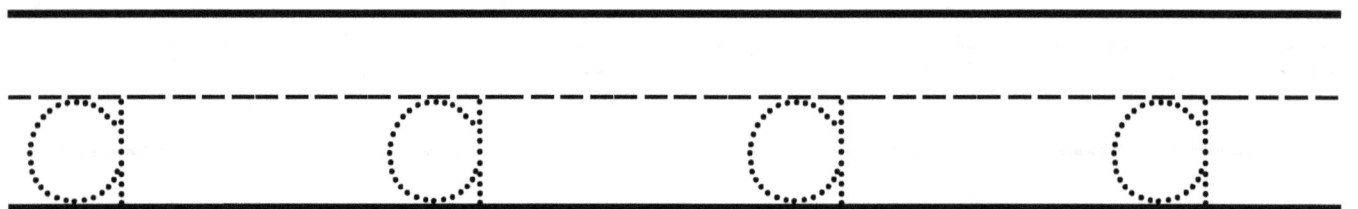

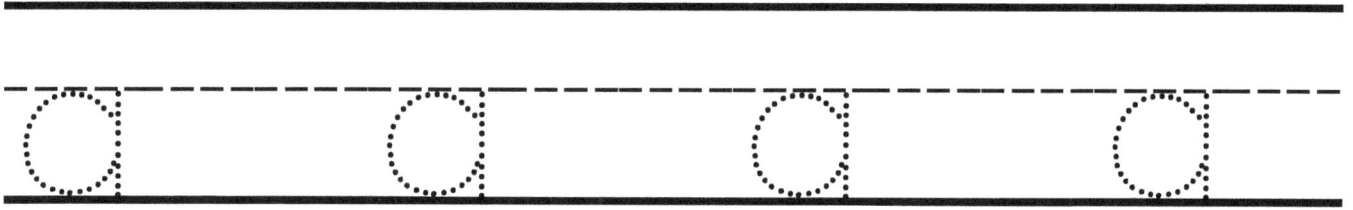

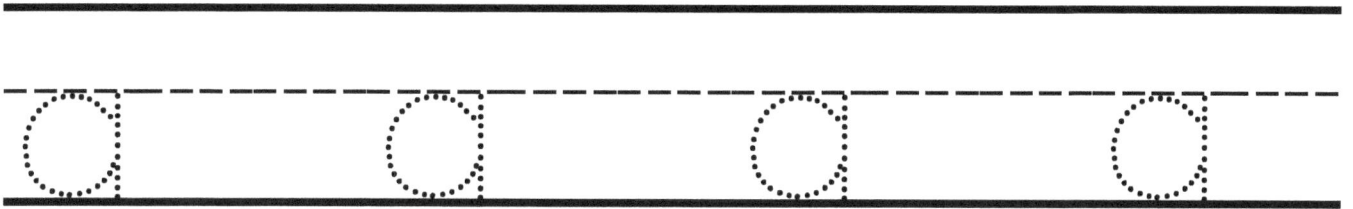

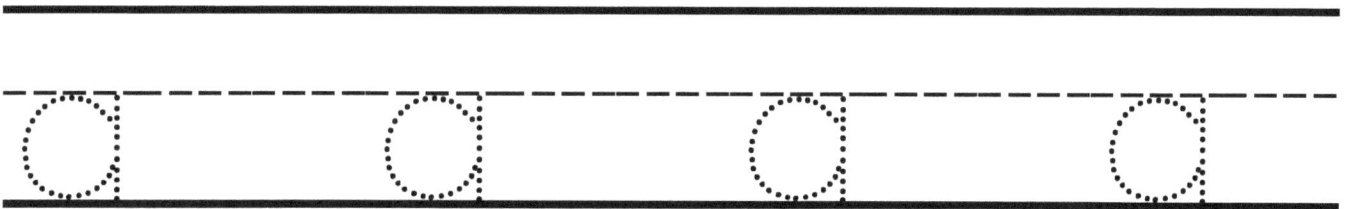

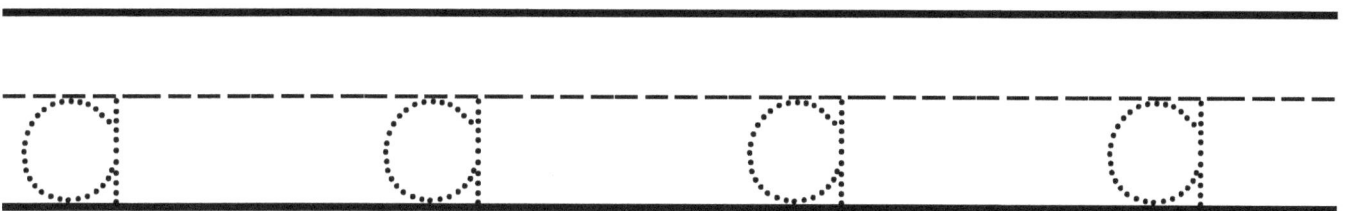

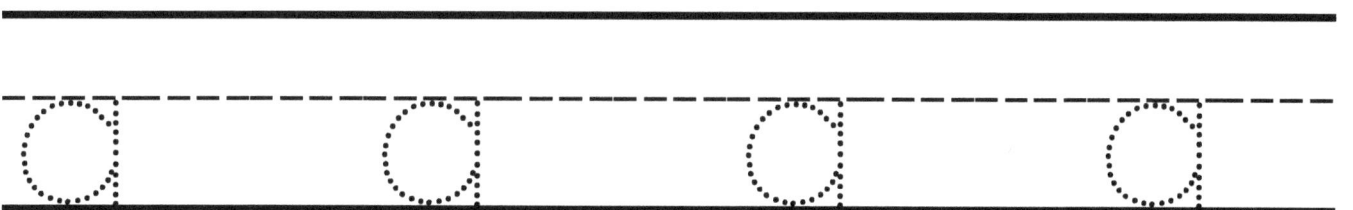

B for Banana

Bb

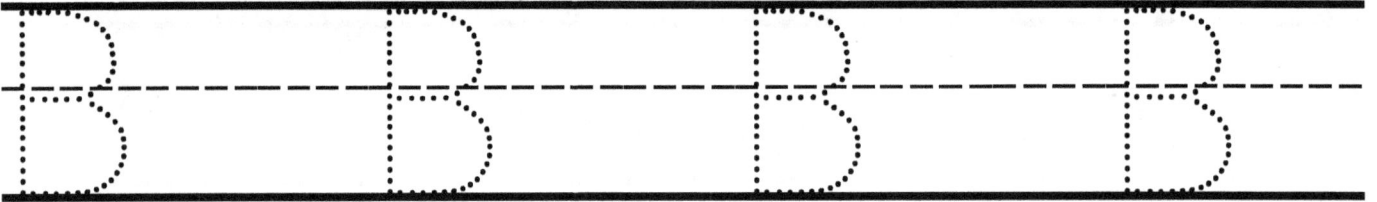

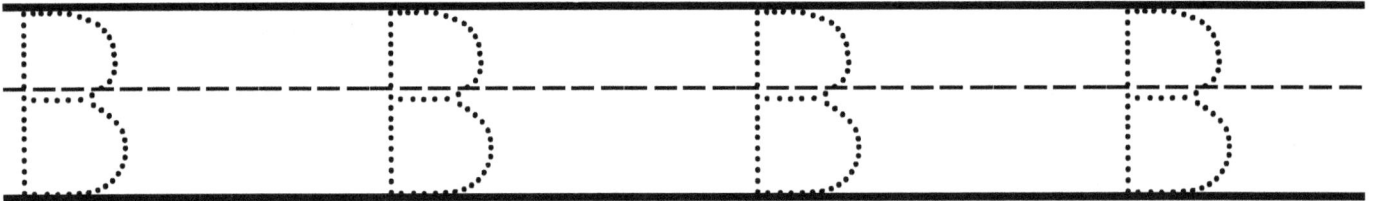

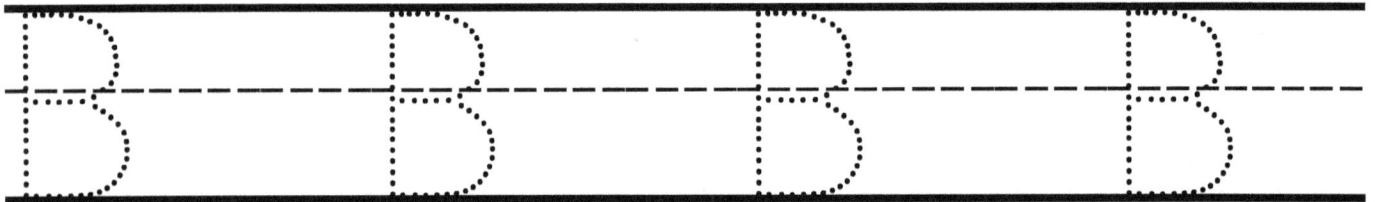

B B B B

B B B B

B B B B

B B B B

B B B B

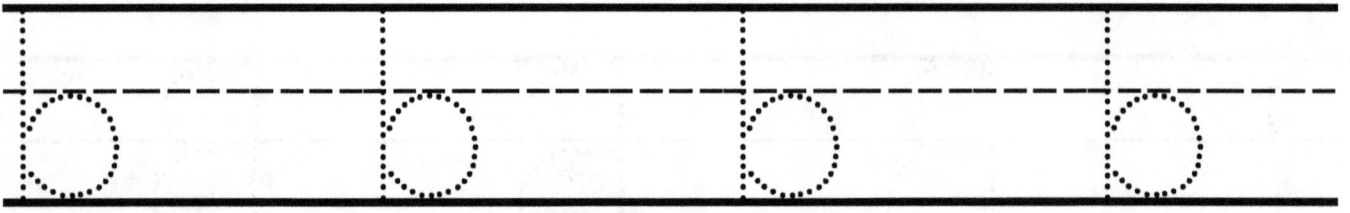

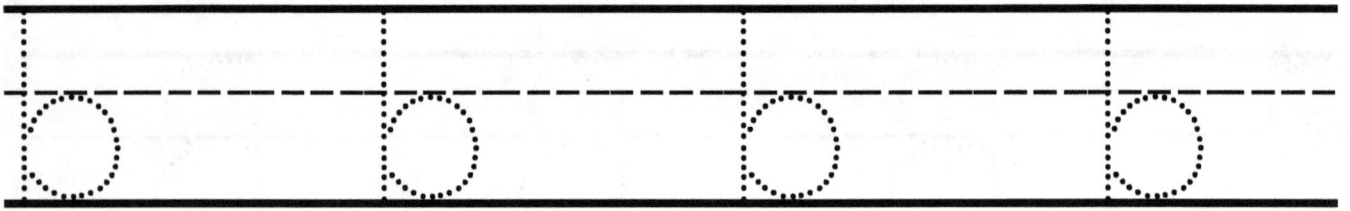

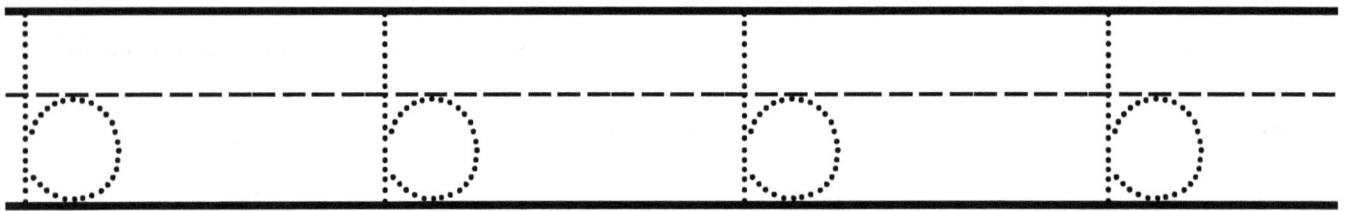

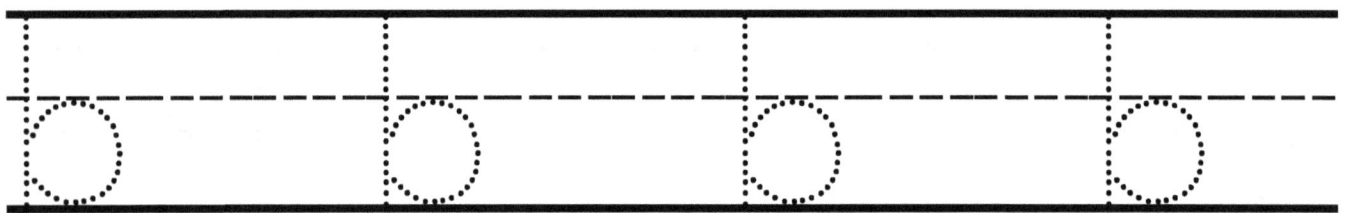

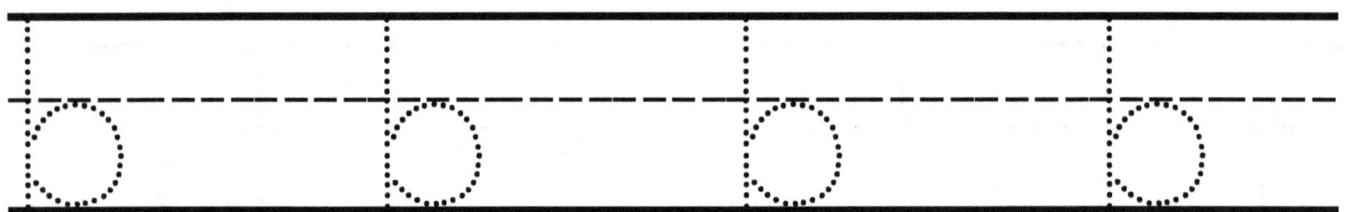

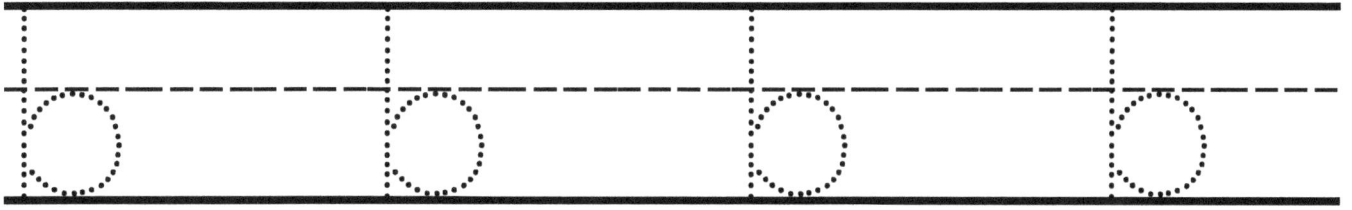

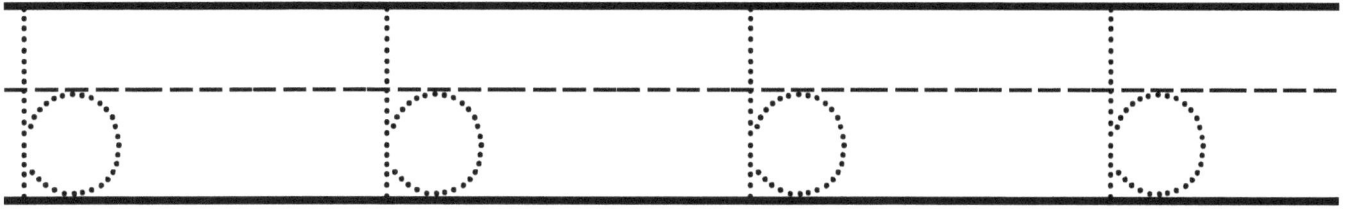

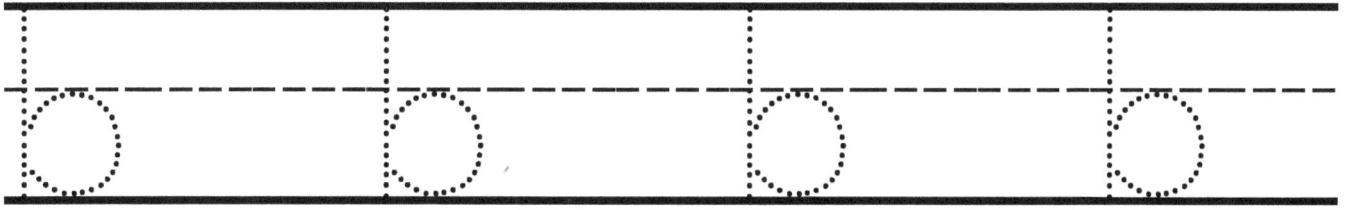

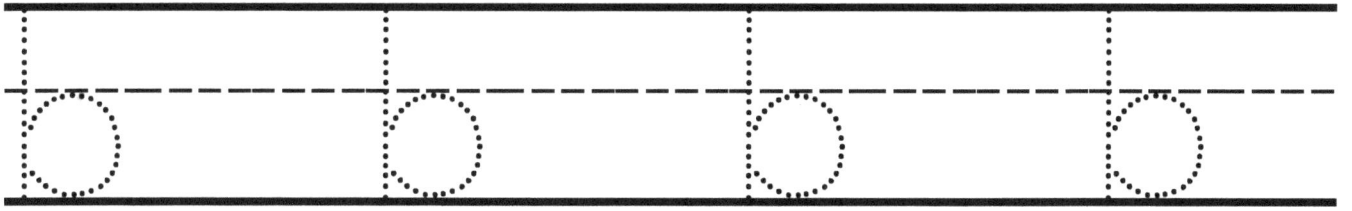

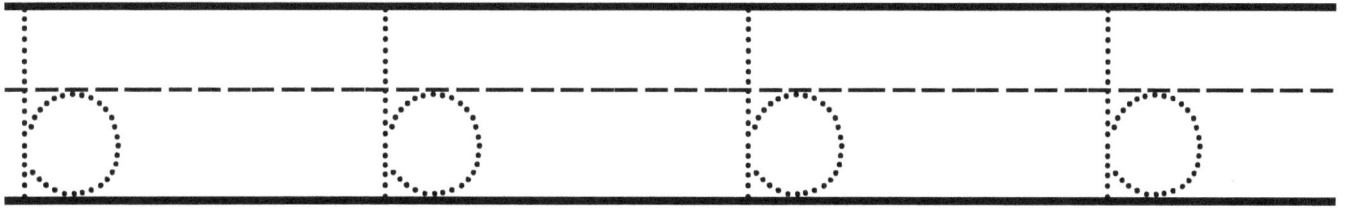

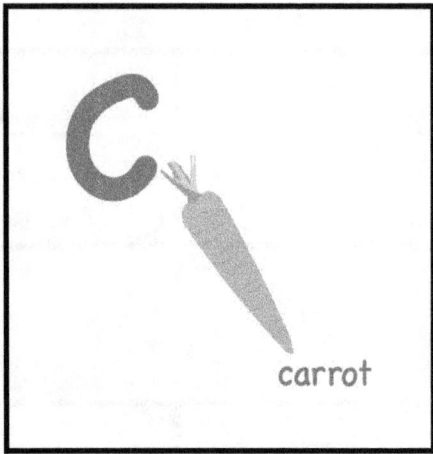

carrot

C for Carrot

Cc

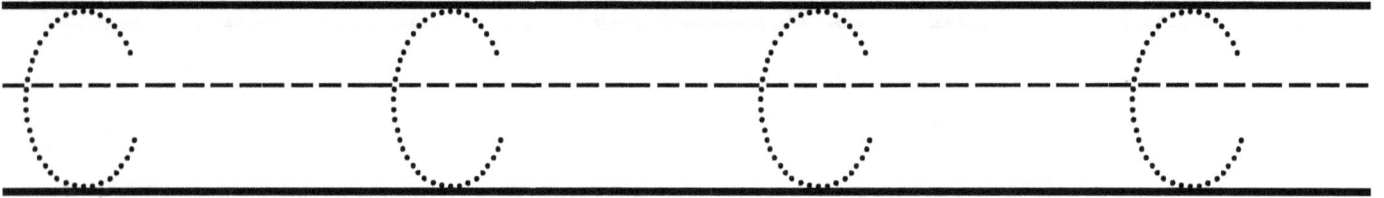

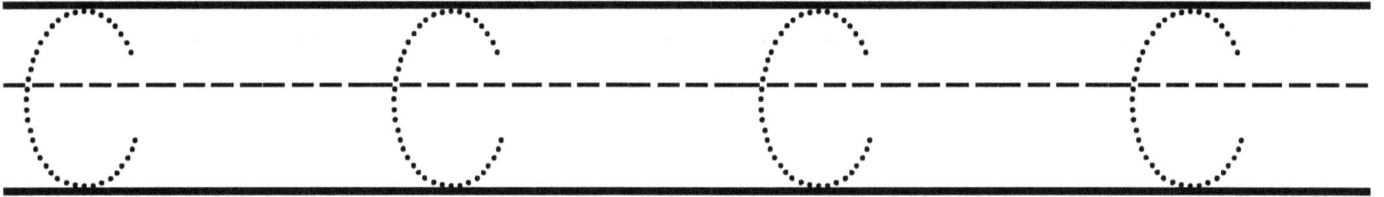

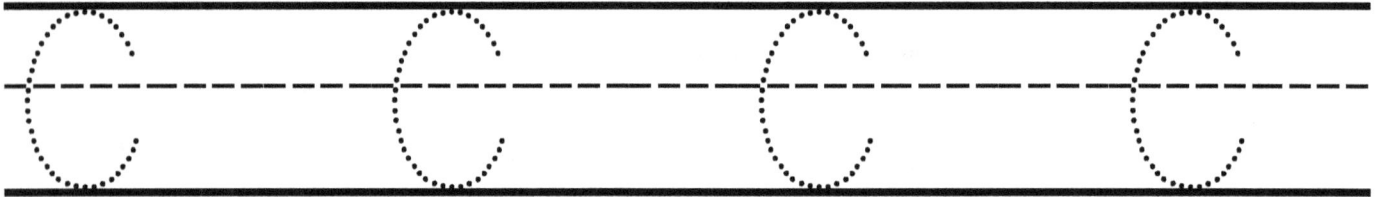

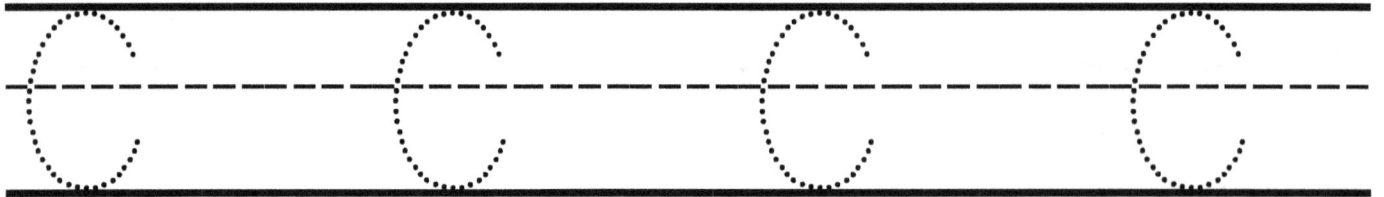

C C C C

C C C C

C C C C

C C C C

C C C C

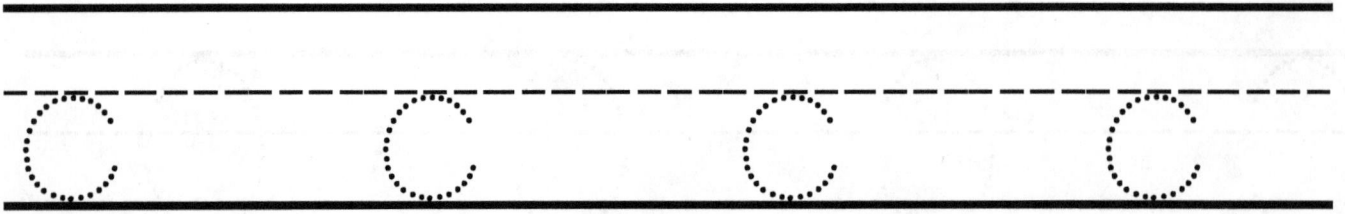

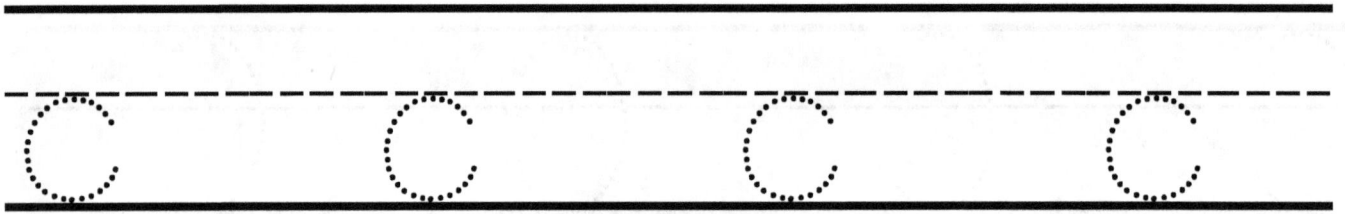

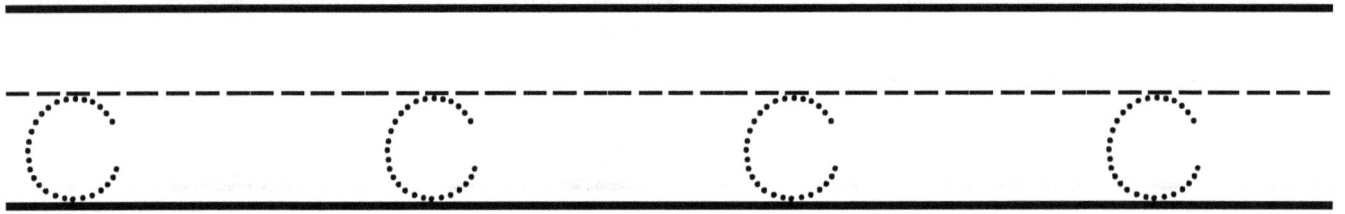

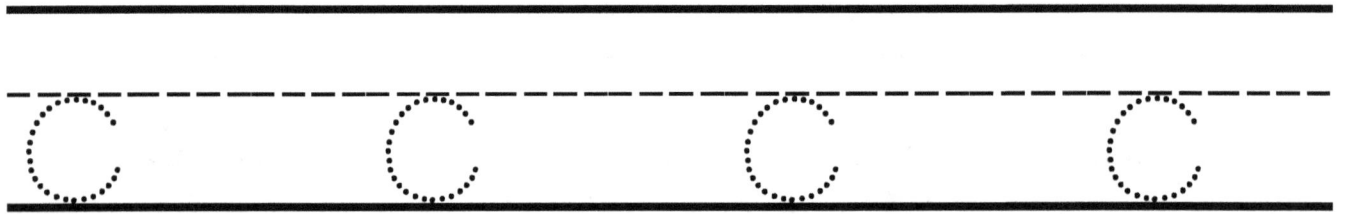

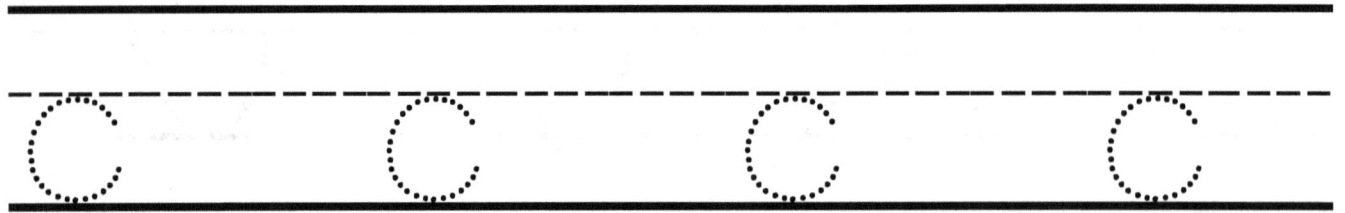

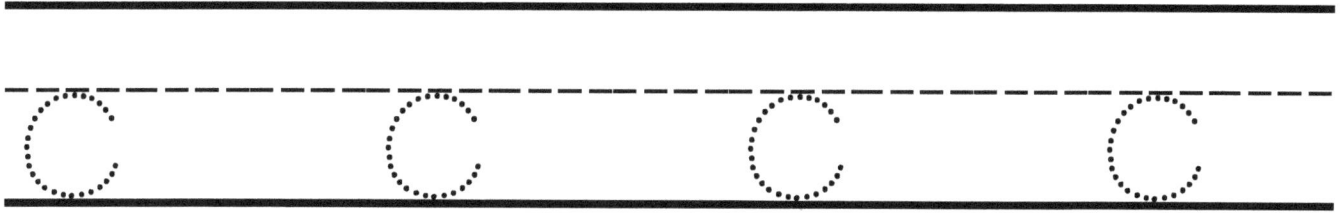

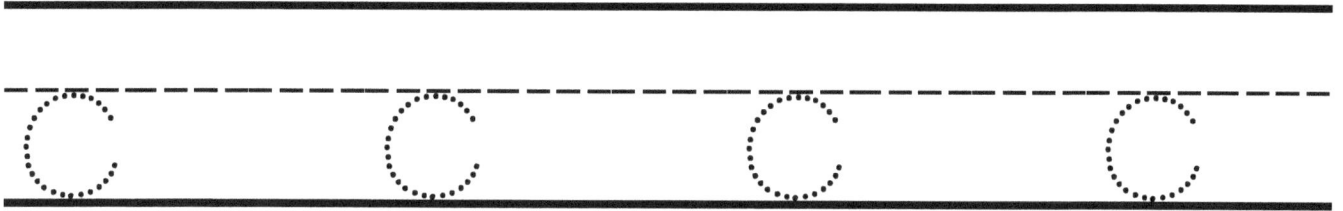

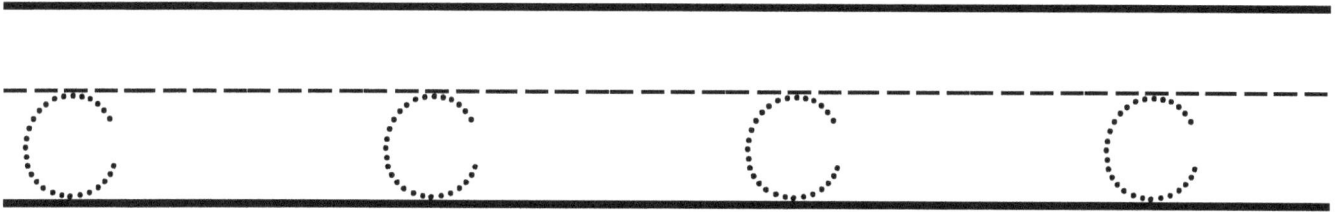

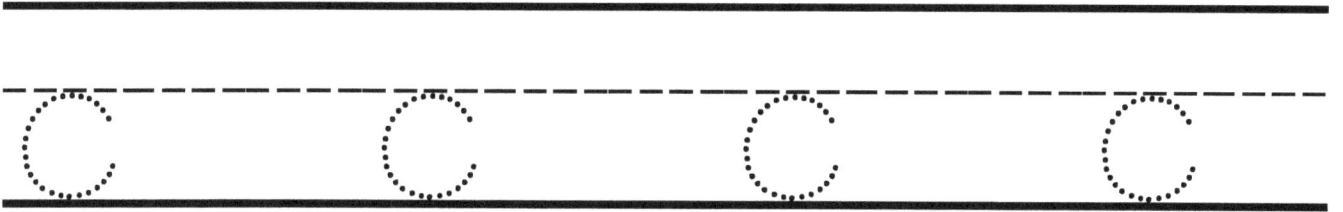

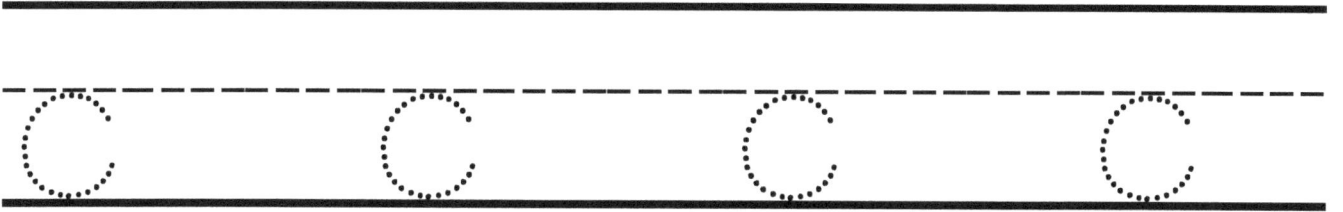

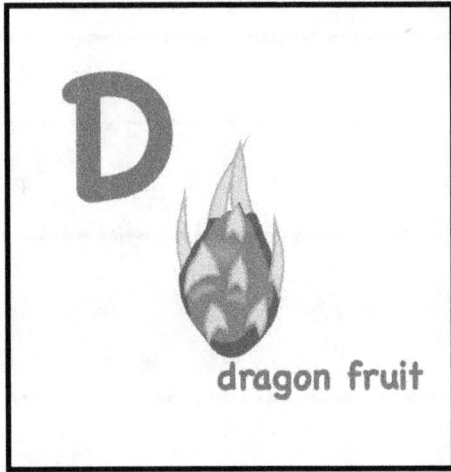

dragon fruit

D for Dragon Fruit

D d

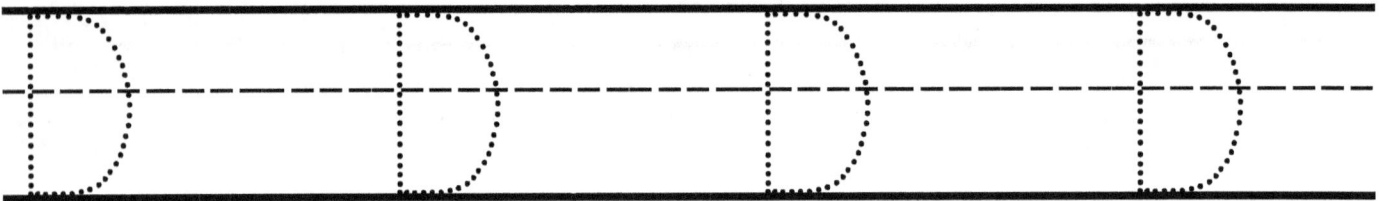

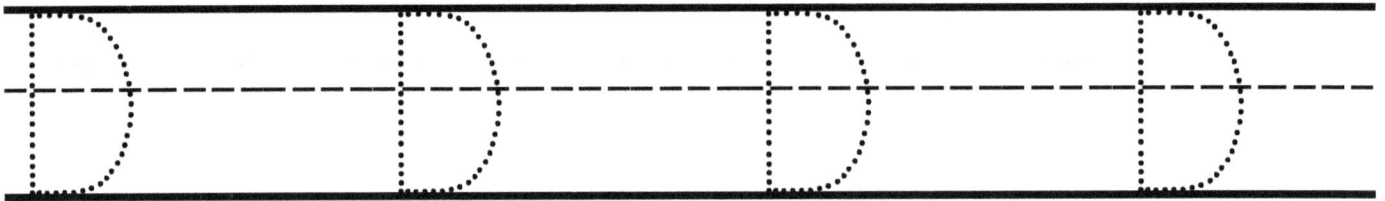

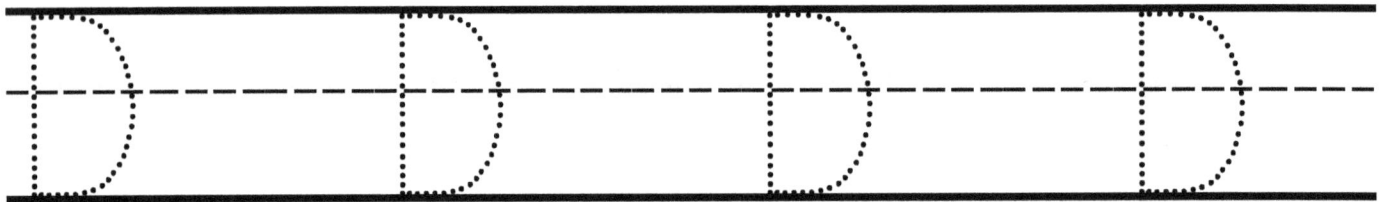

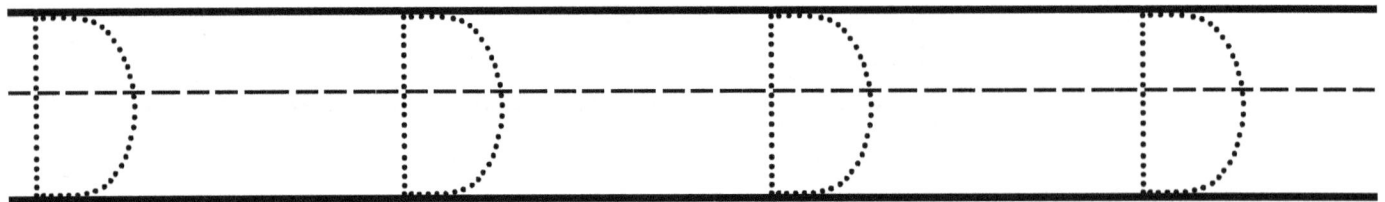

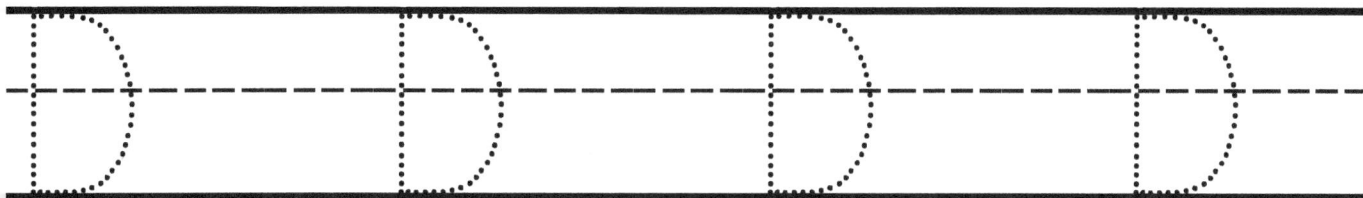

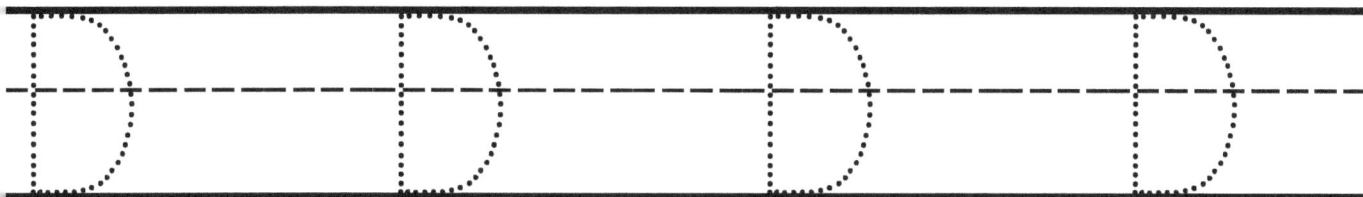

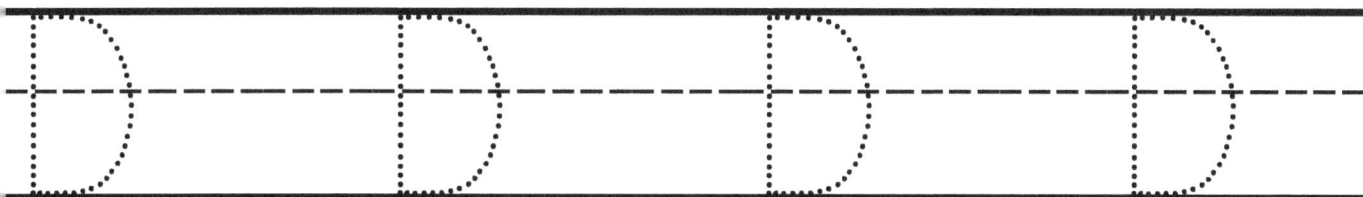

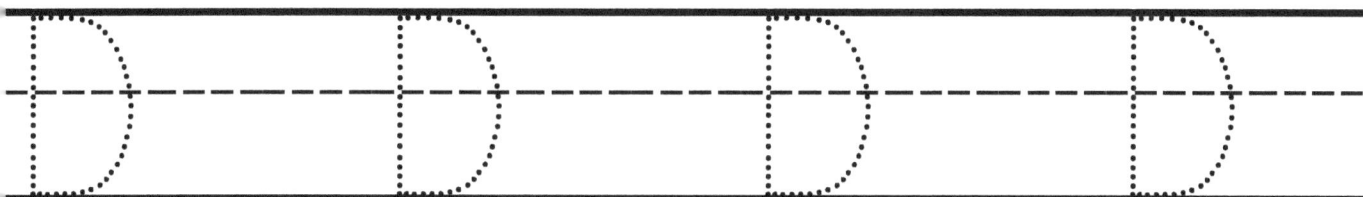

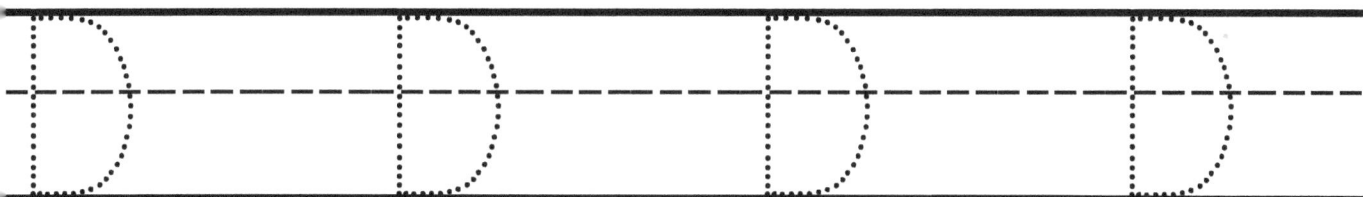

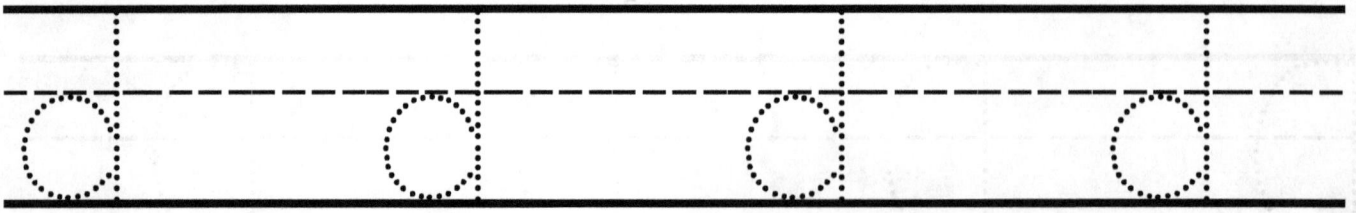

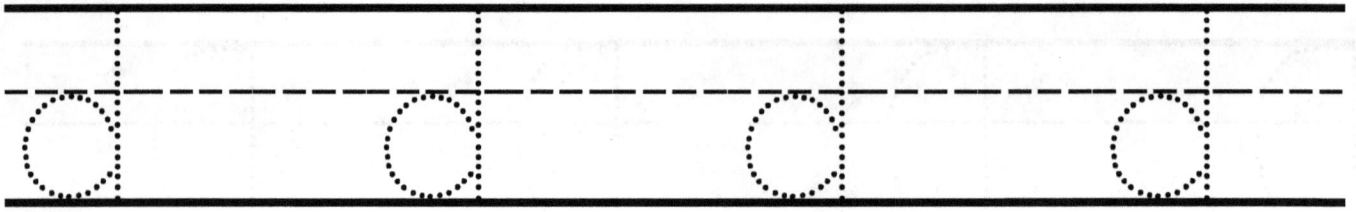

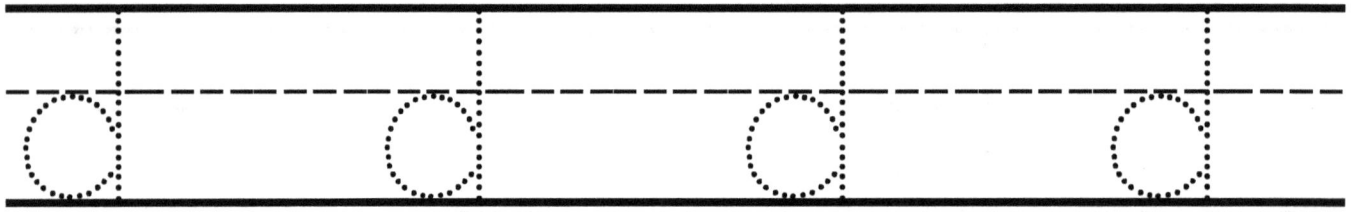

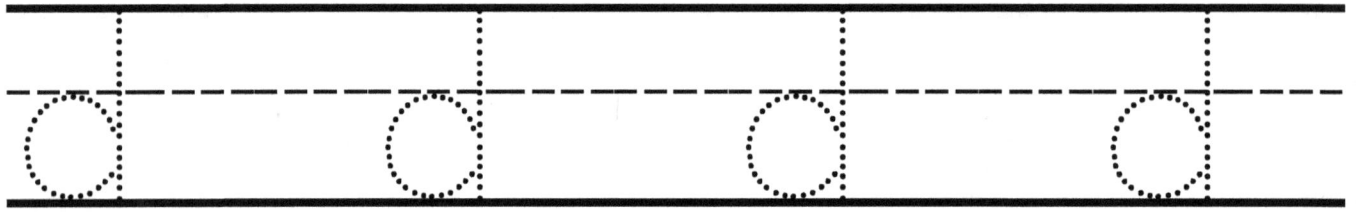

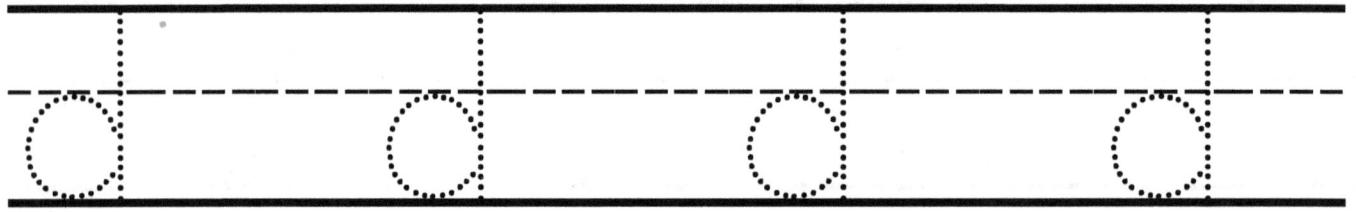

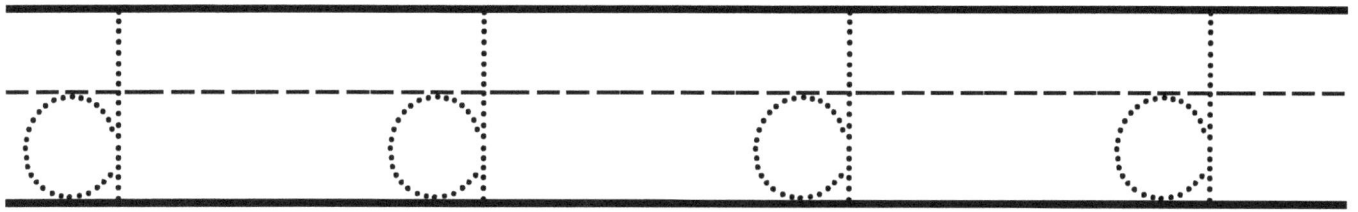

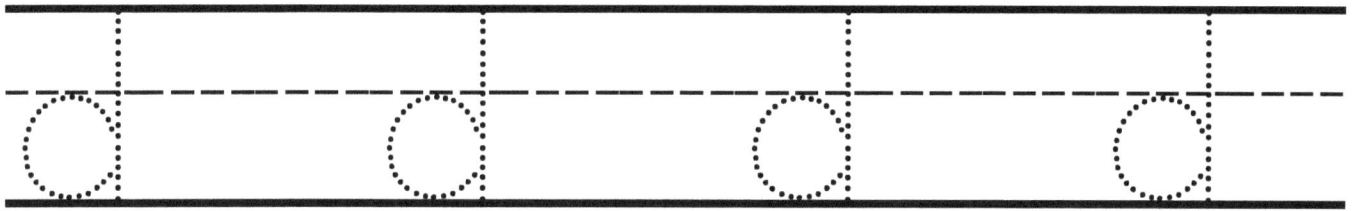

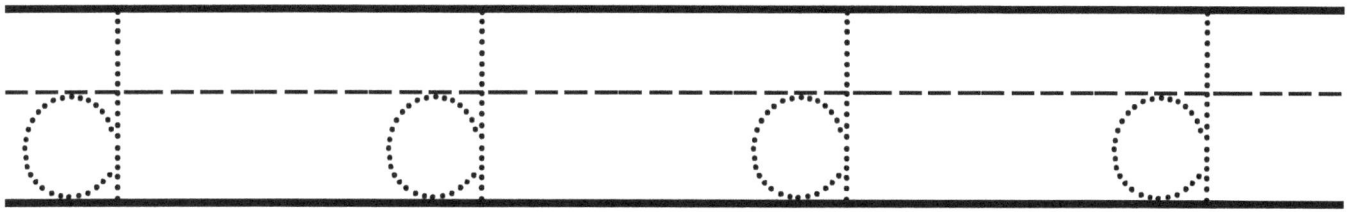

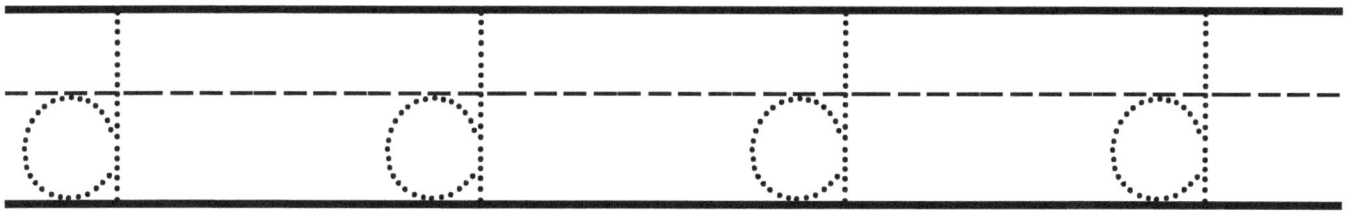

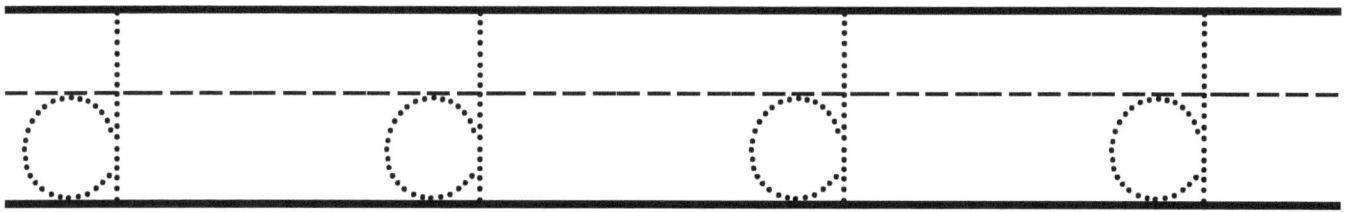

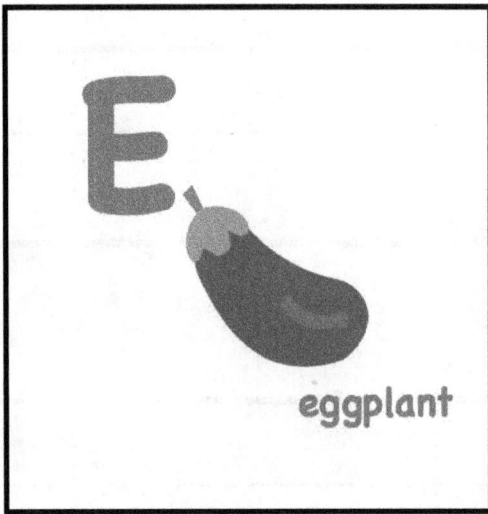

E for Eggplant

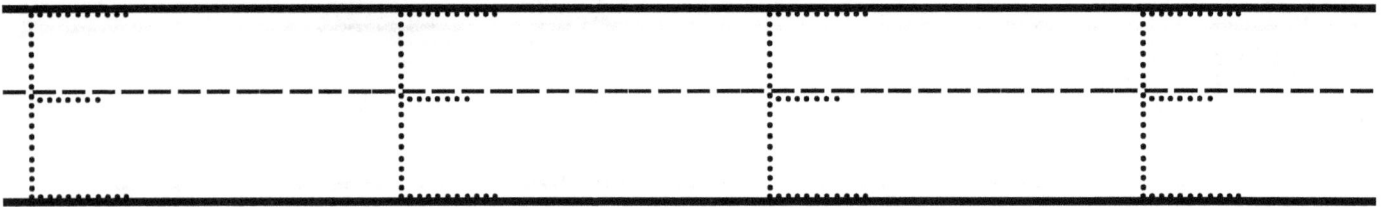

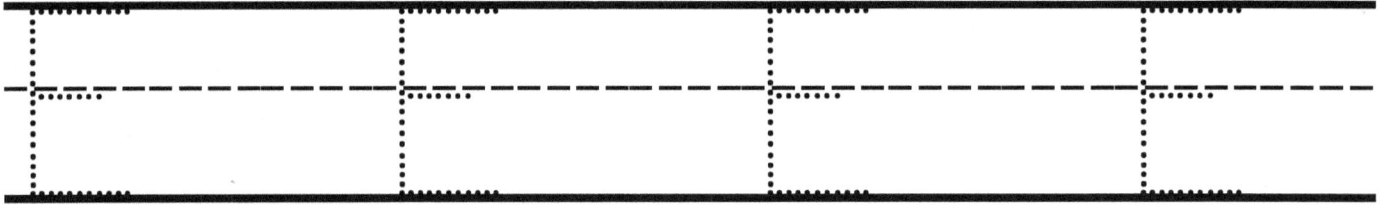

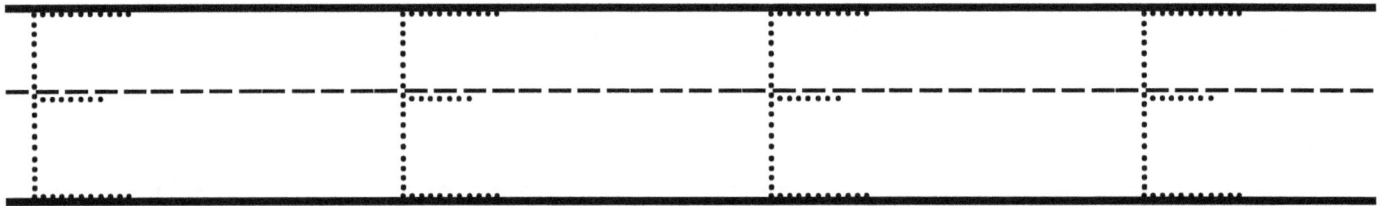

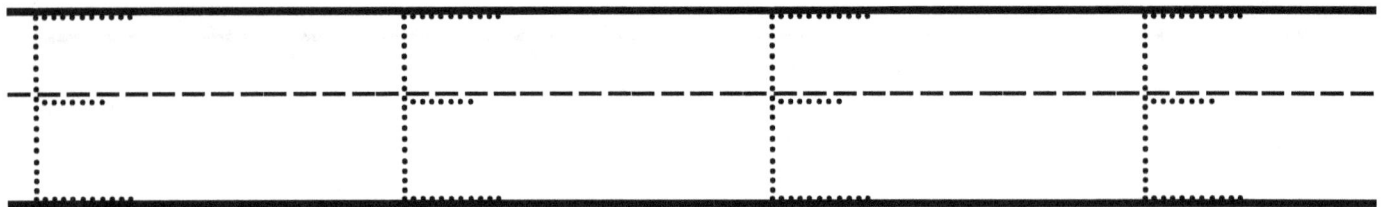

eggplant

E e

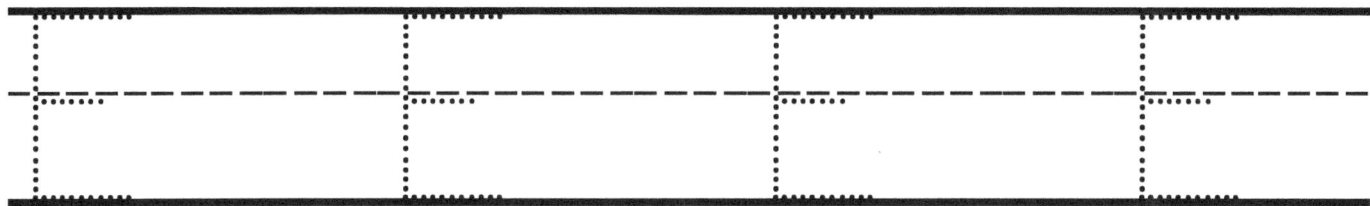

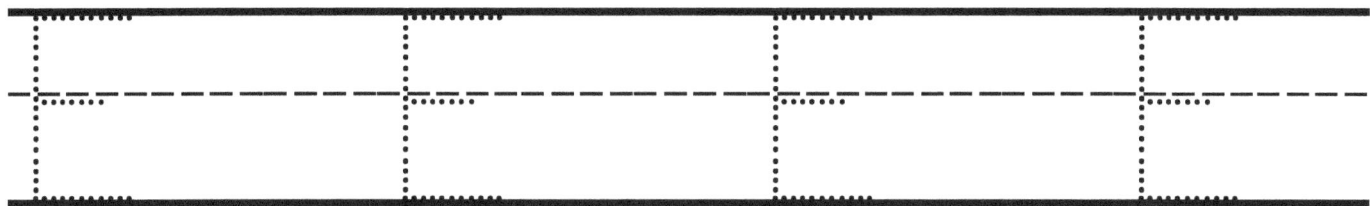

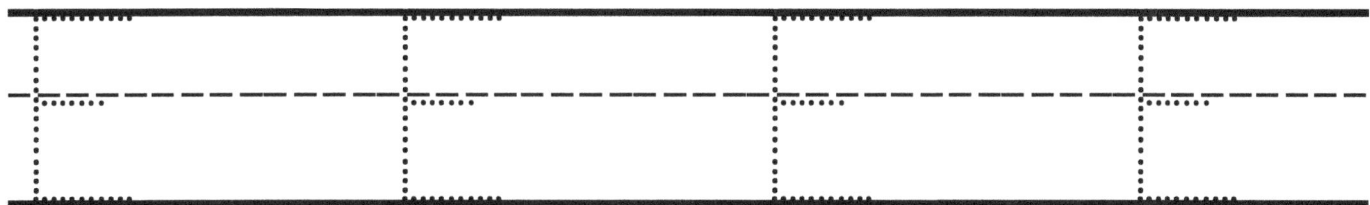

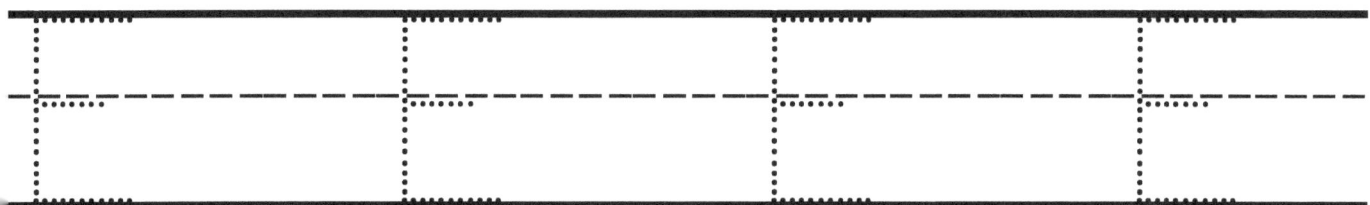

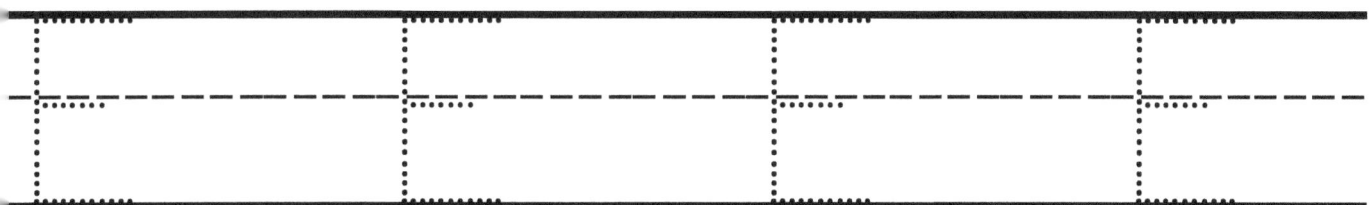

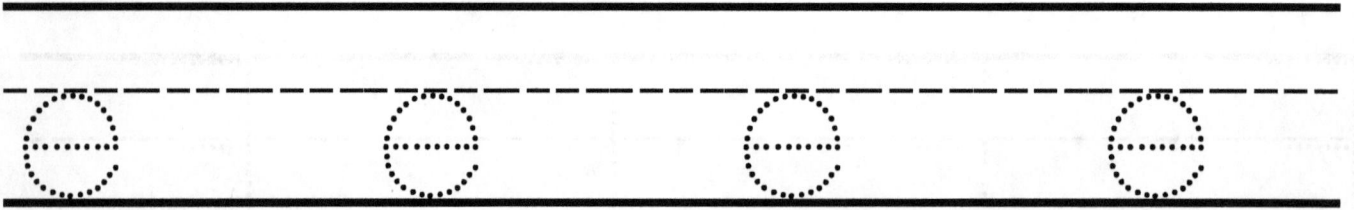

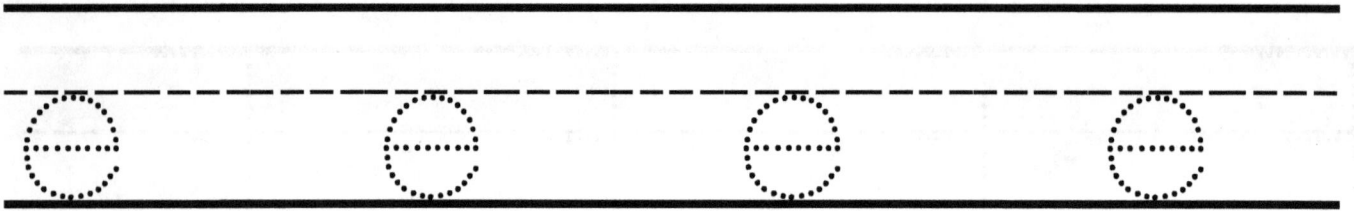

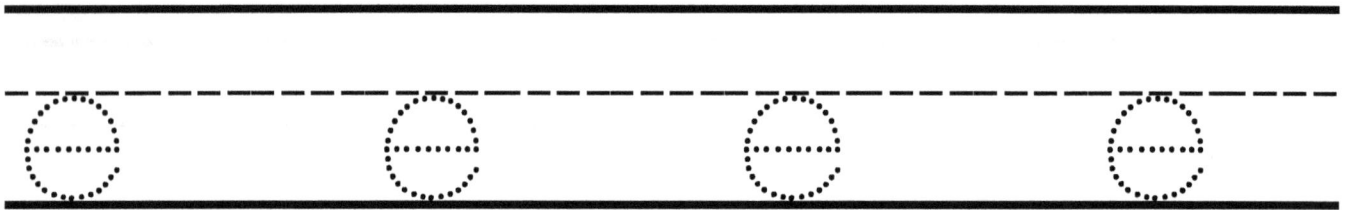

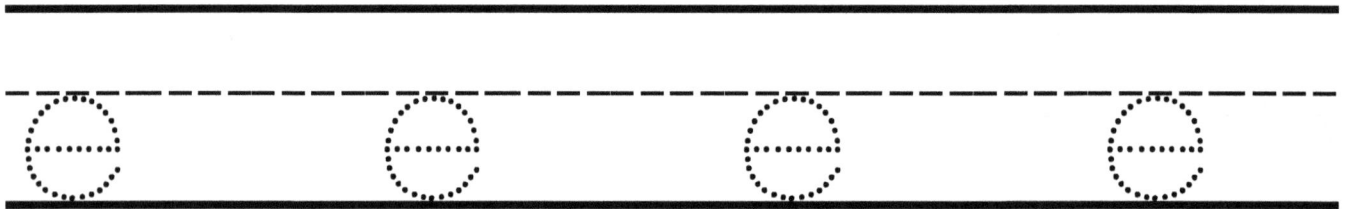

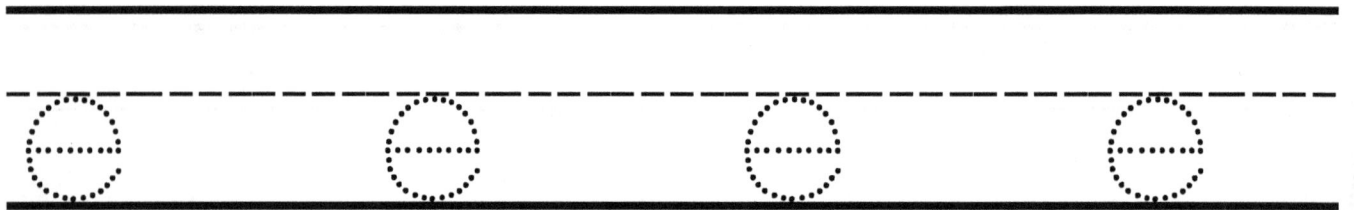

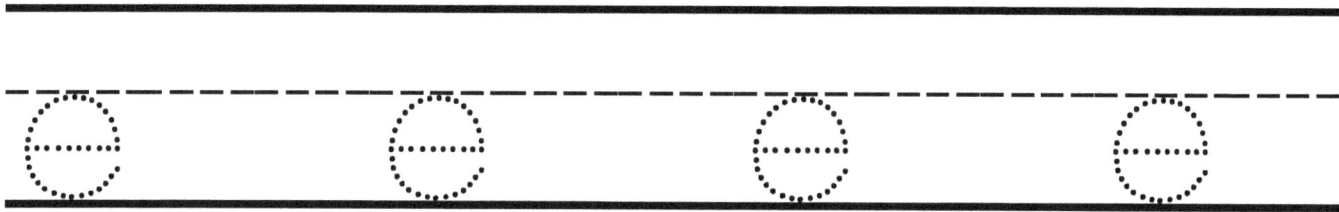

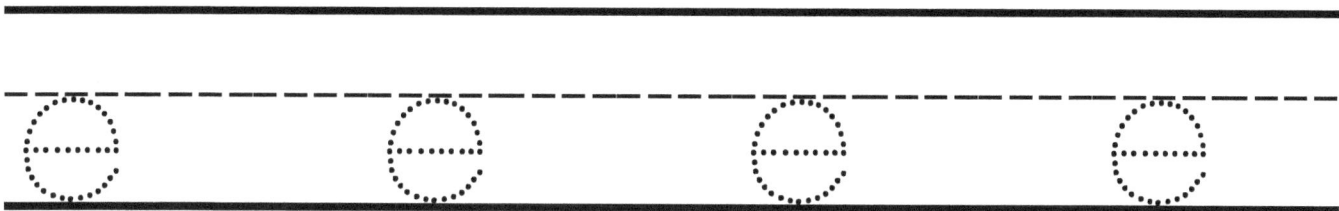

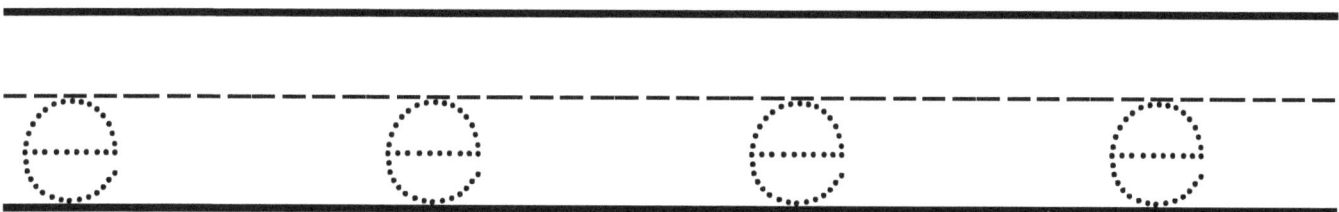

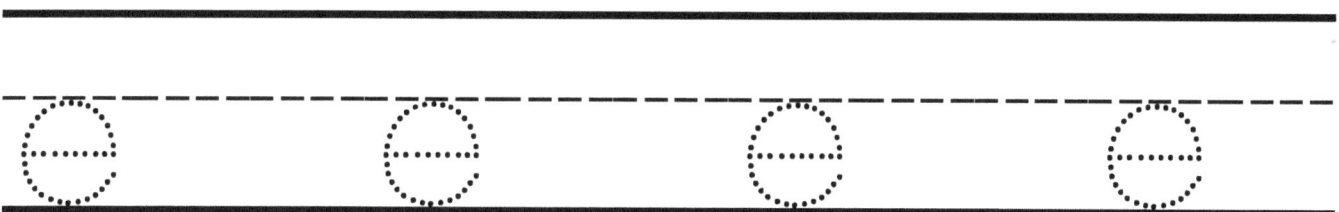

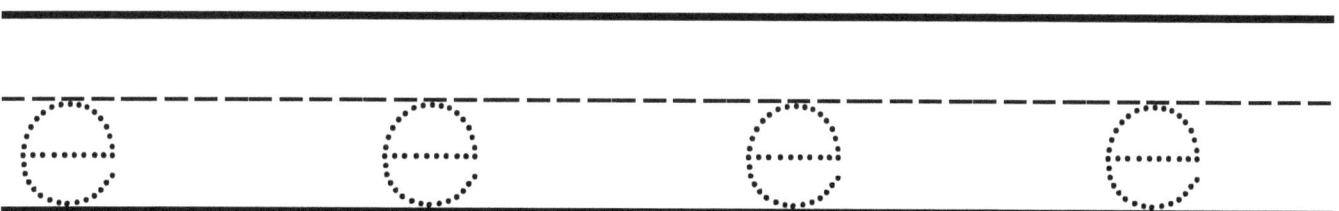

F for Fig

fig

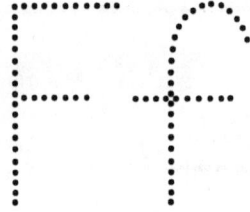

Ff

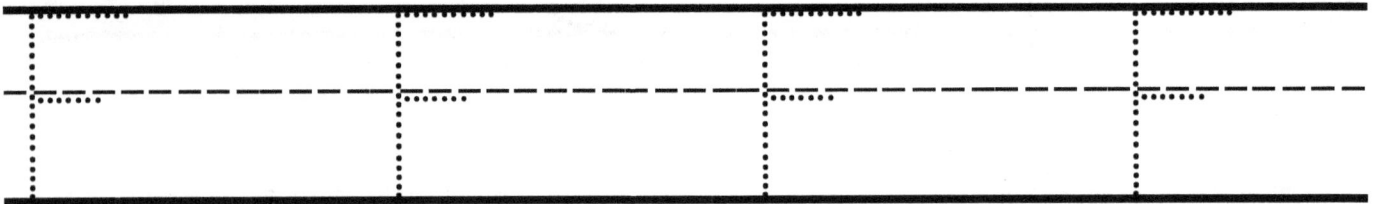

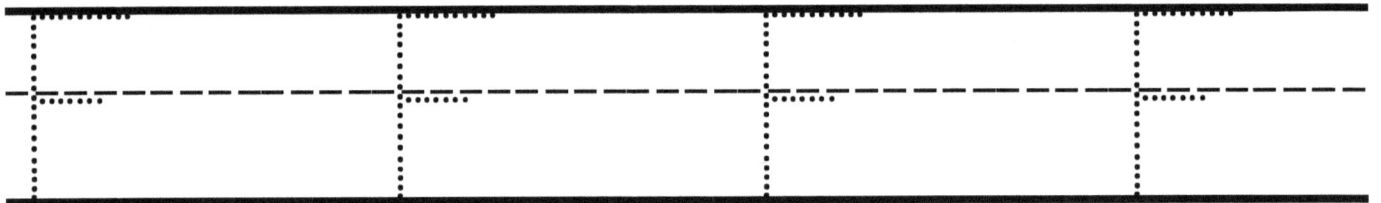

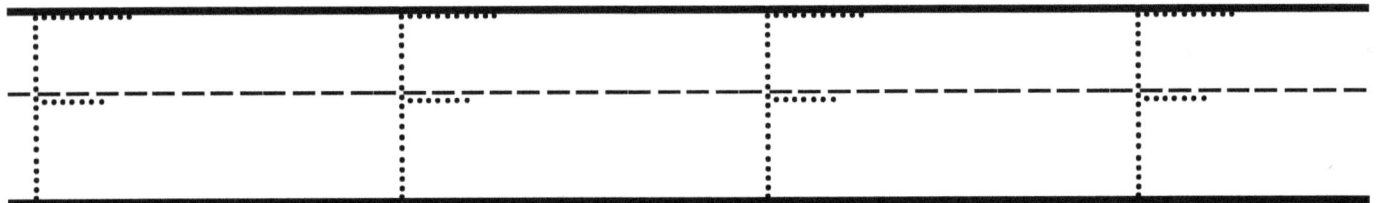

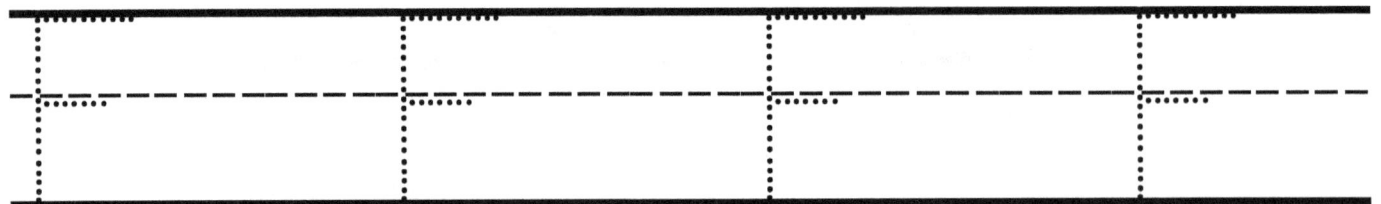

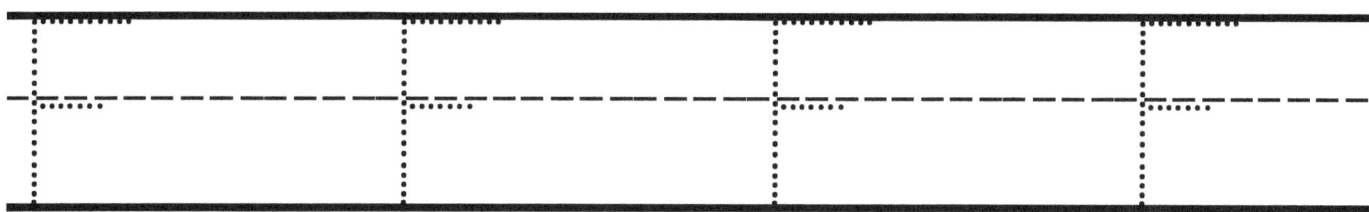

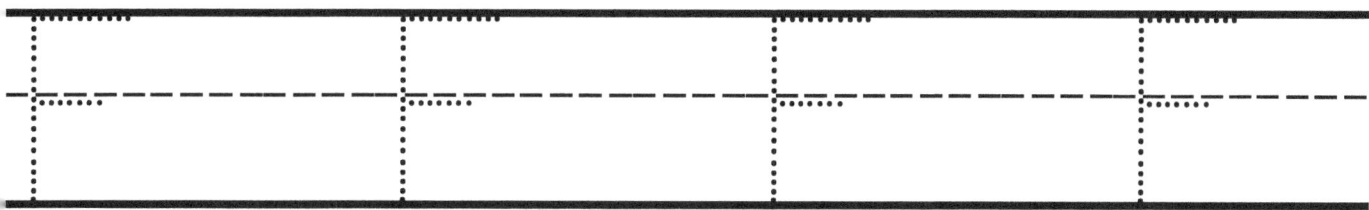

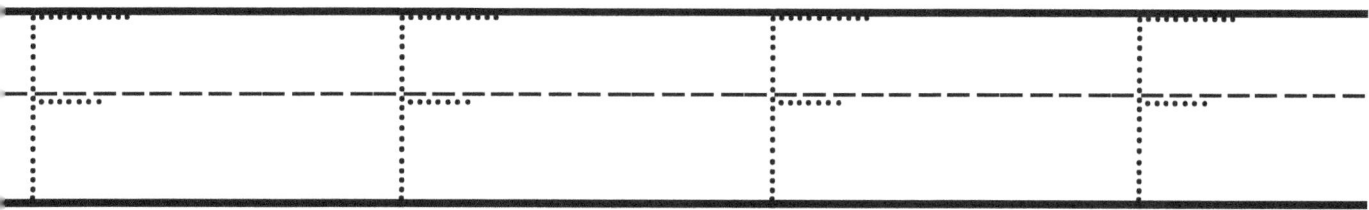

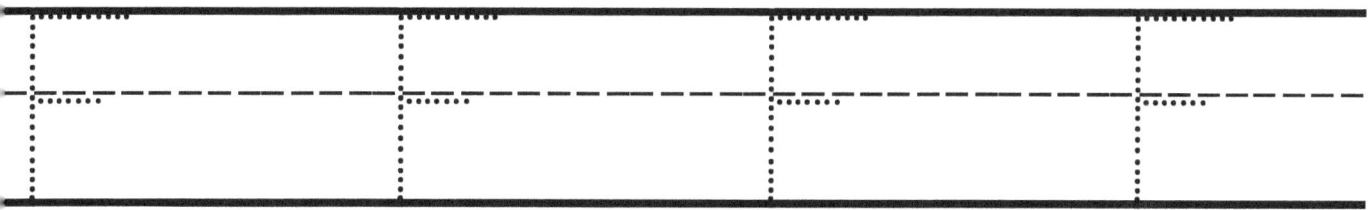

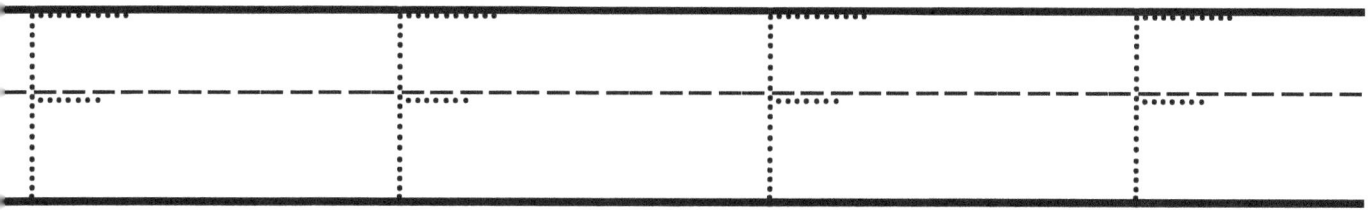

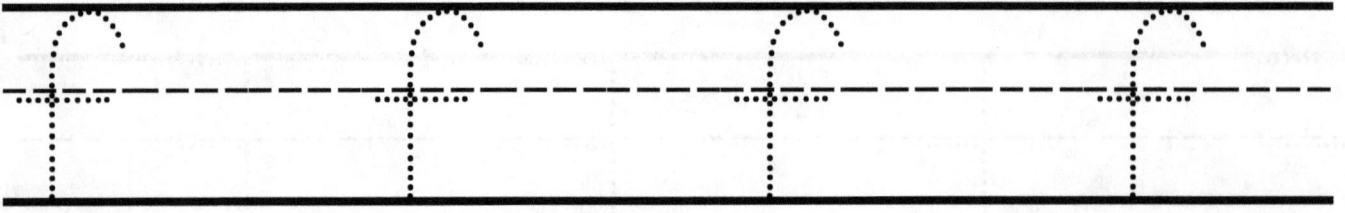

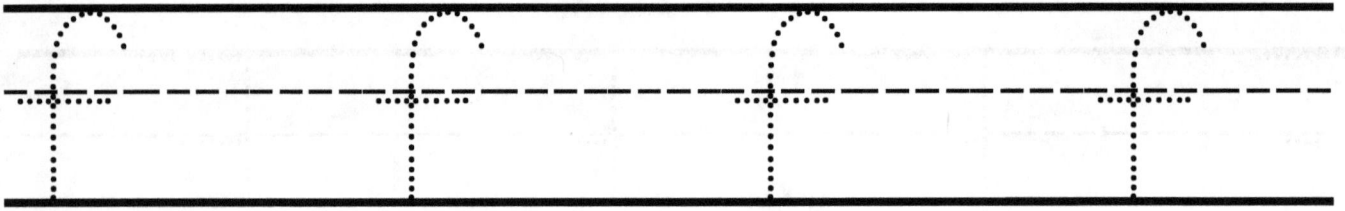

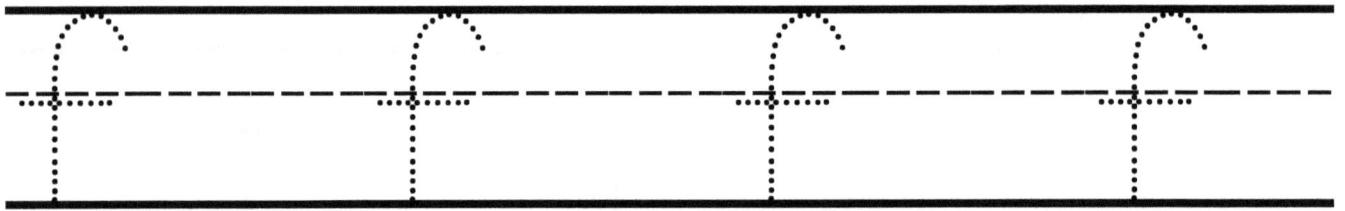

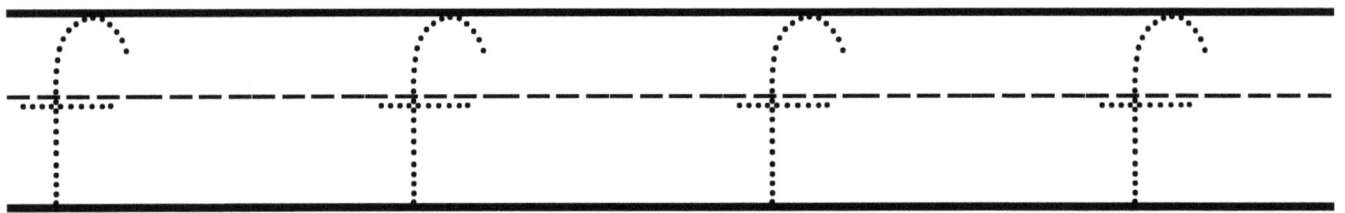

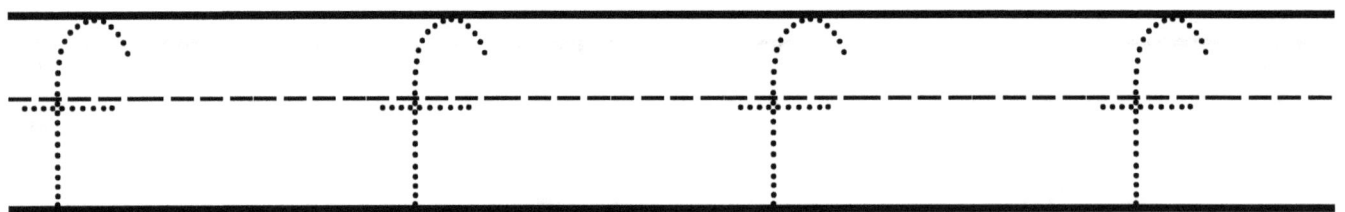

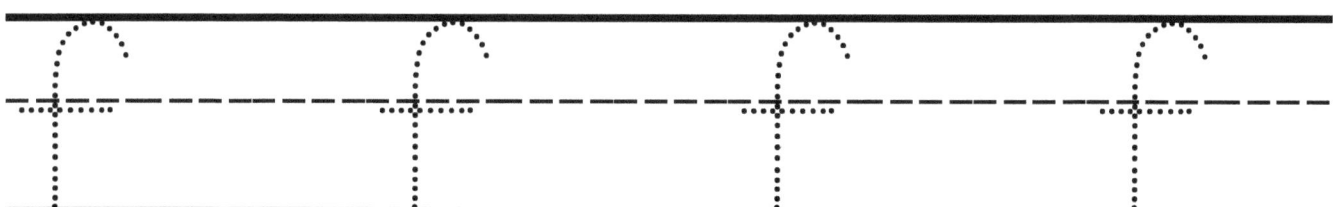

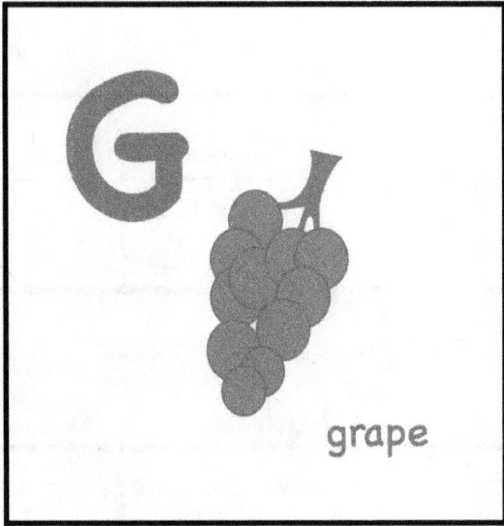

grape

G for Grape

Gg

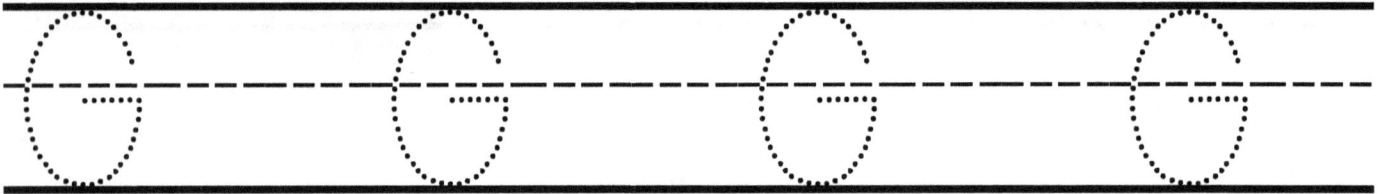

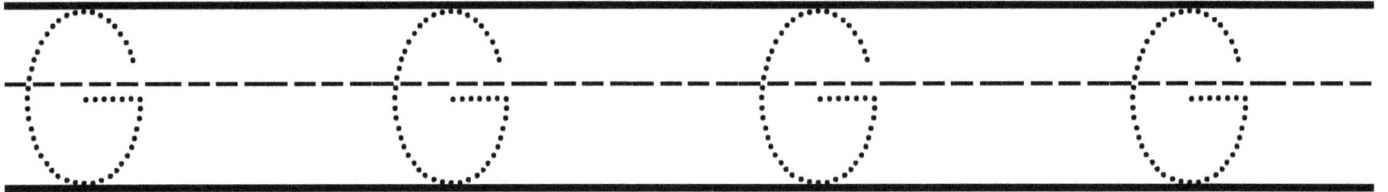

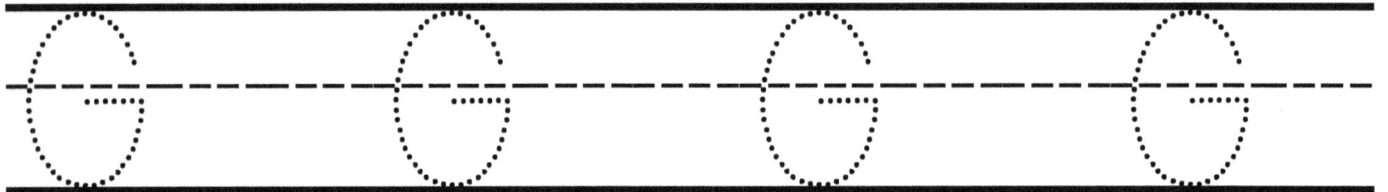

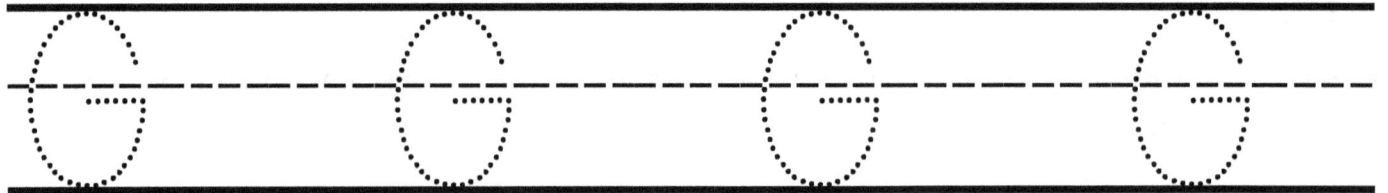

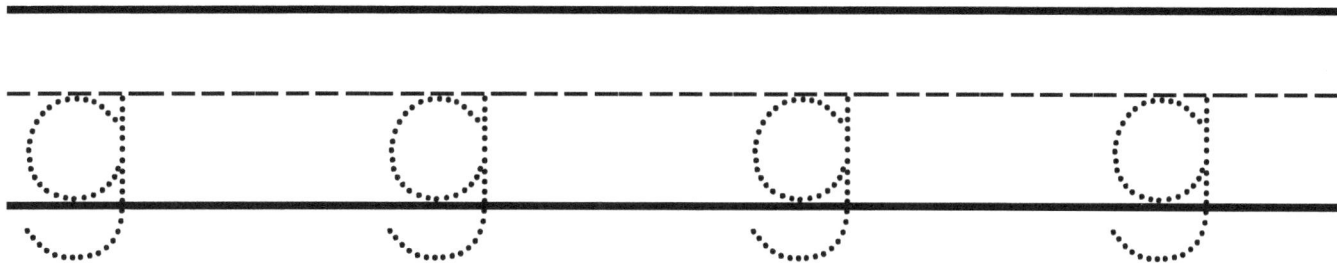

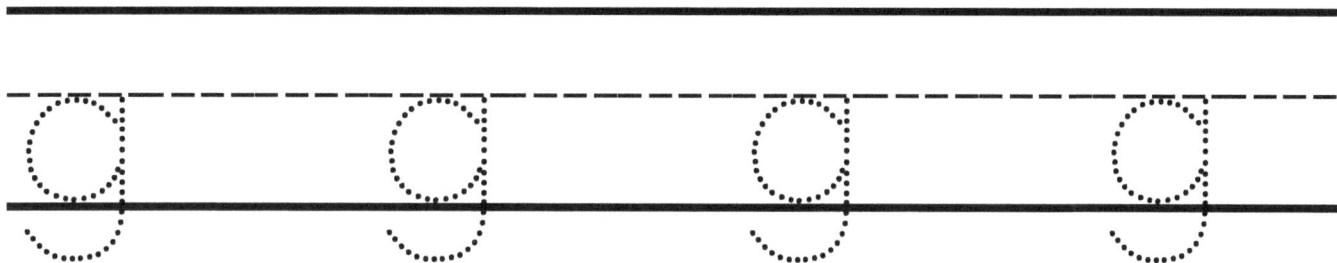

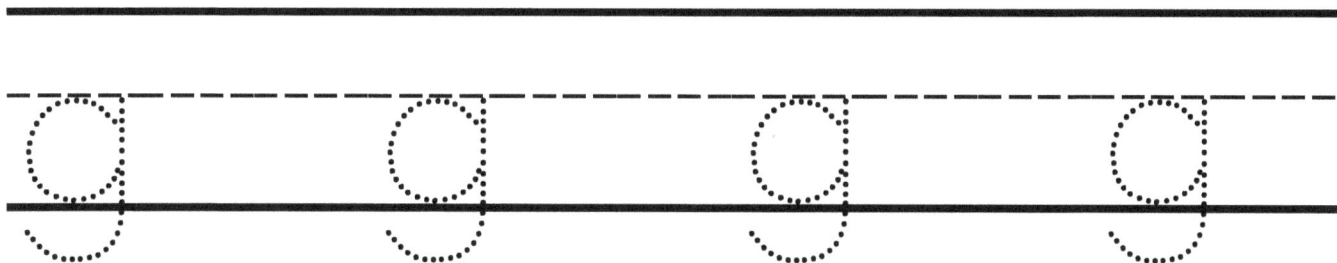

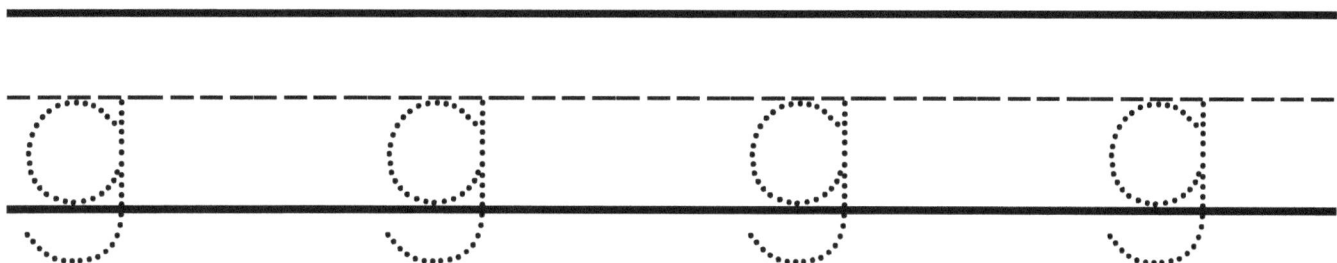

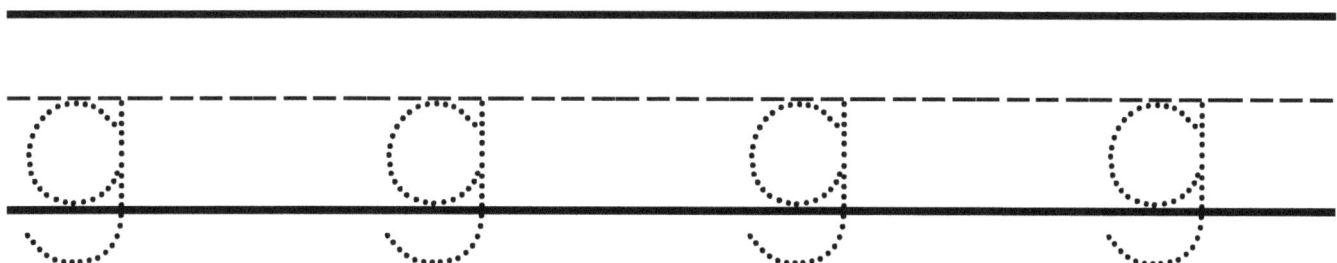

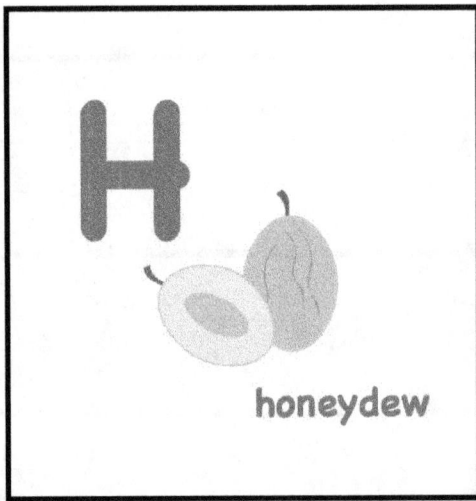

honeydew

H for Honeydew

Hh

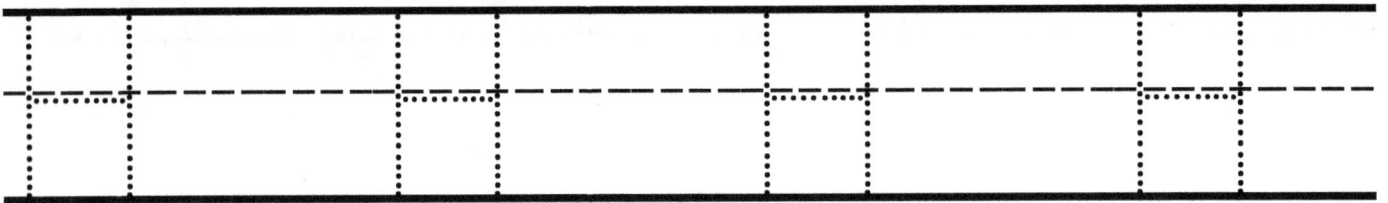

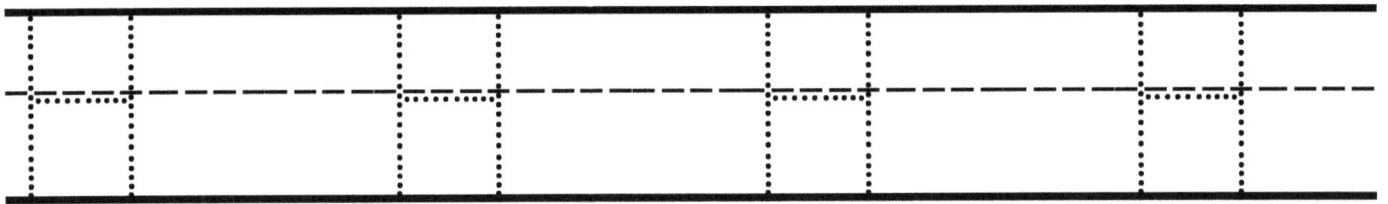

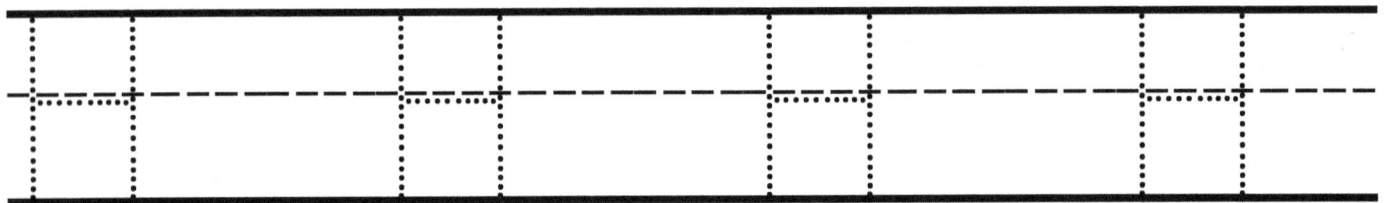

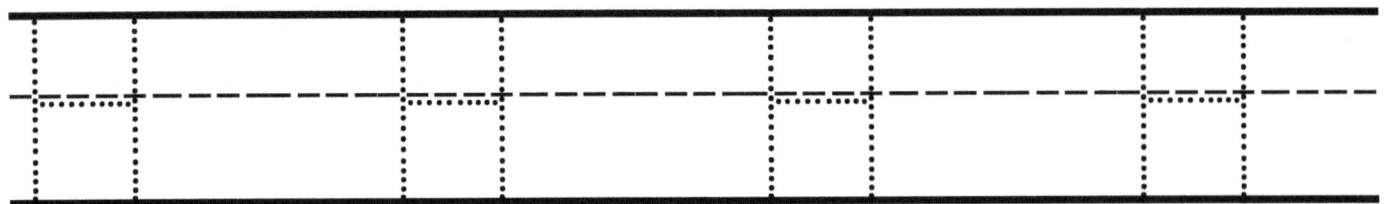

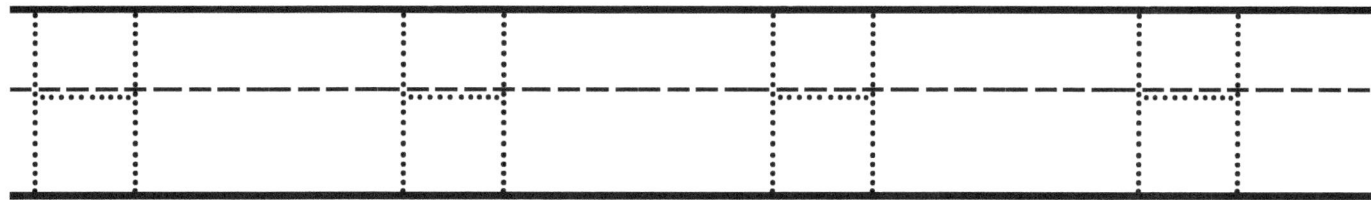

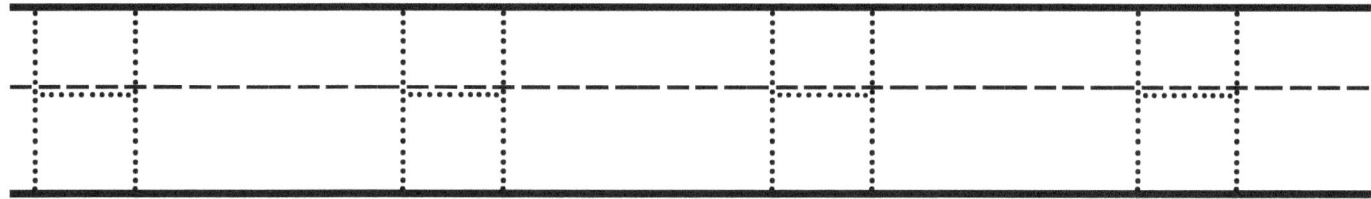

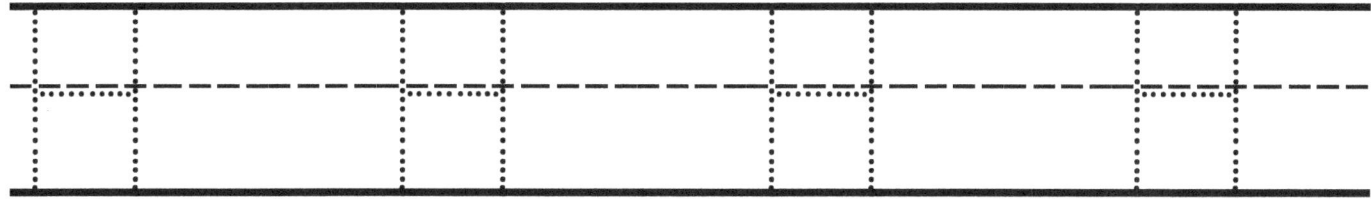

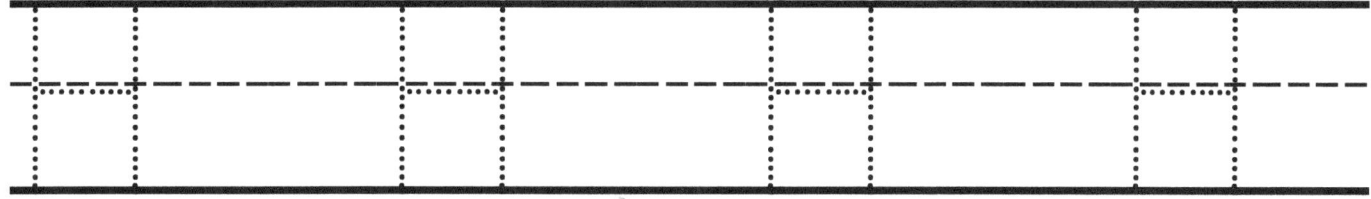

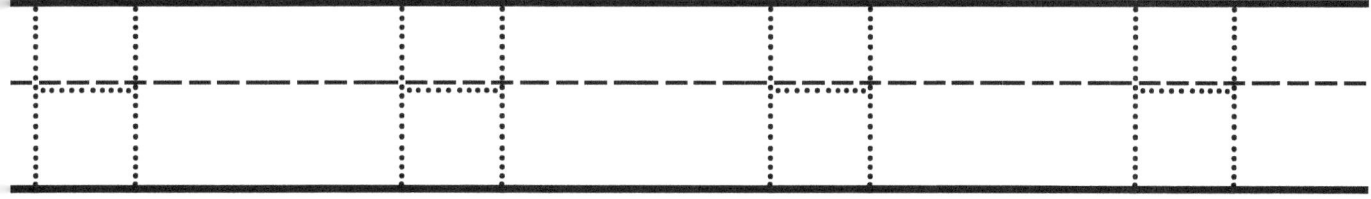

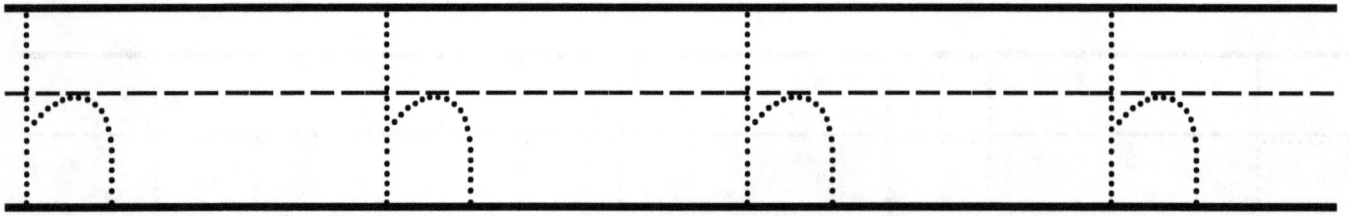

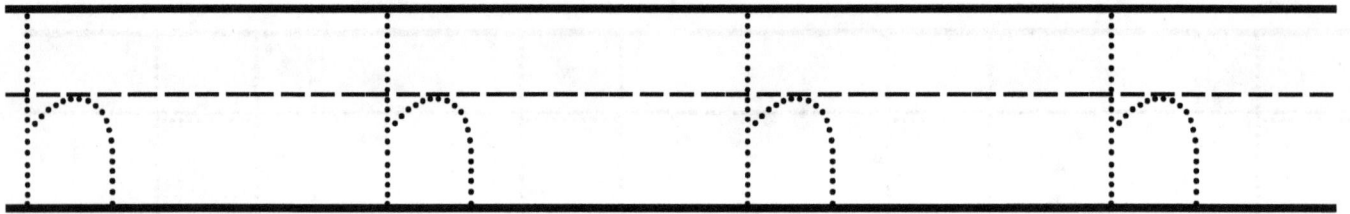

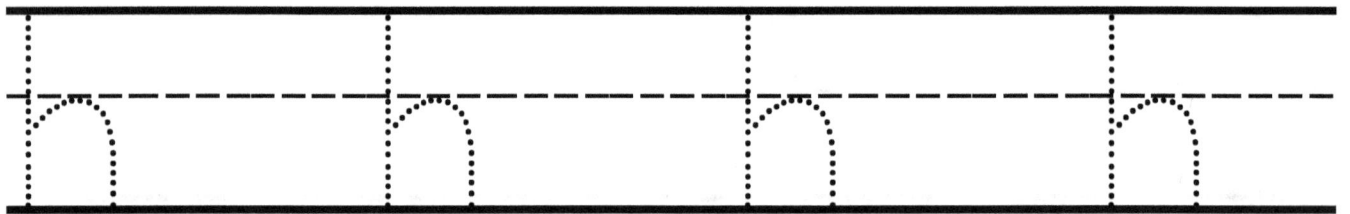

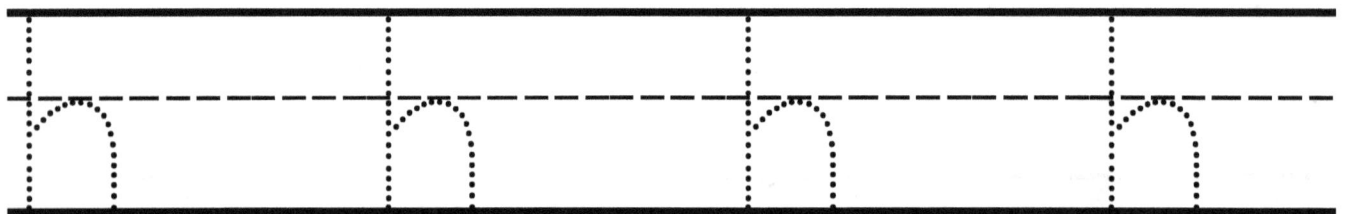

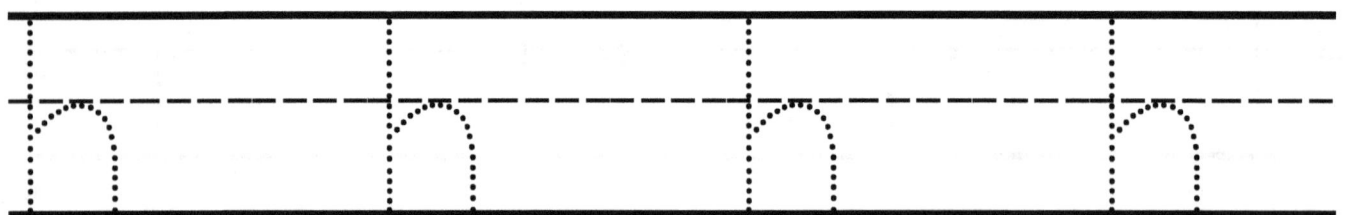

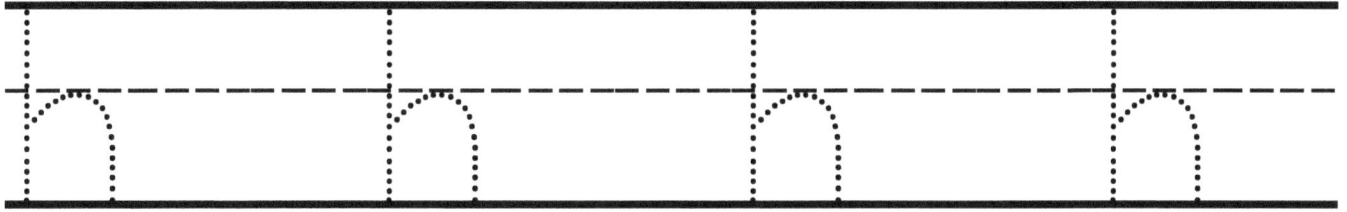

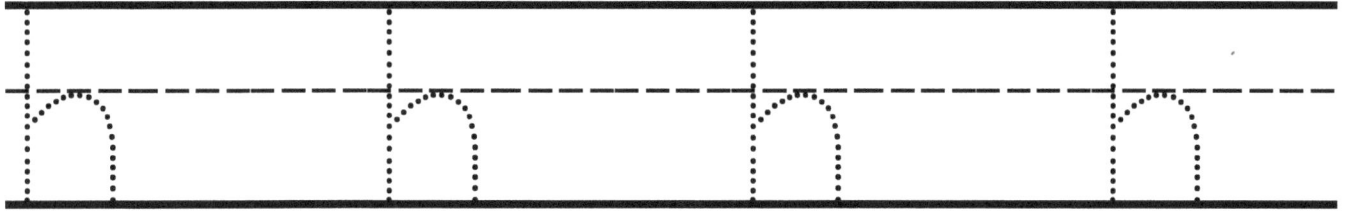

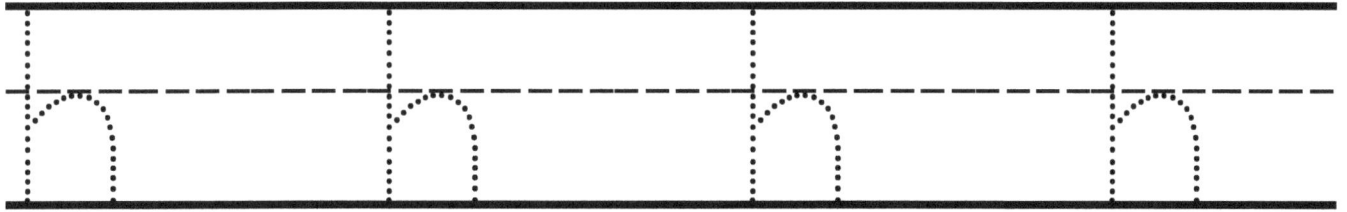

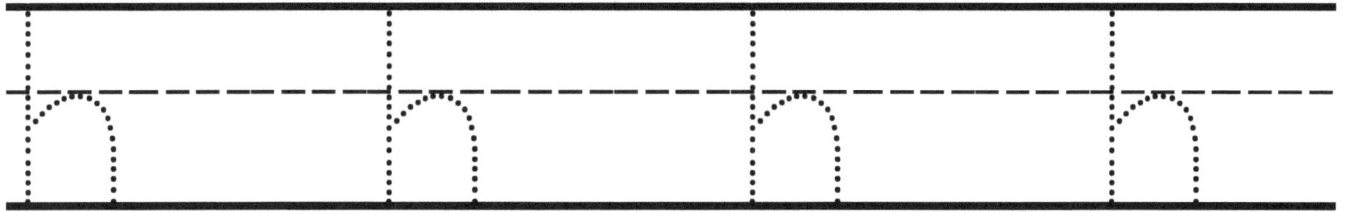

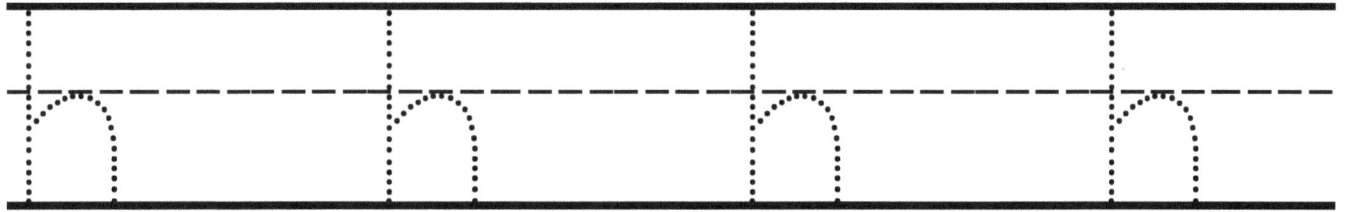

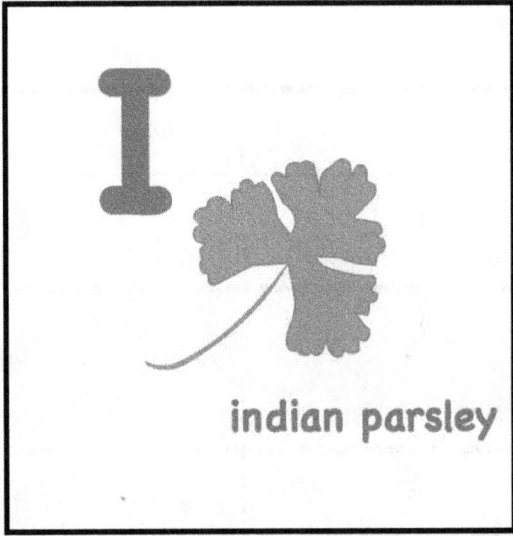

indian parsley

I for Indian Parsely

I i

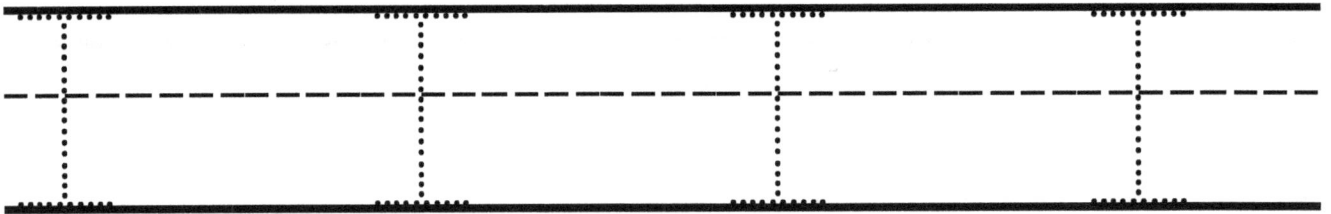

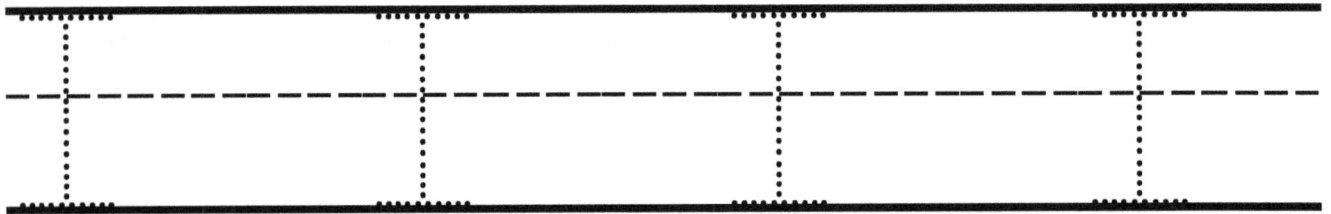

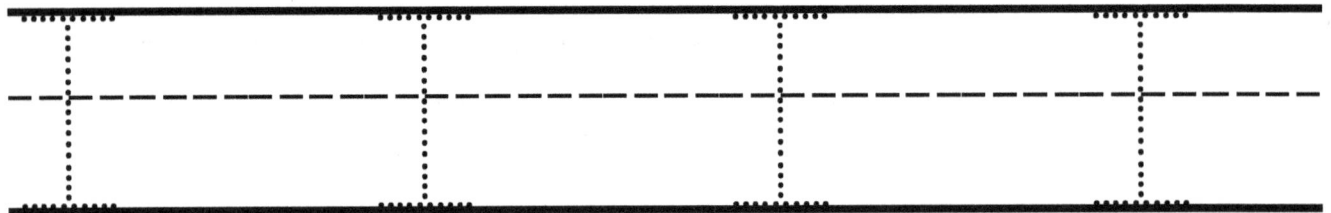

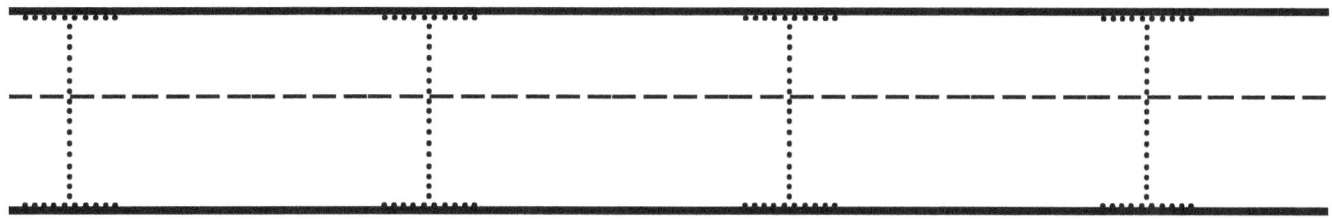

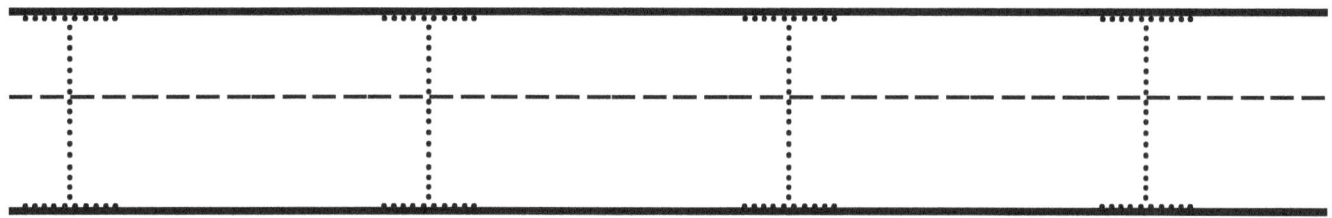

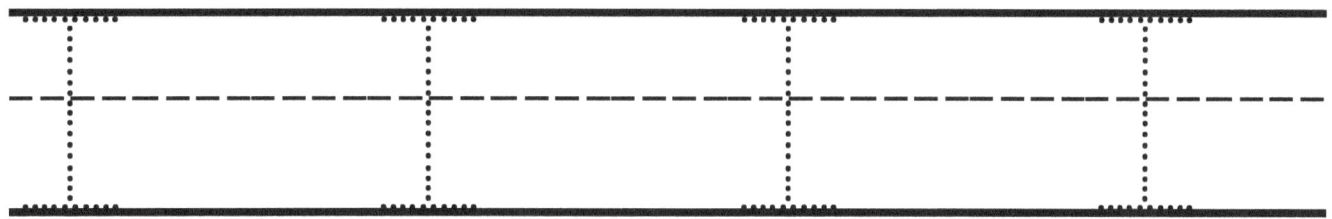

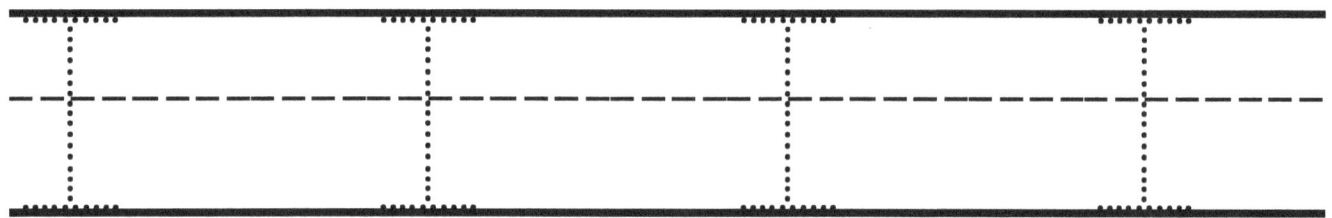

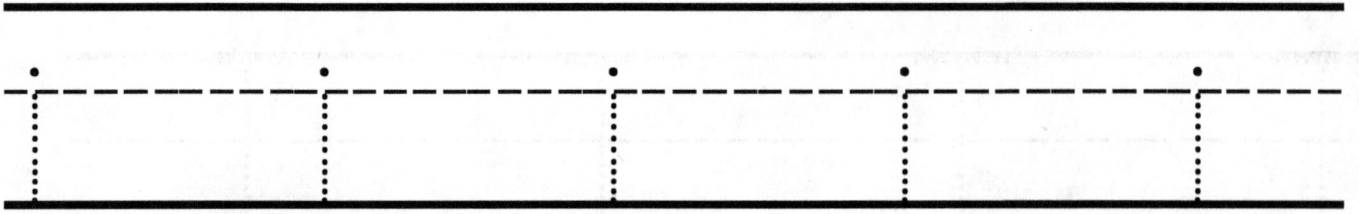

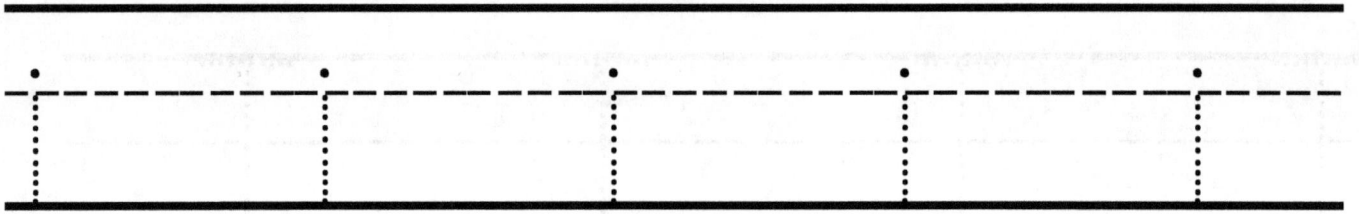

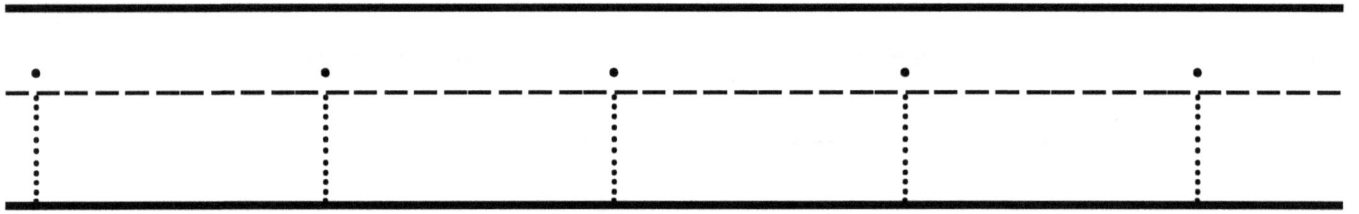

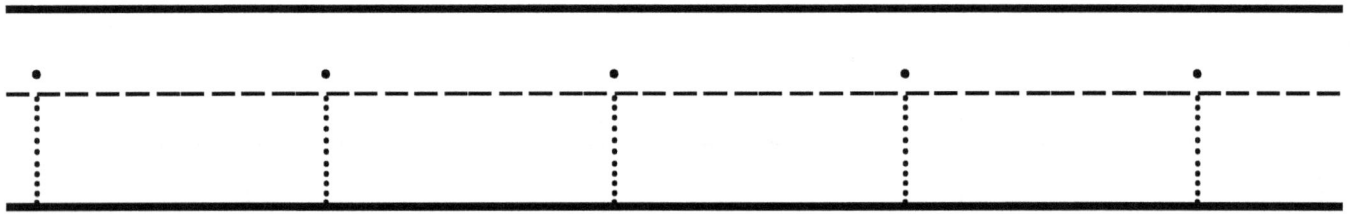

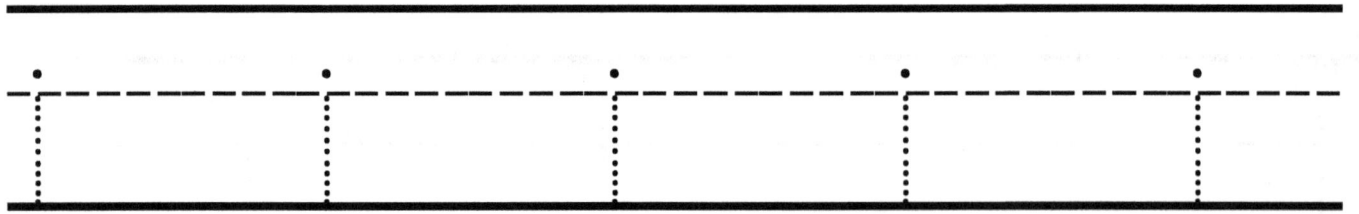

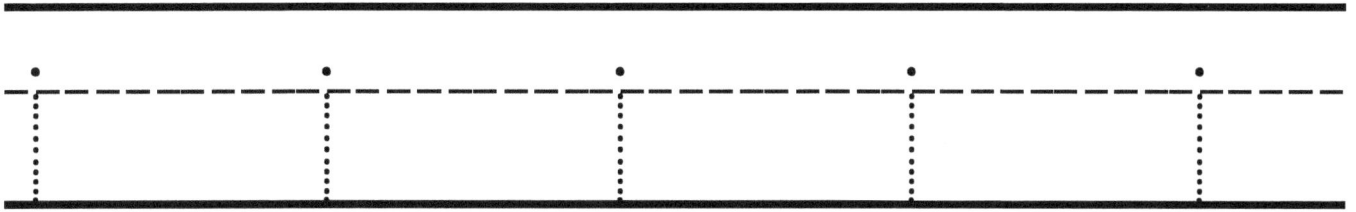

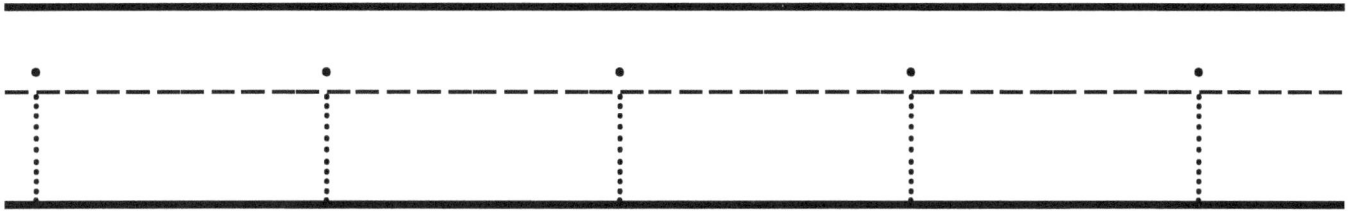

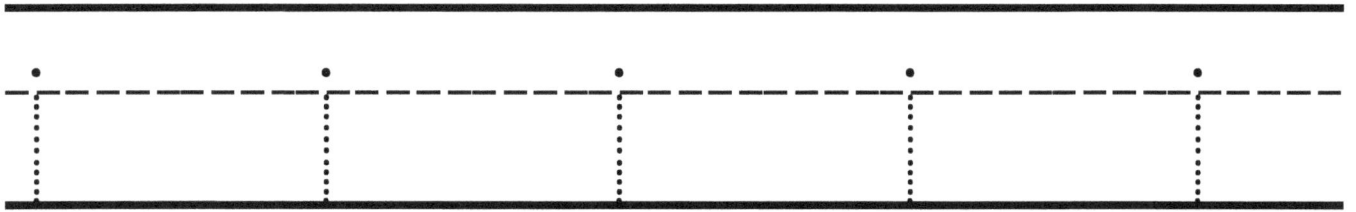

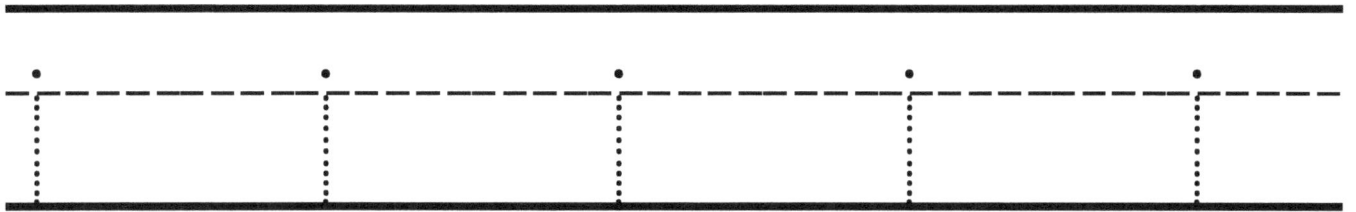

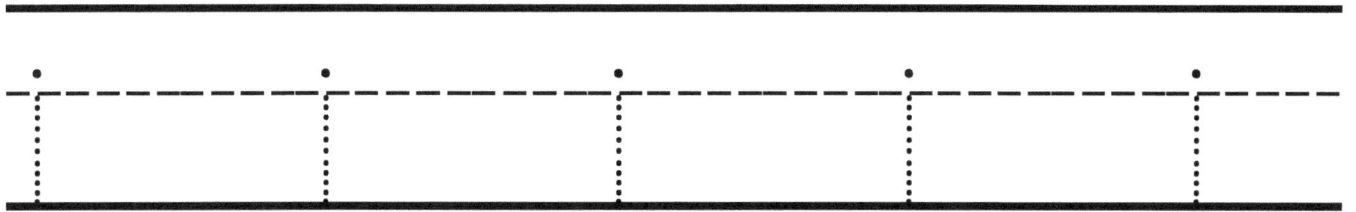

J for Jalapeno

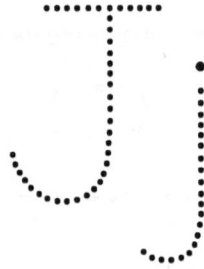

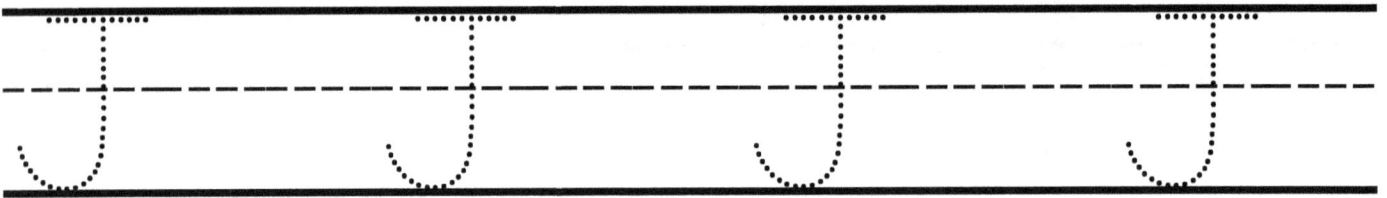

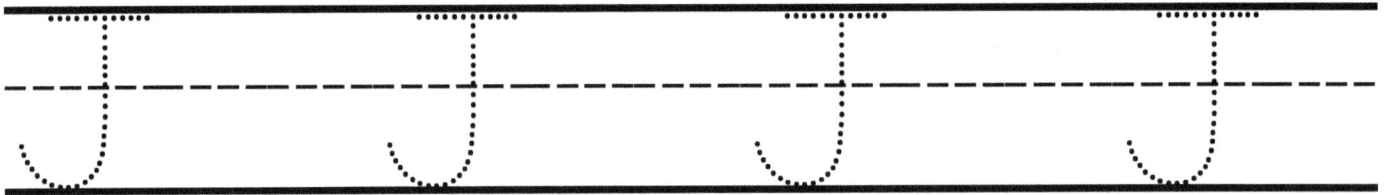

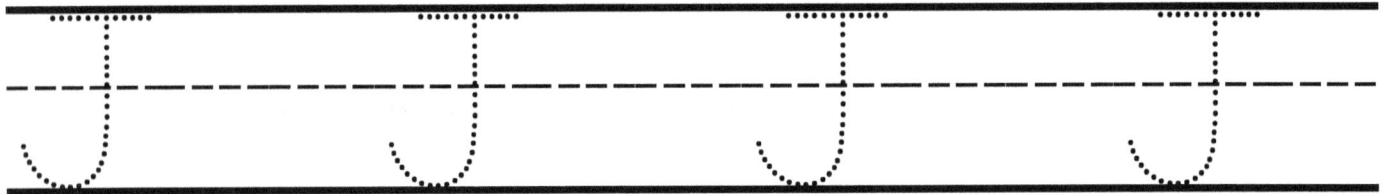

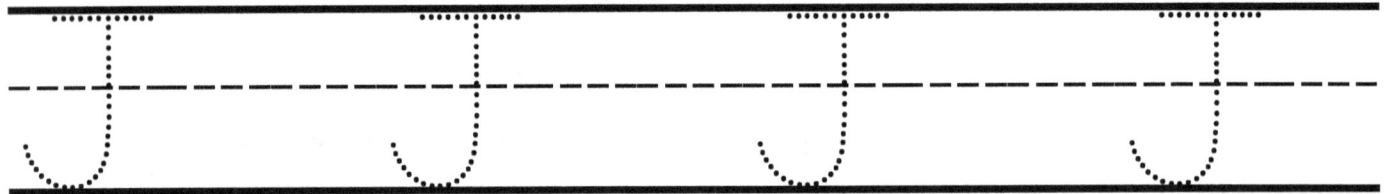

J

jalapeno

J j

J J J J

J J J J

J J J J

J J J J

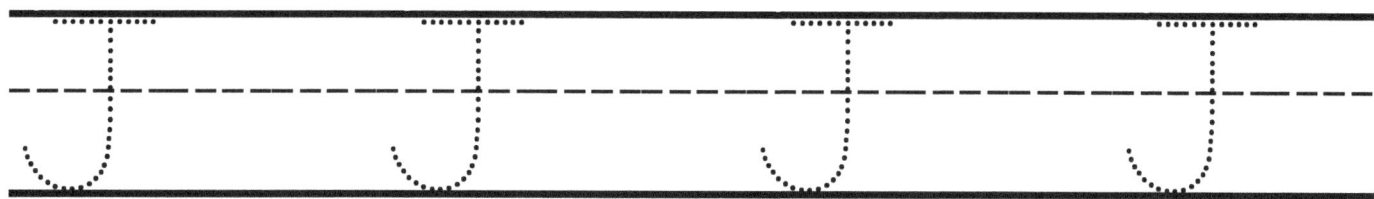

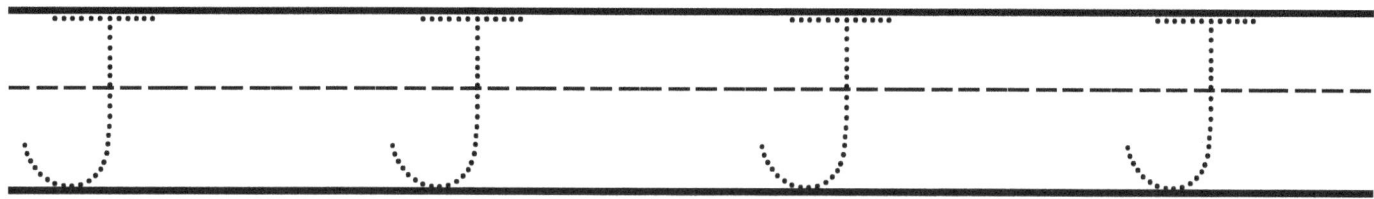

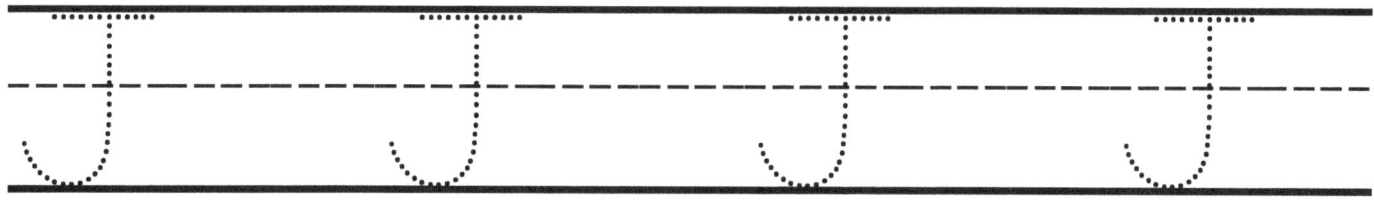

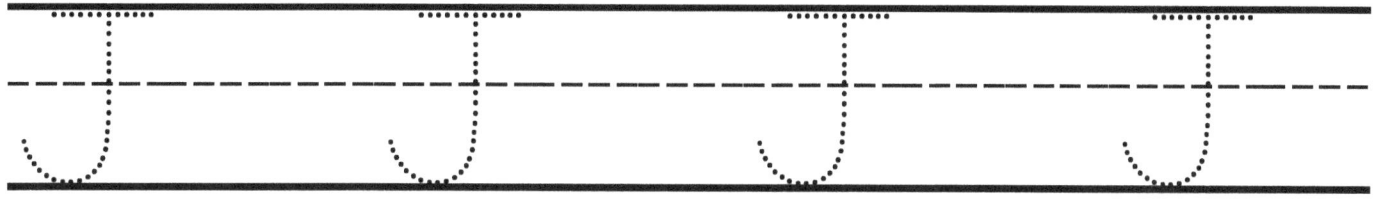

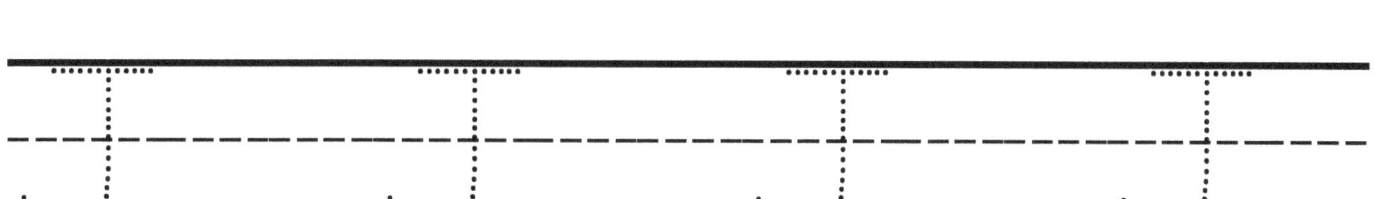

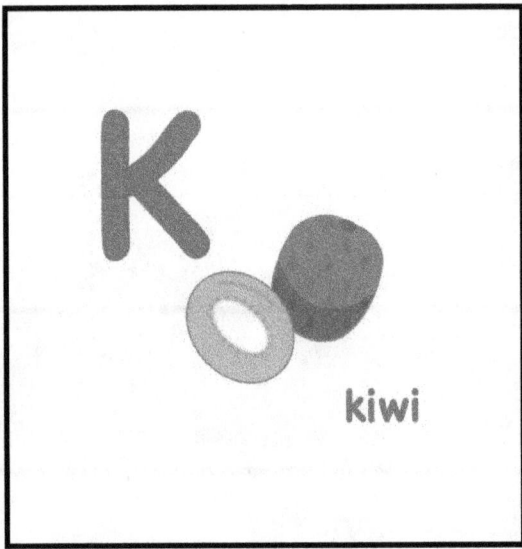

kiwi

K for Kiwi

Kk

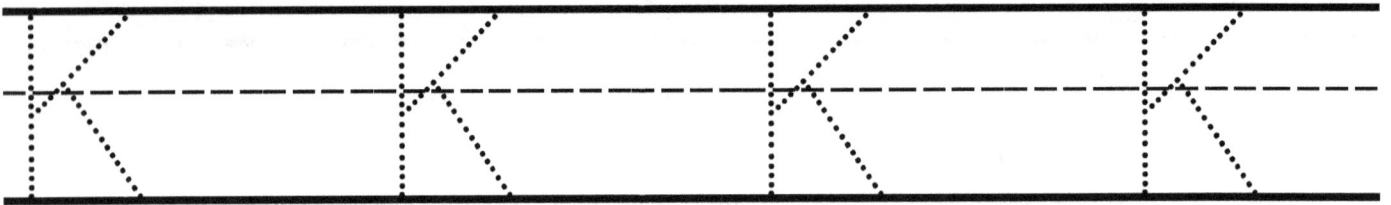

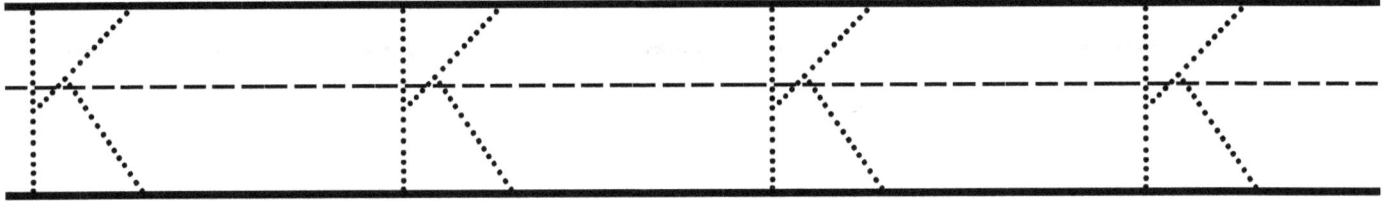

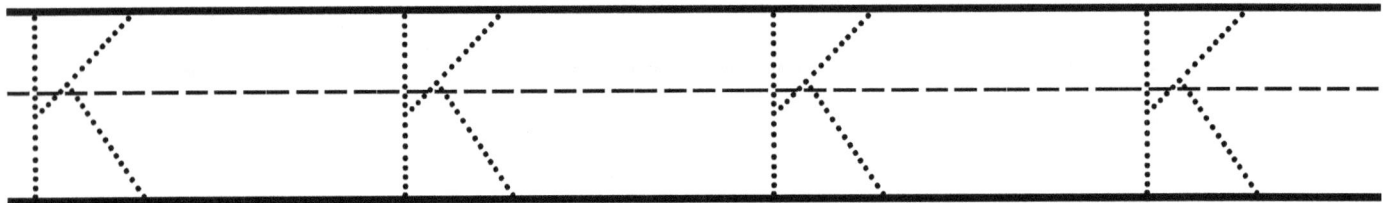

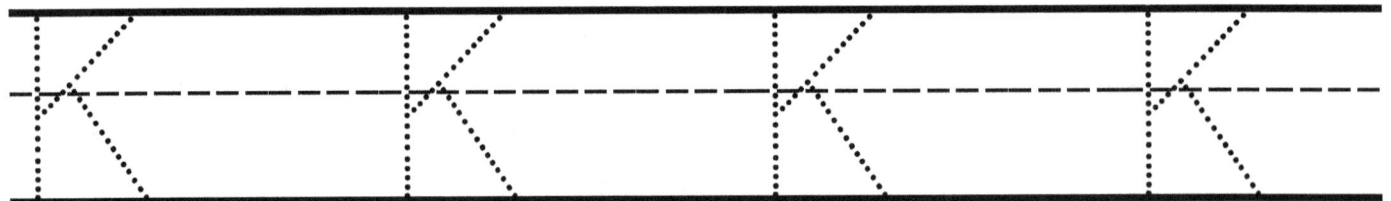

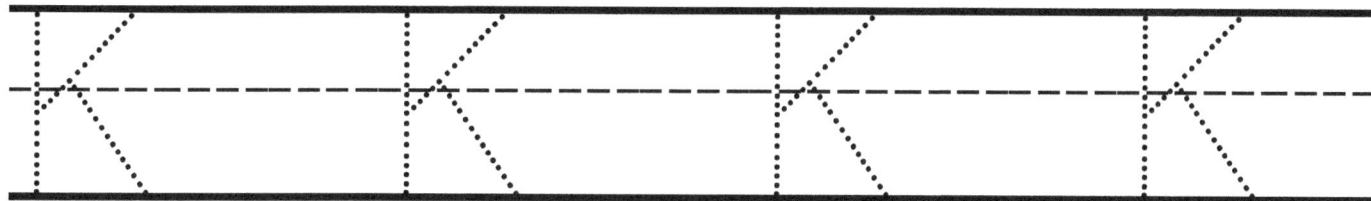

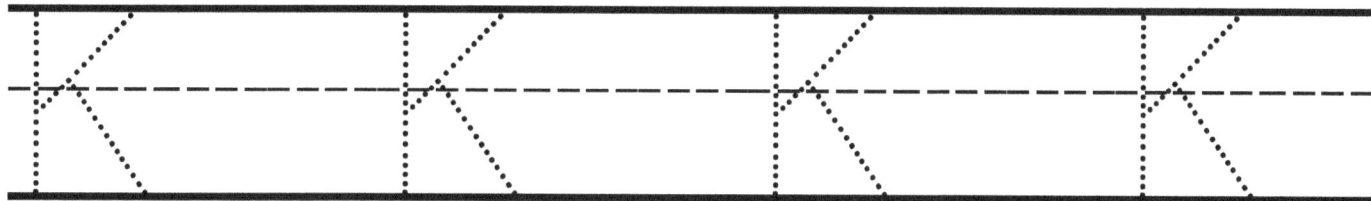

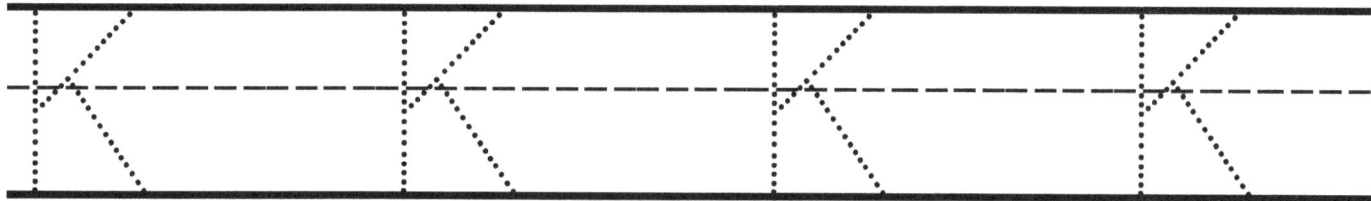

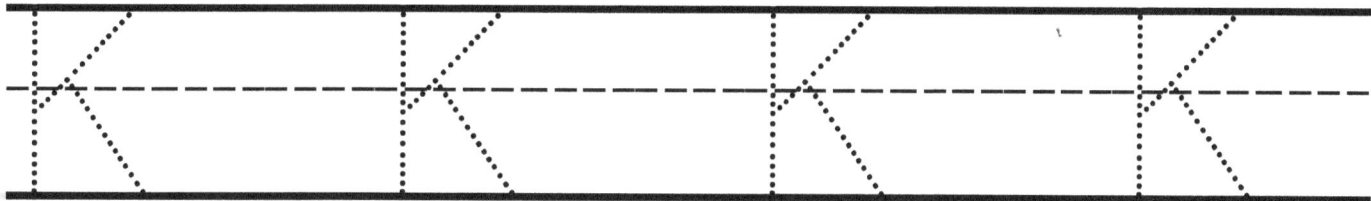

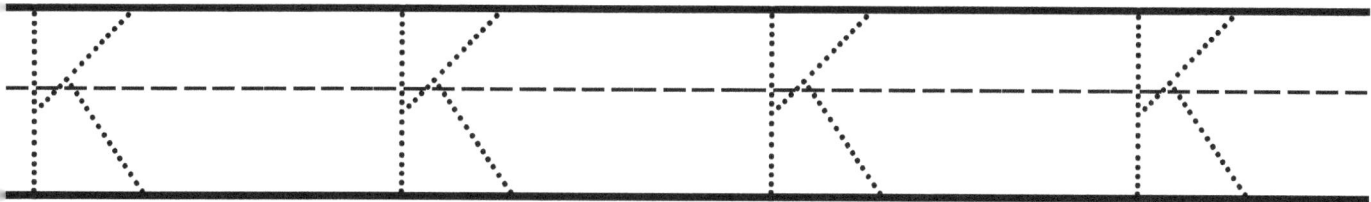

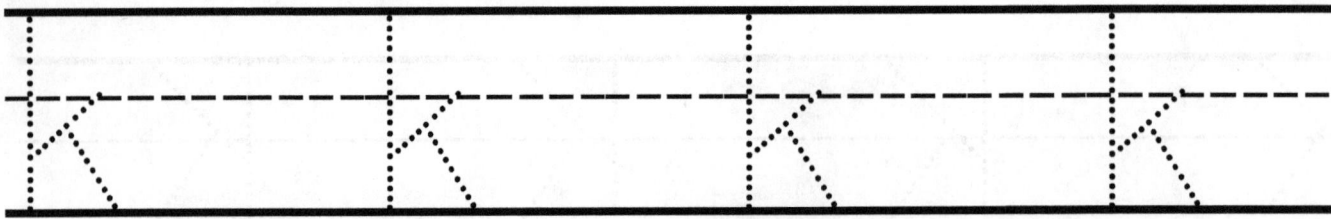

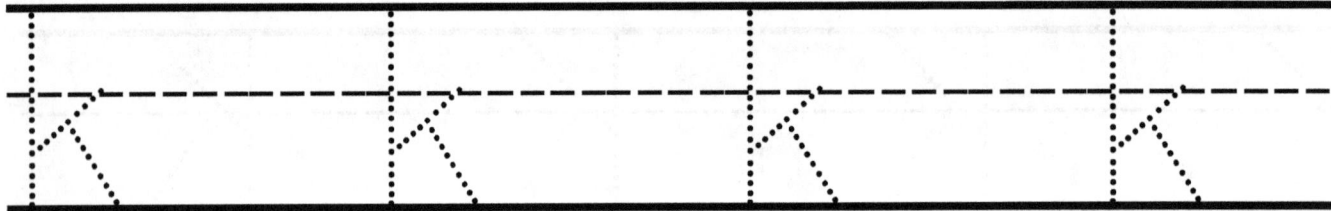

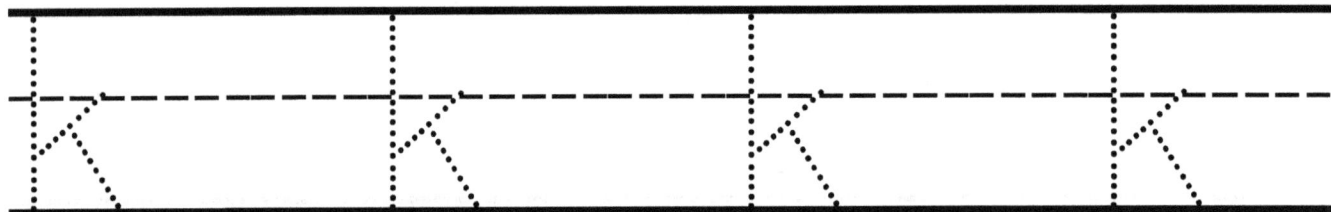

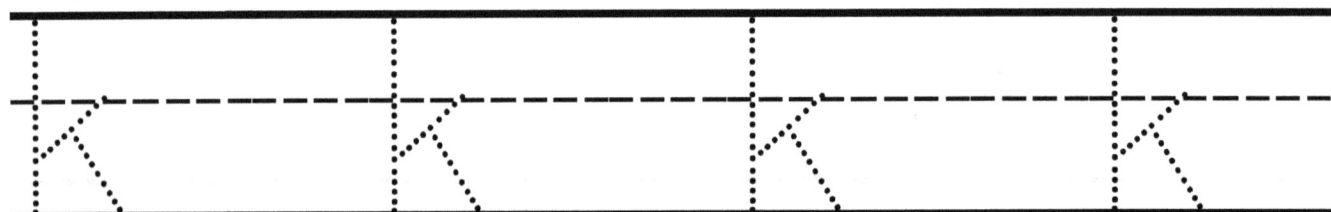

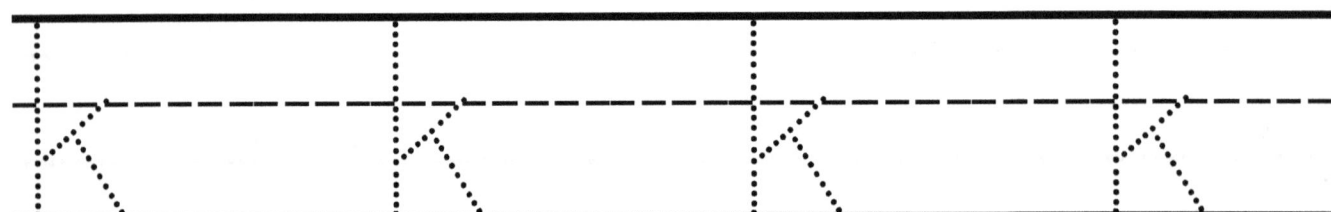

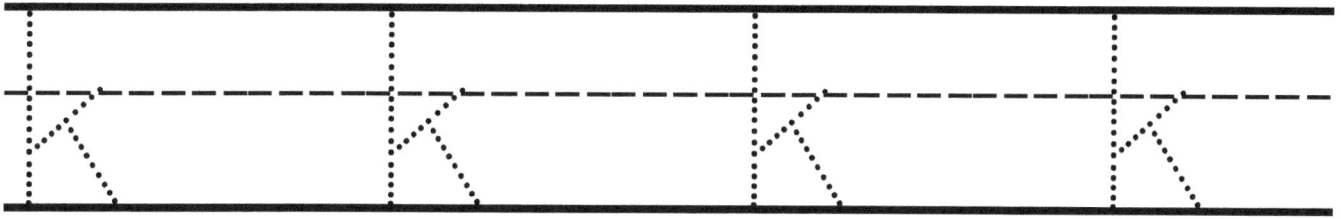

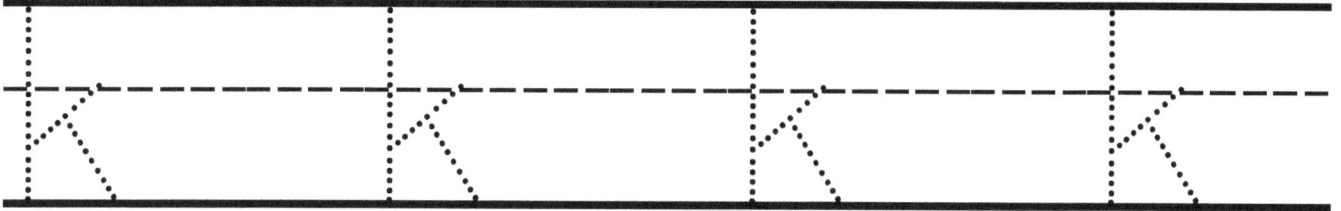

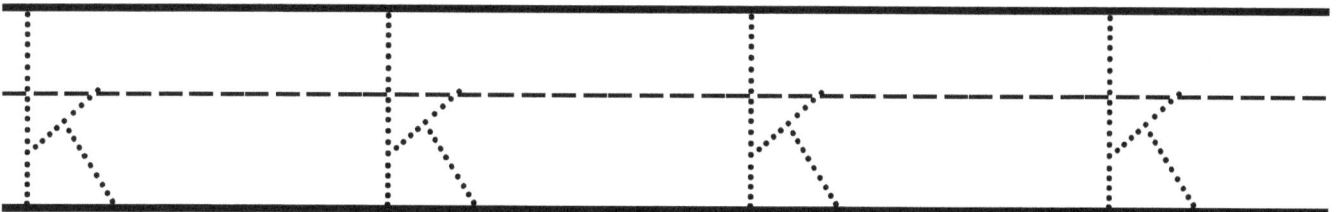

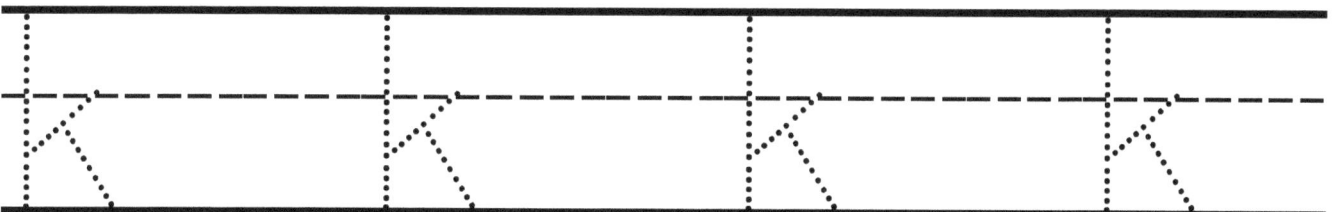

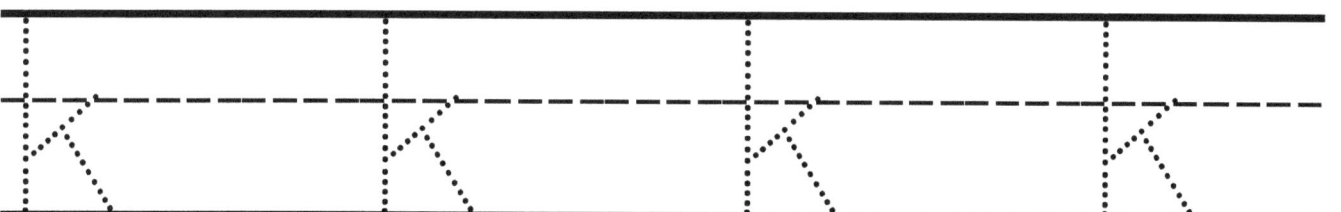

lemon

L for lemon

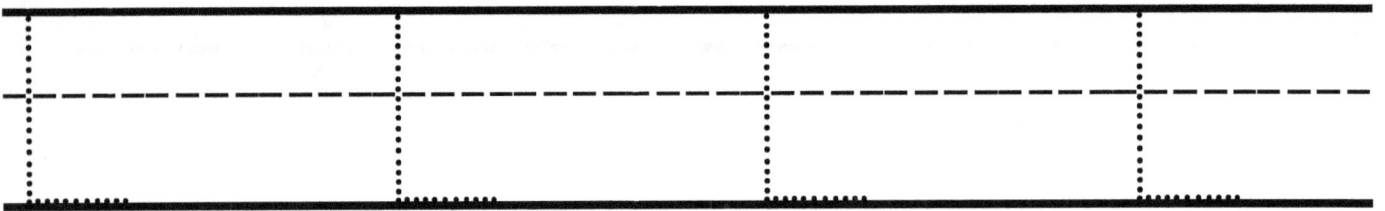

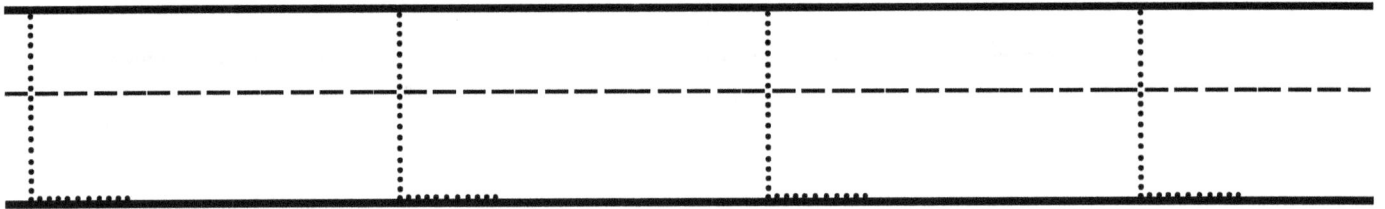

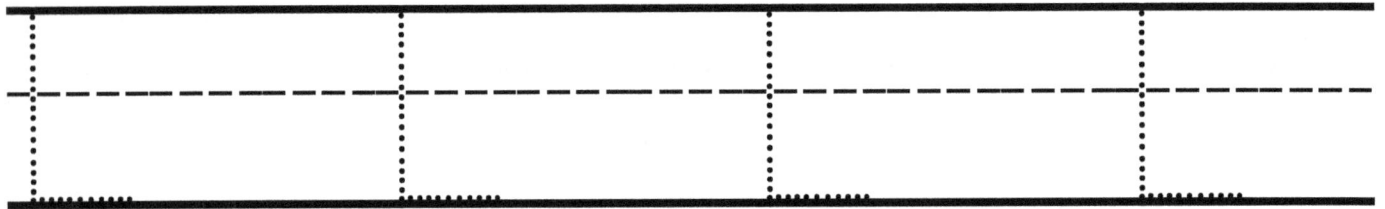

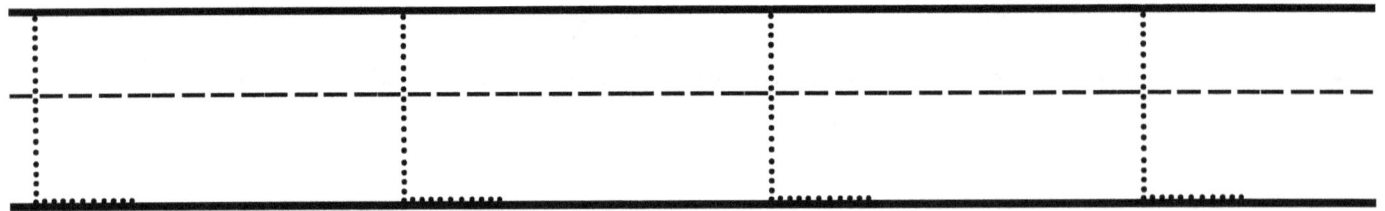

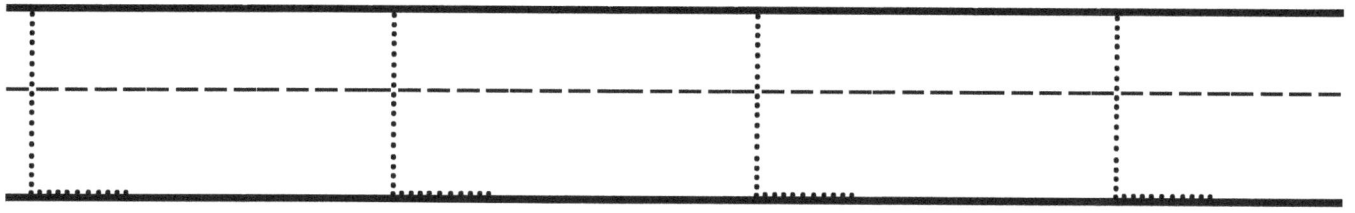

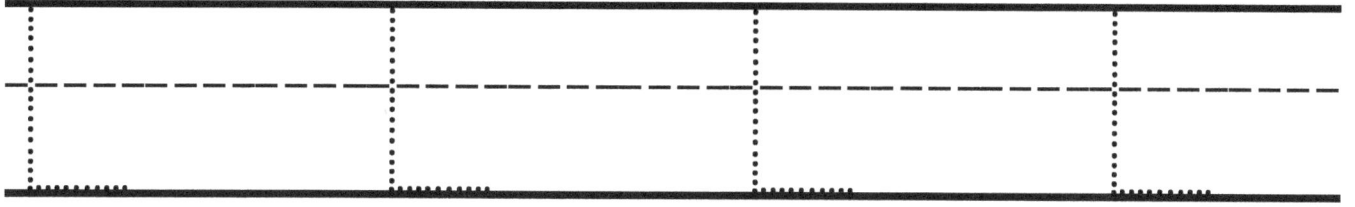

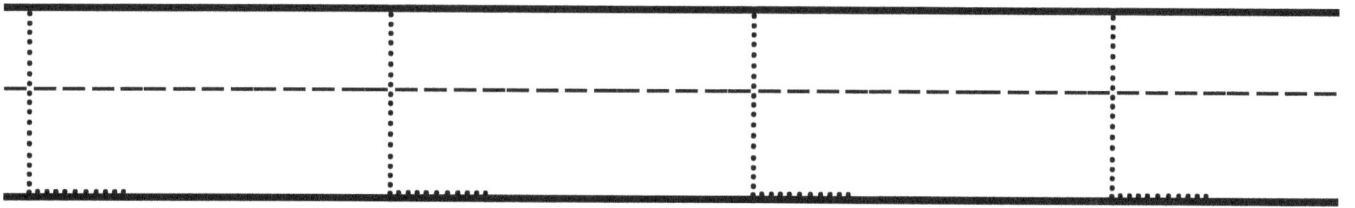

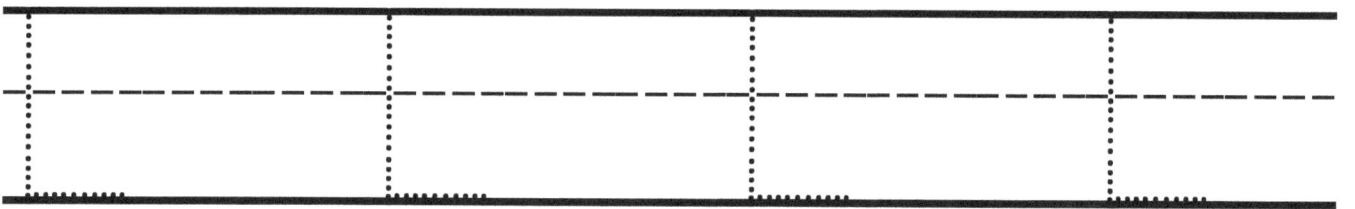

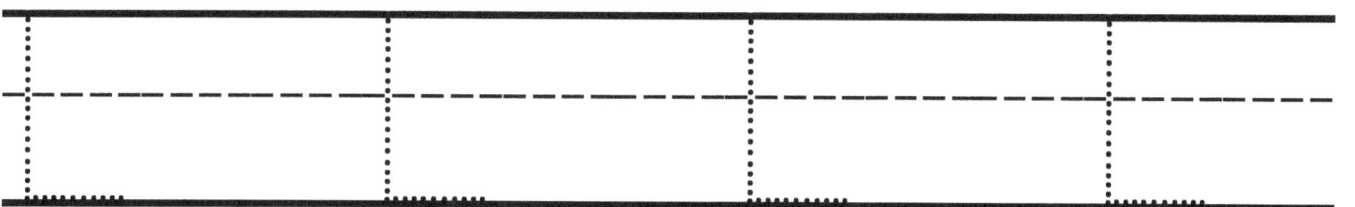

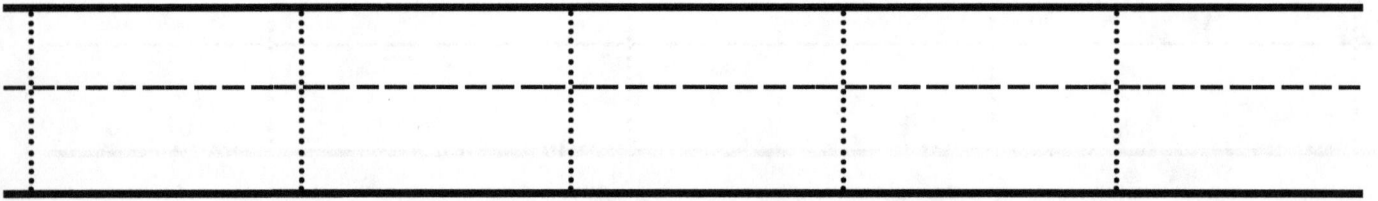

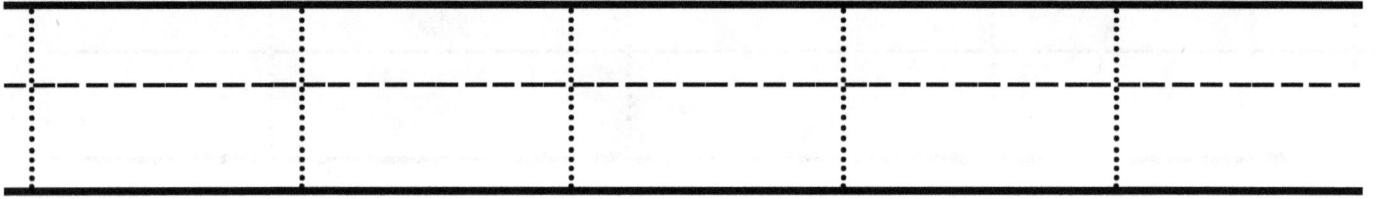

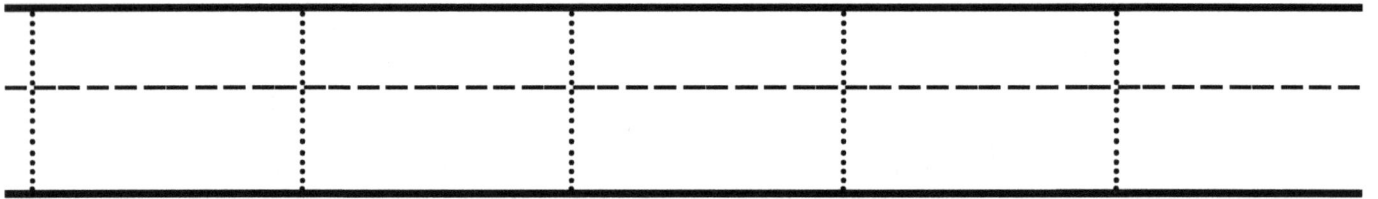

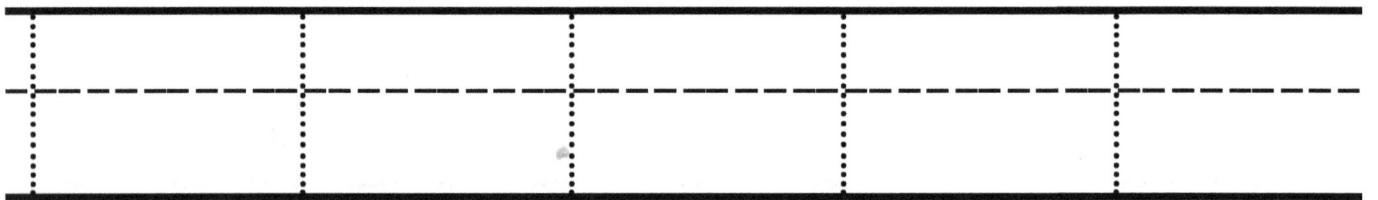

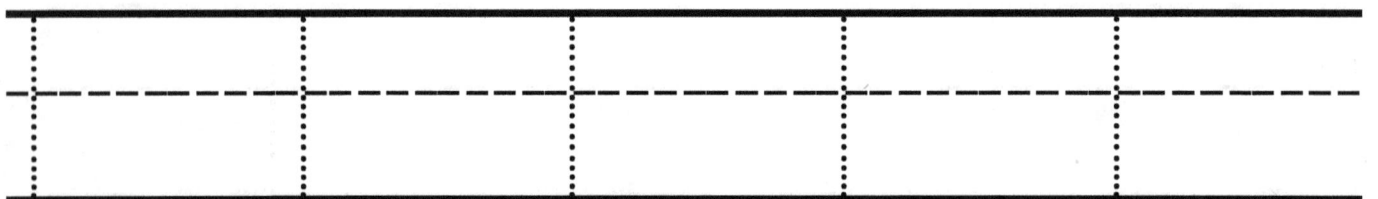

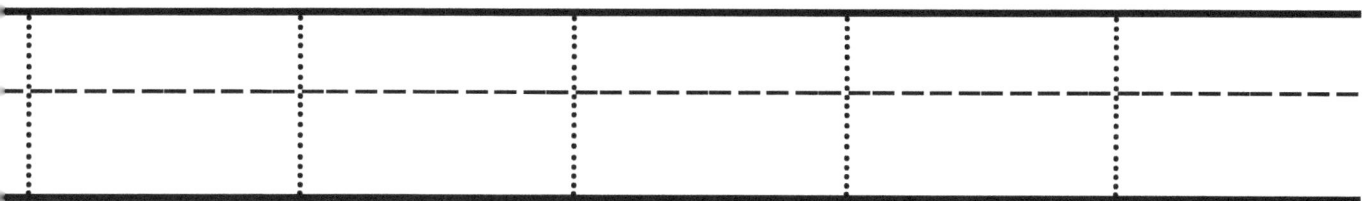

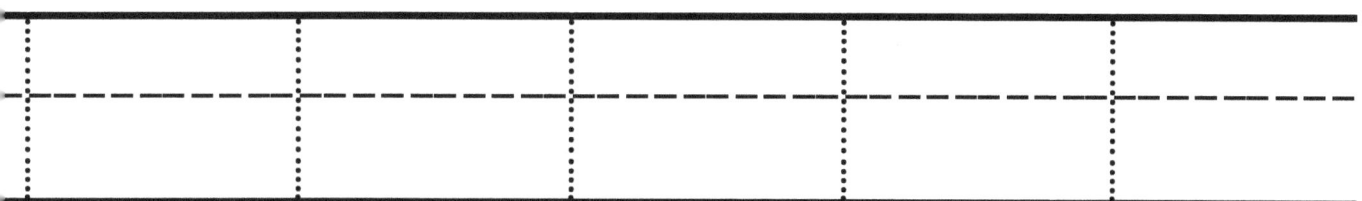

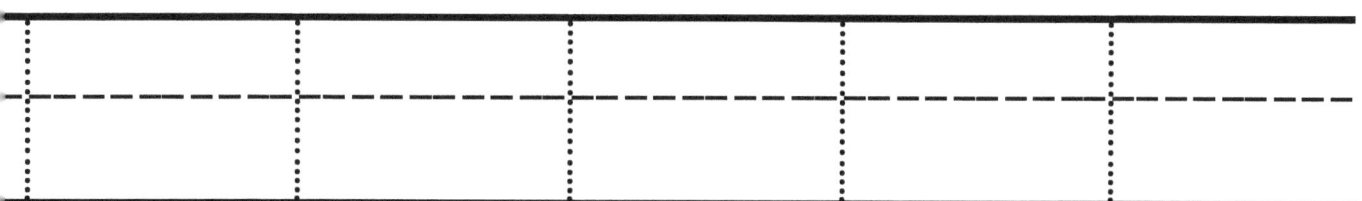

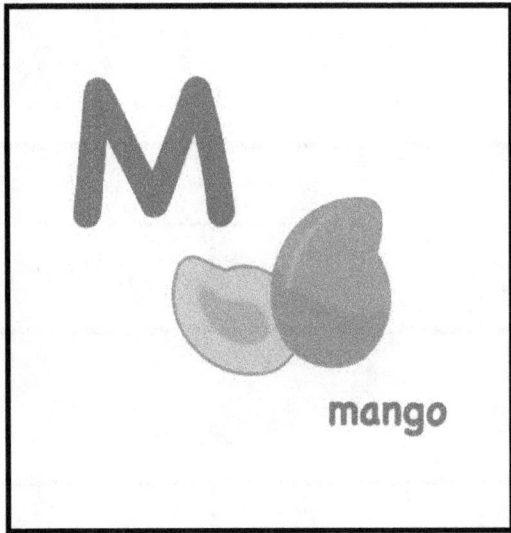

mango

M for Mango

Mm

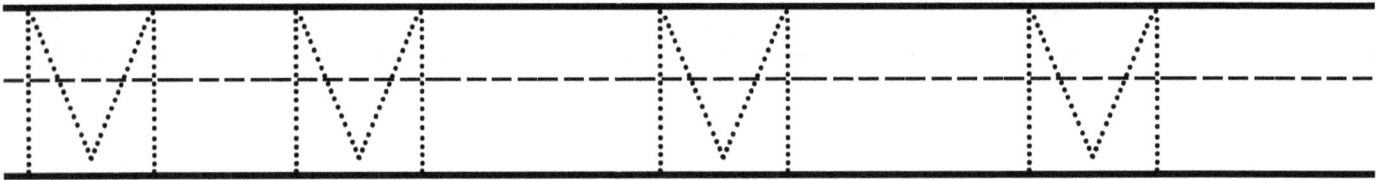

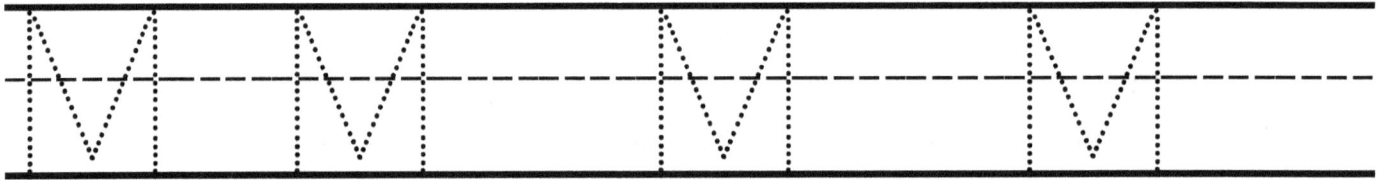

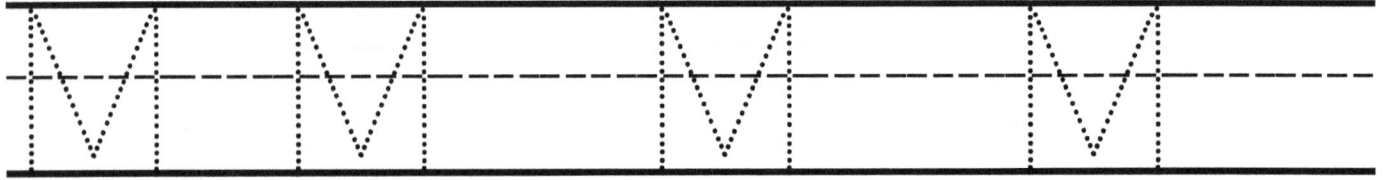

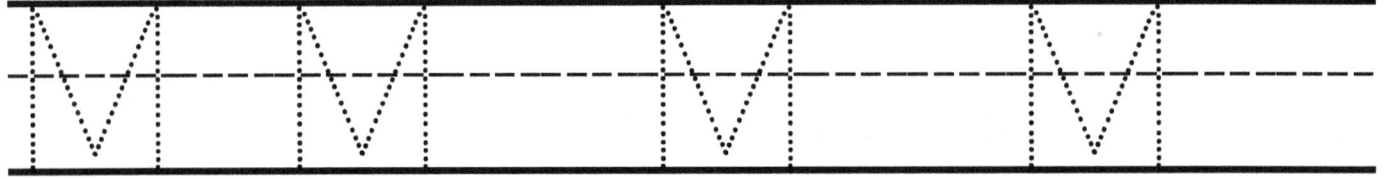

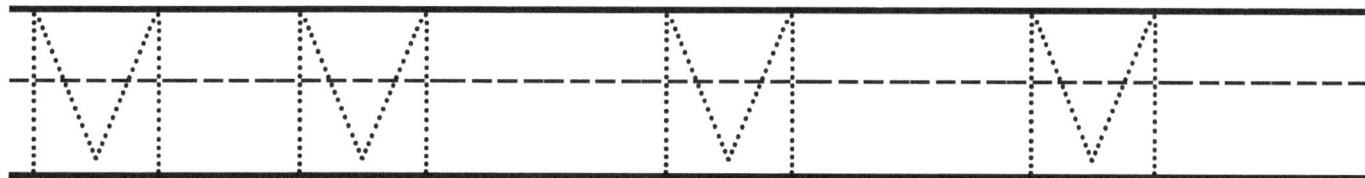

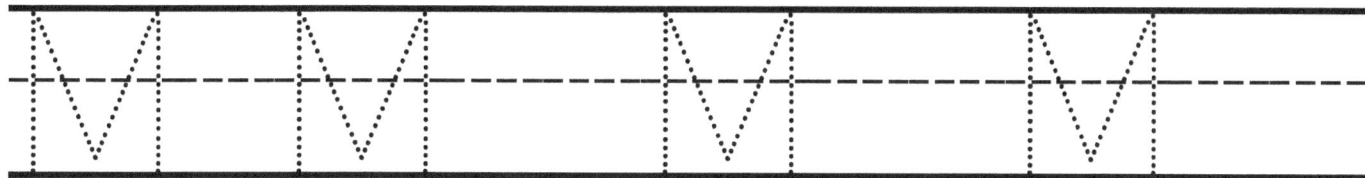

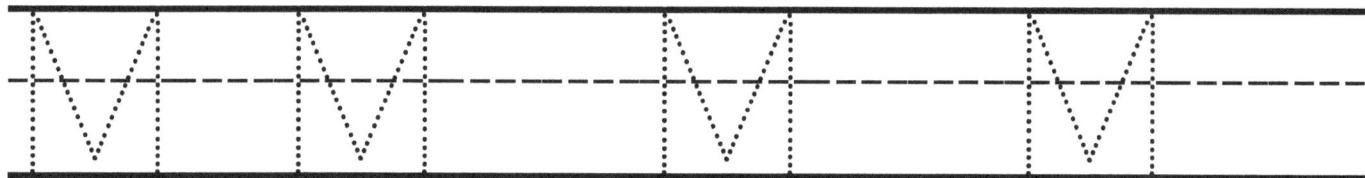

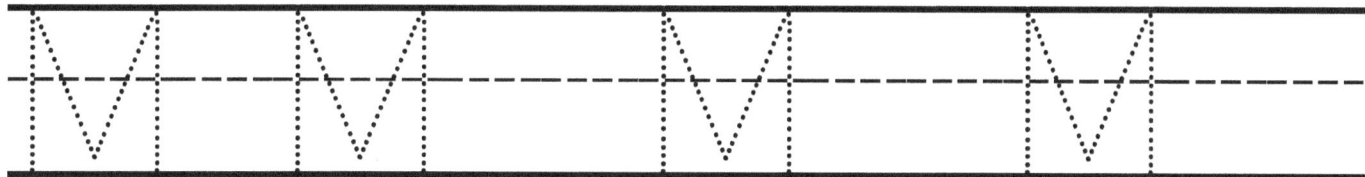

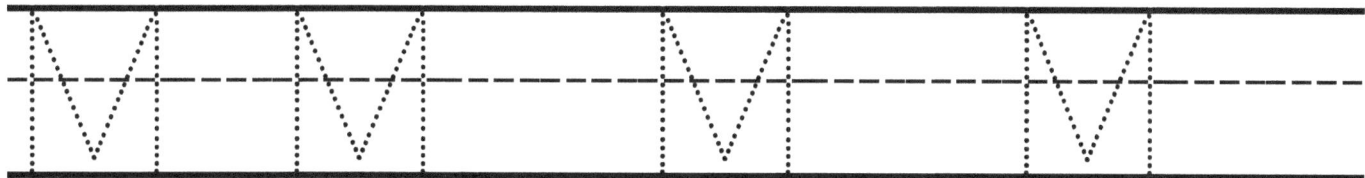

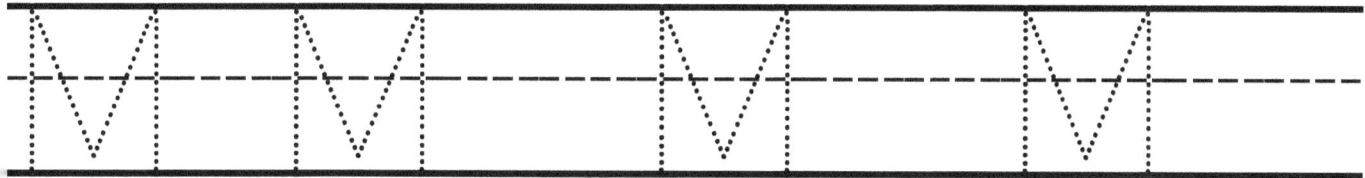

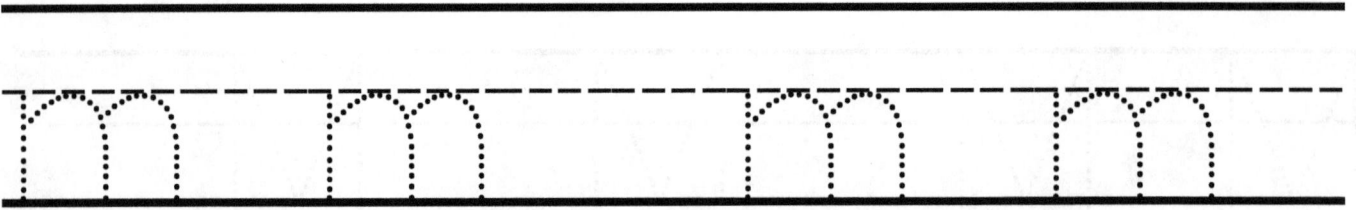

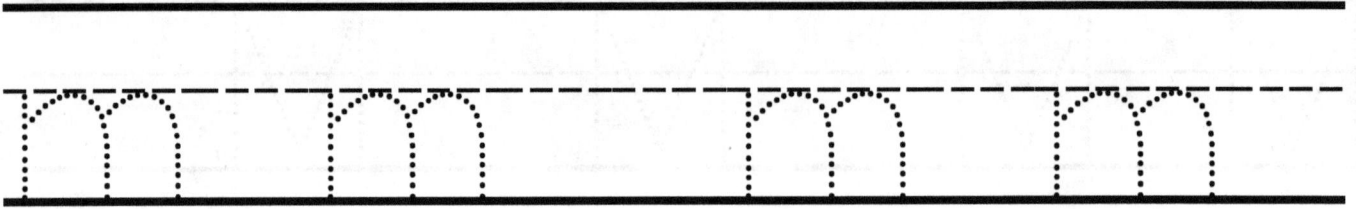

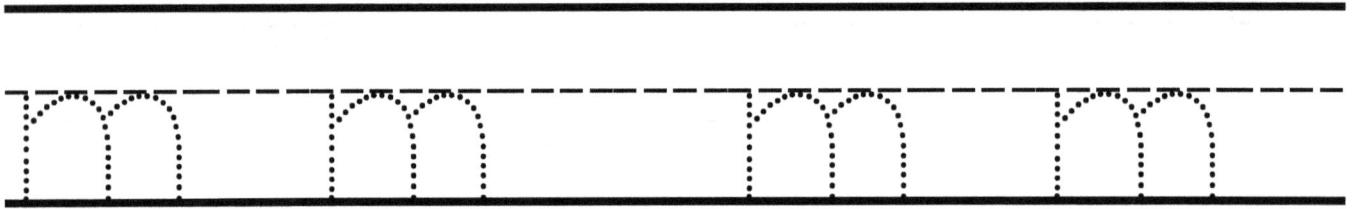

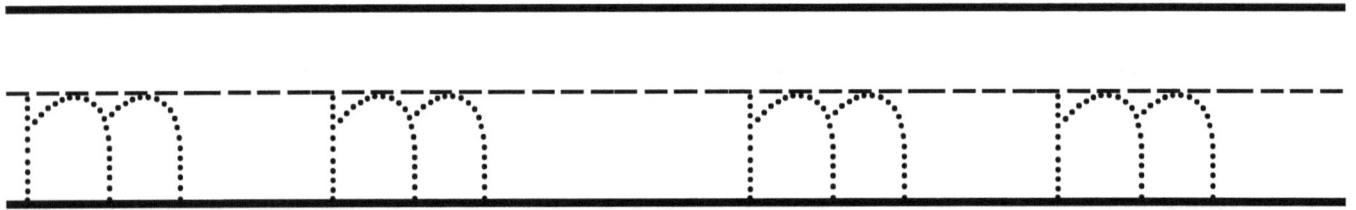

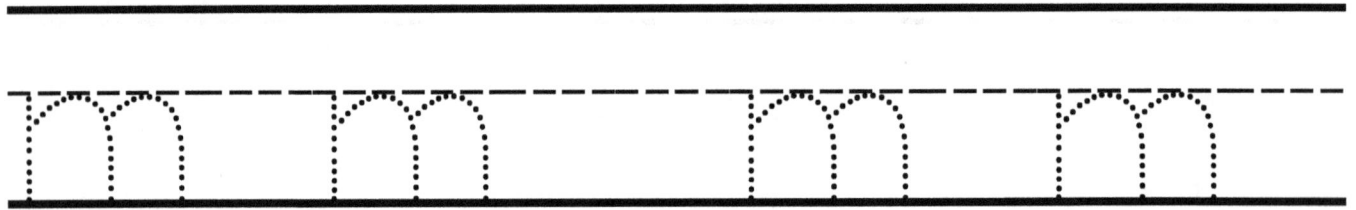

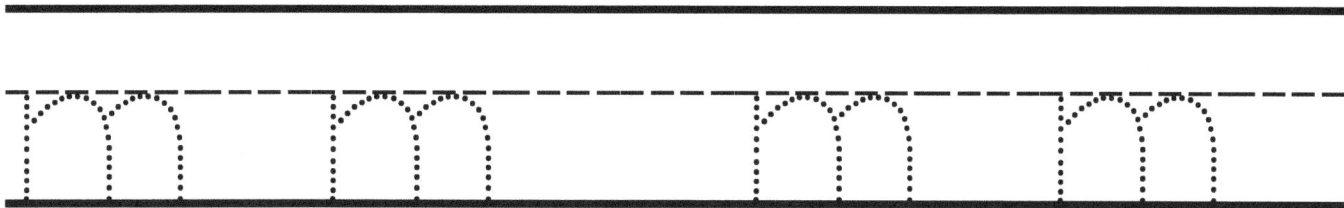

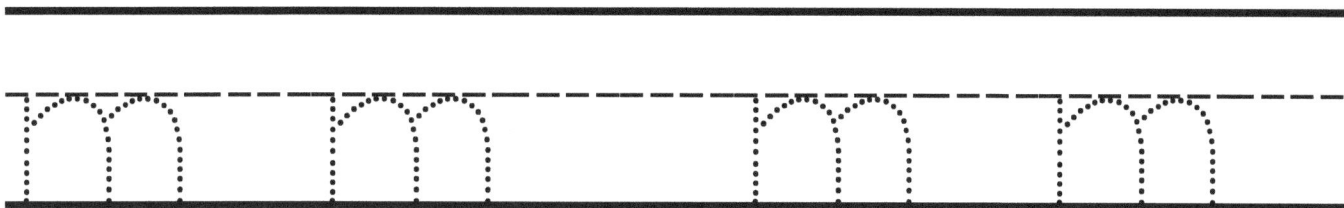

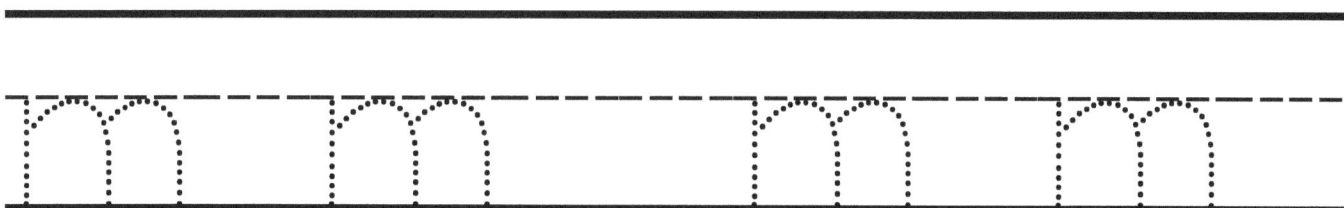

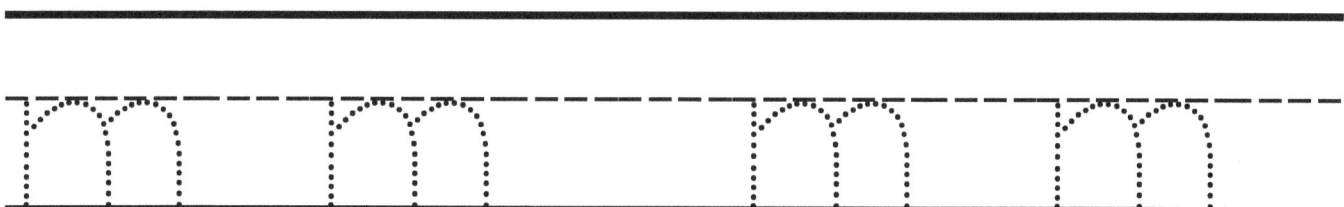

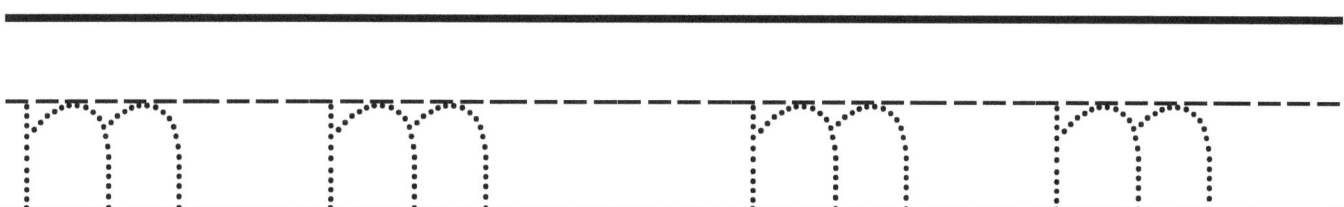

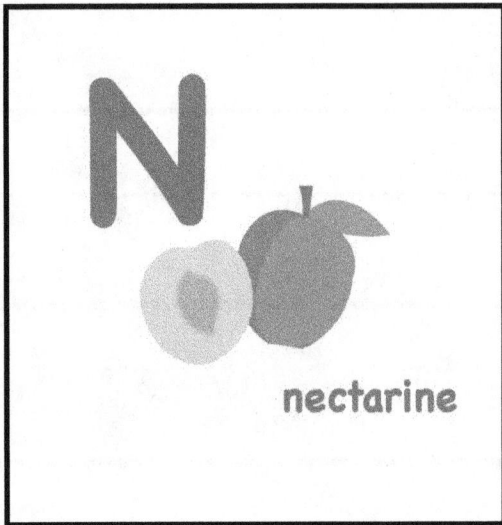

nectarine

N for
Nectarine

Nn

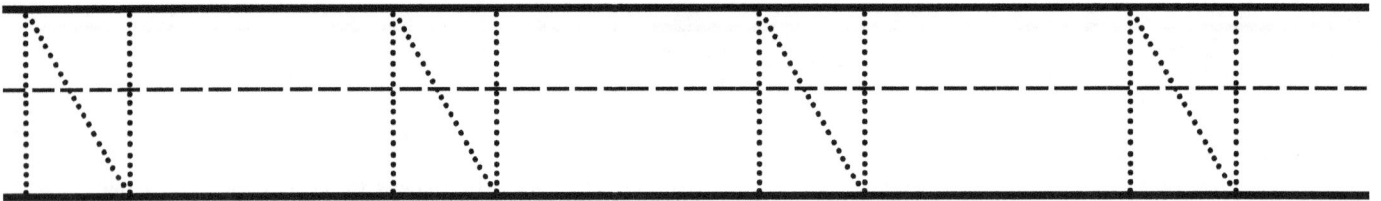

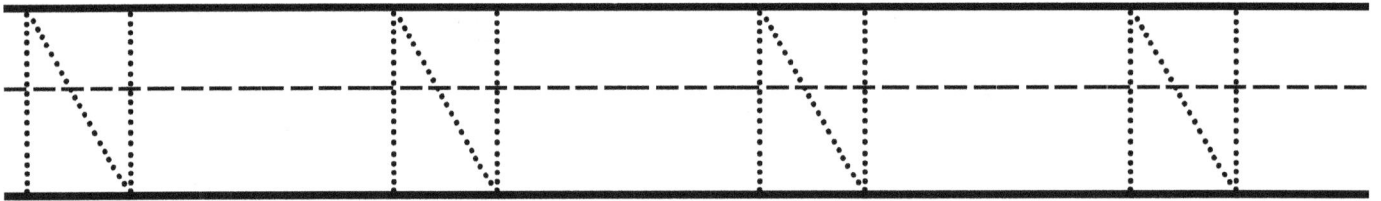

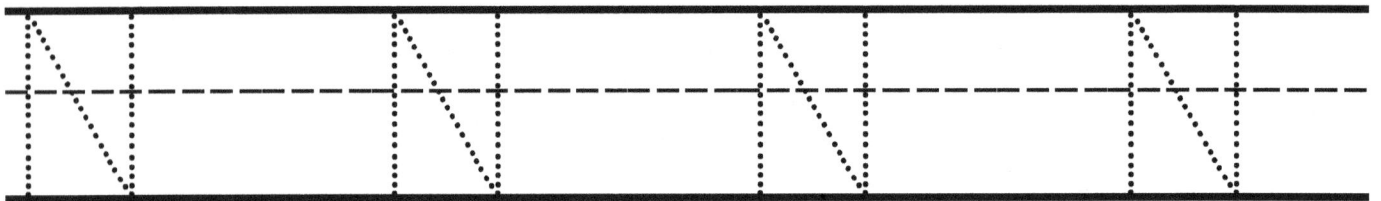

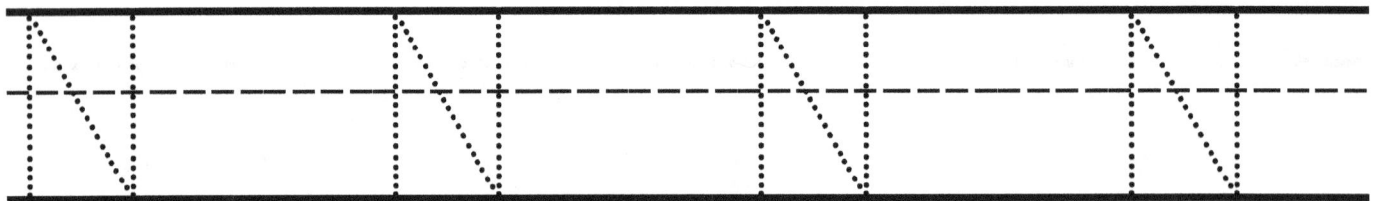

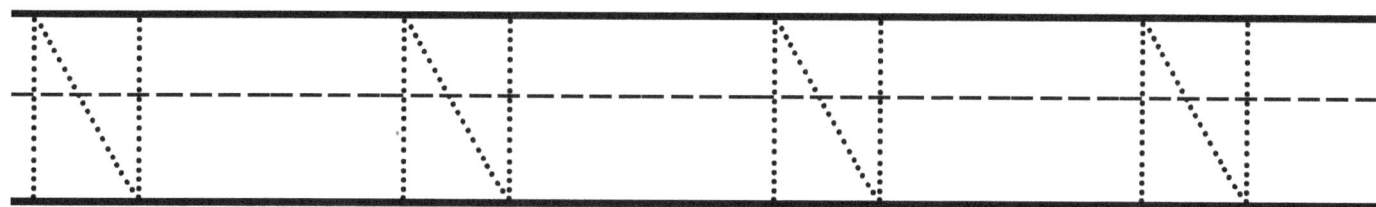

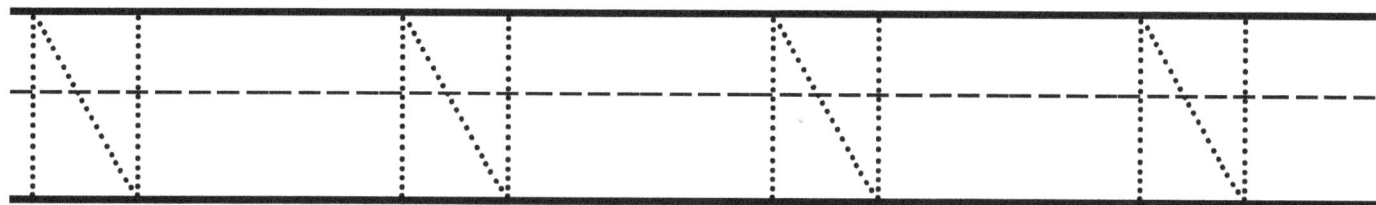

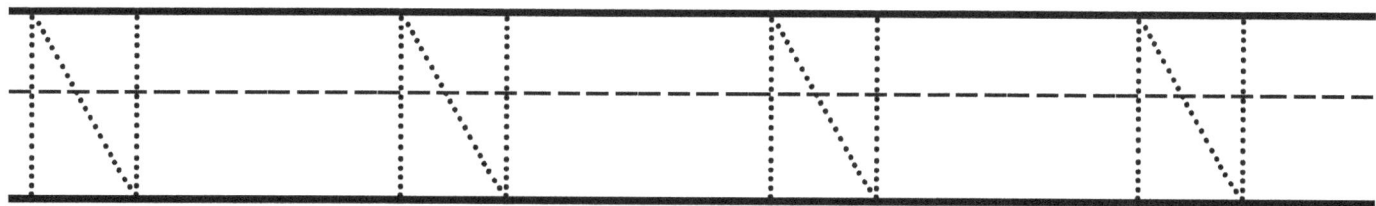

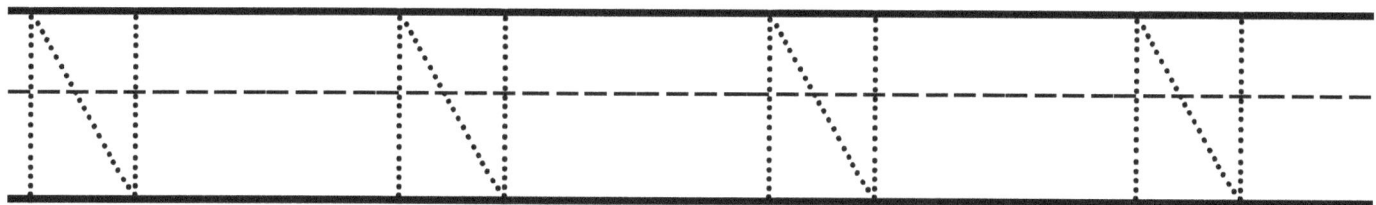

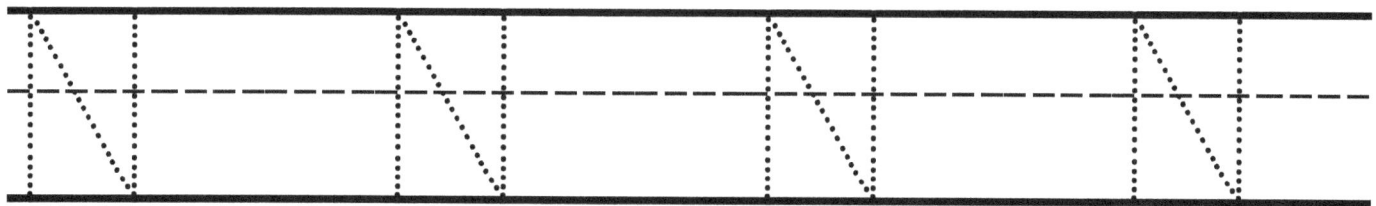

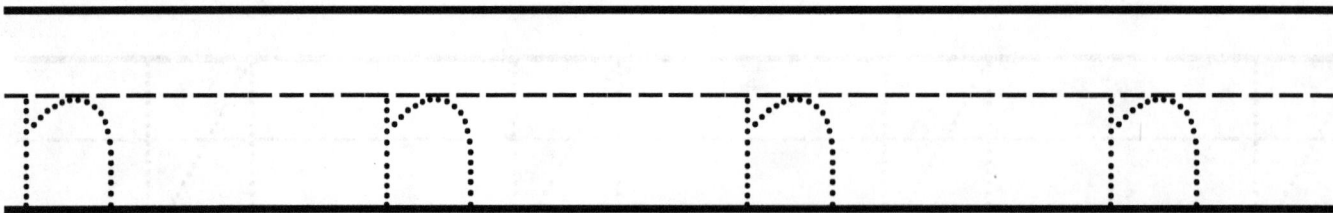

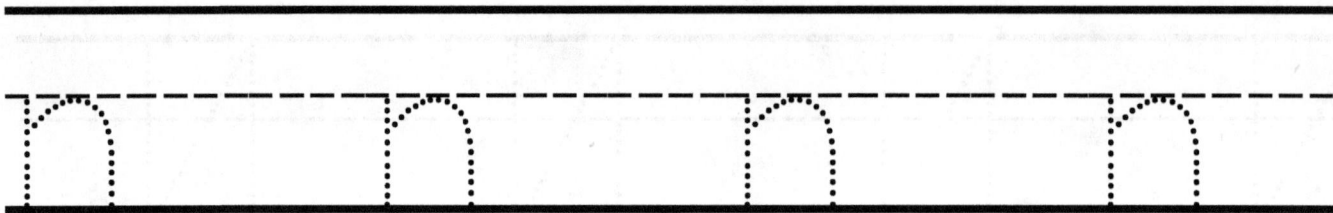

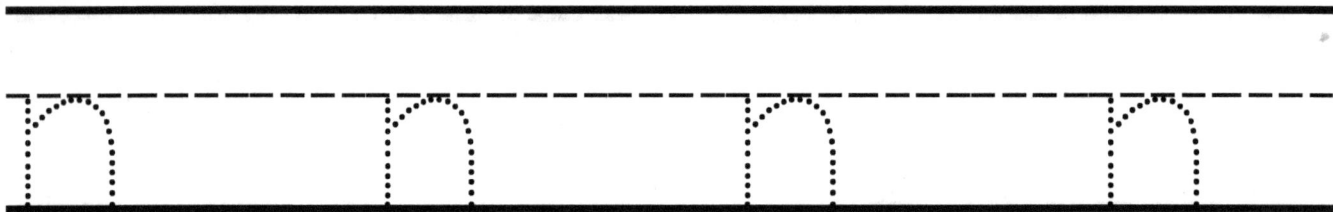

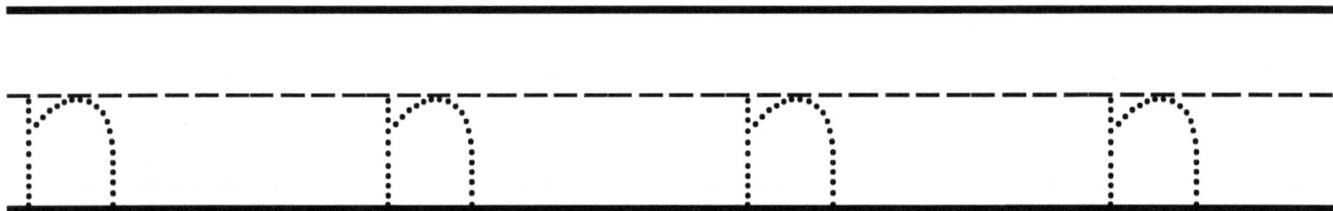

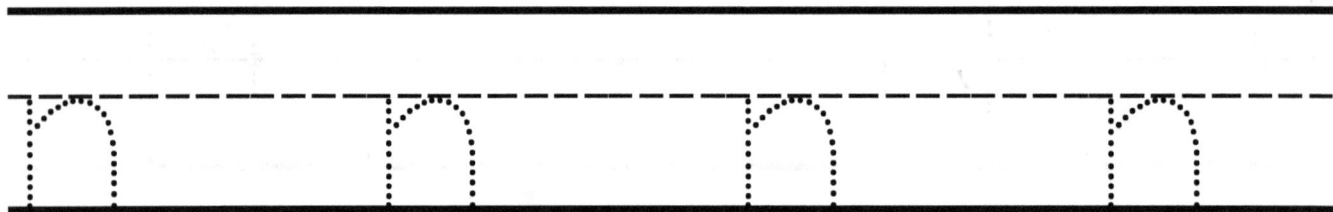

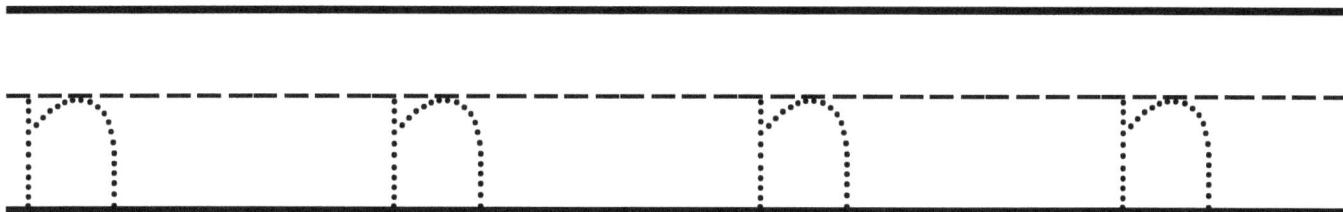

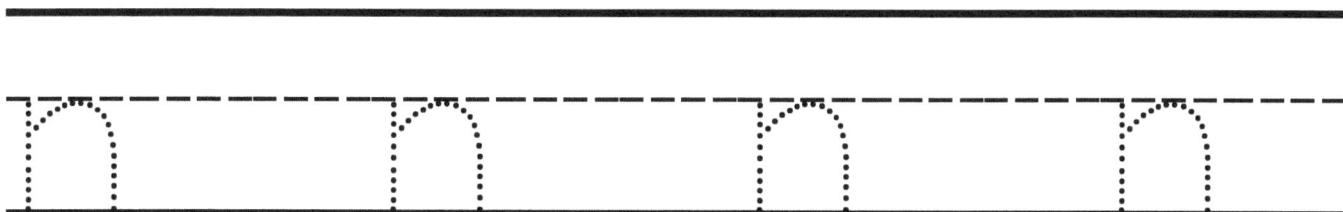

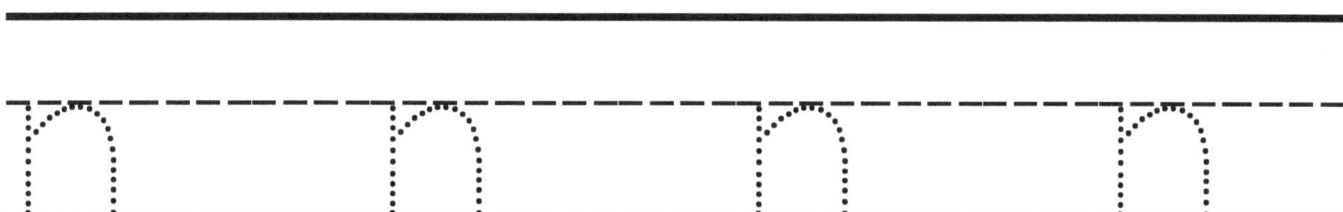

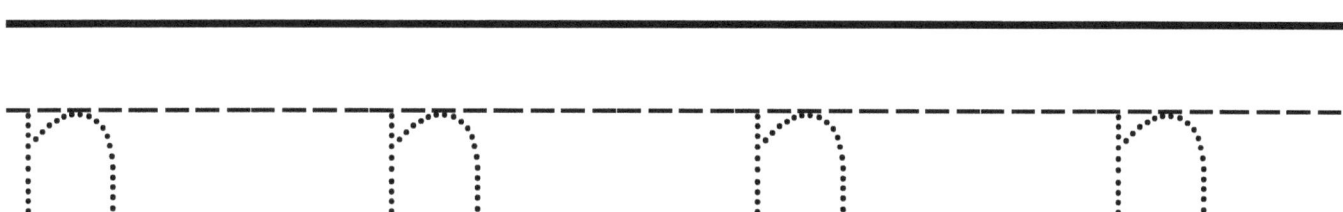

O for Olives

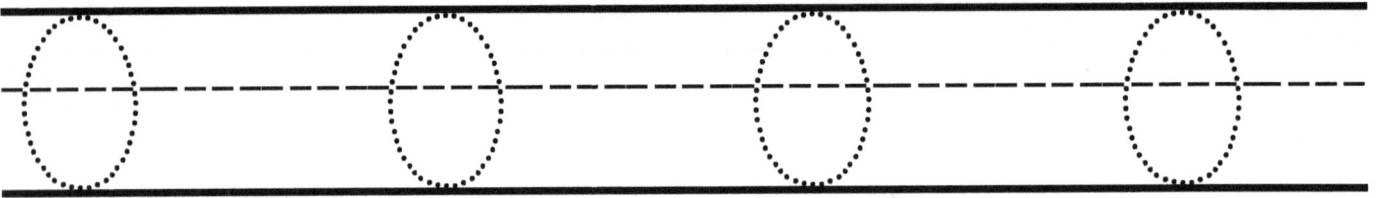

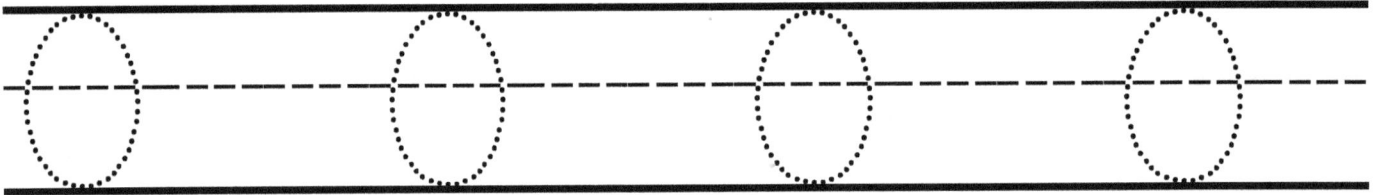

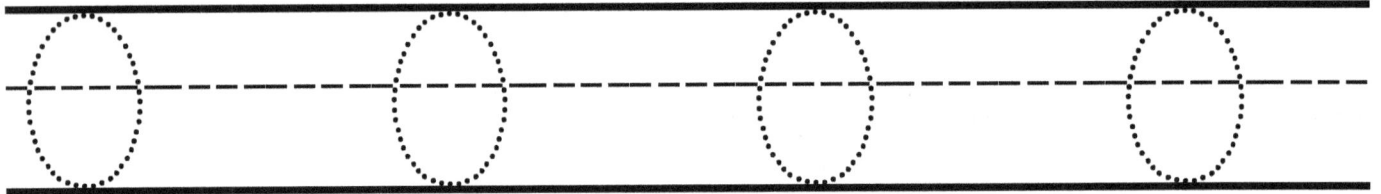

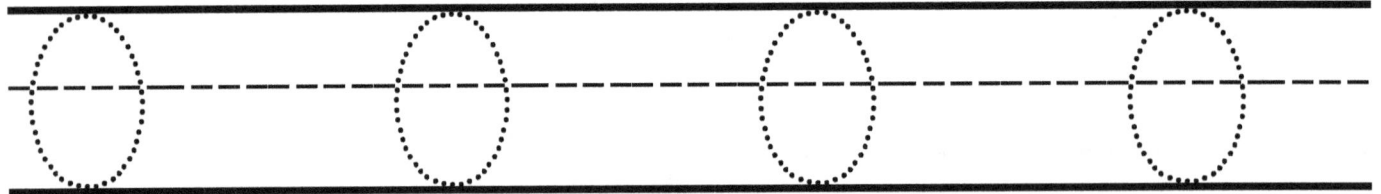

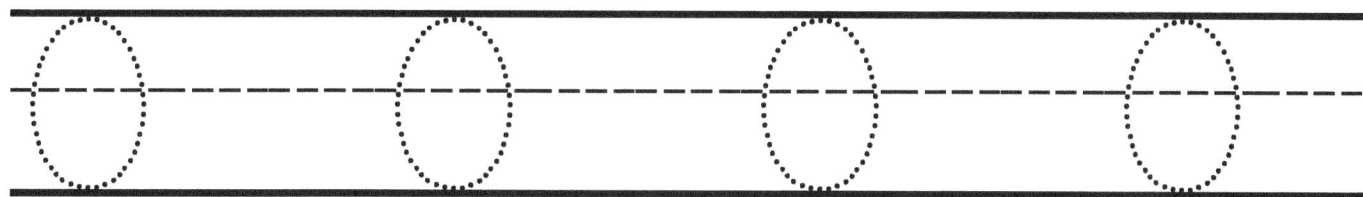

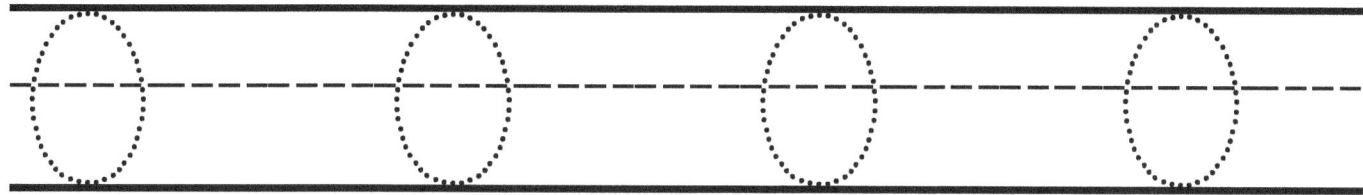

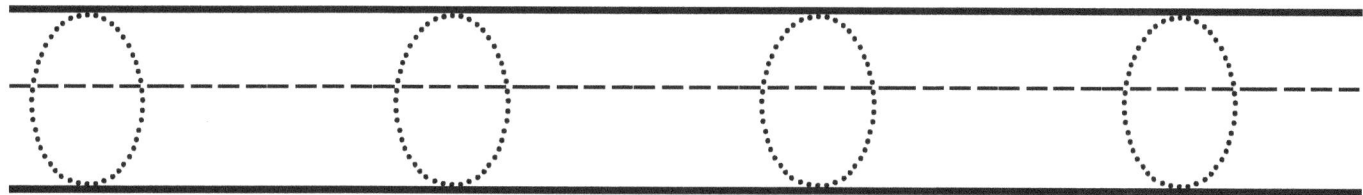

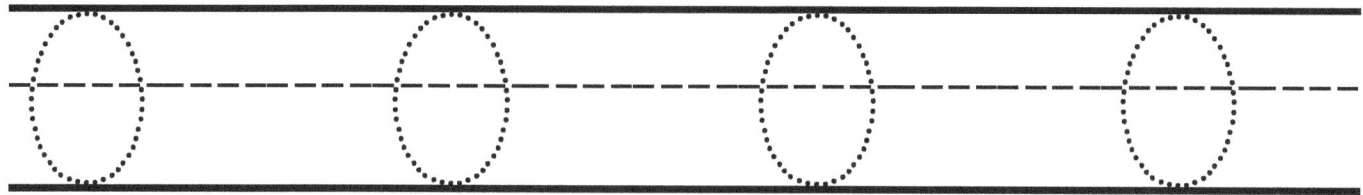

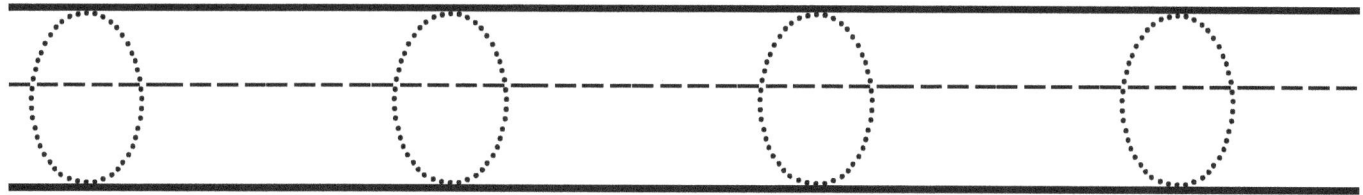

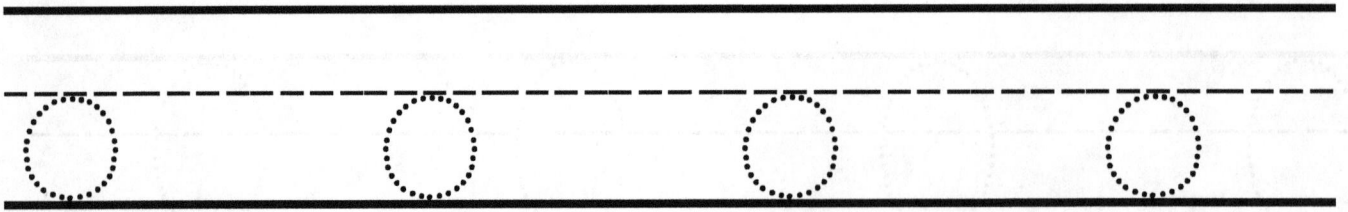

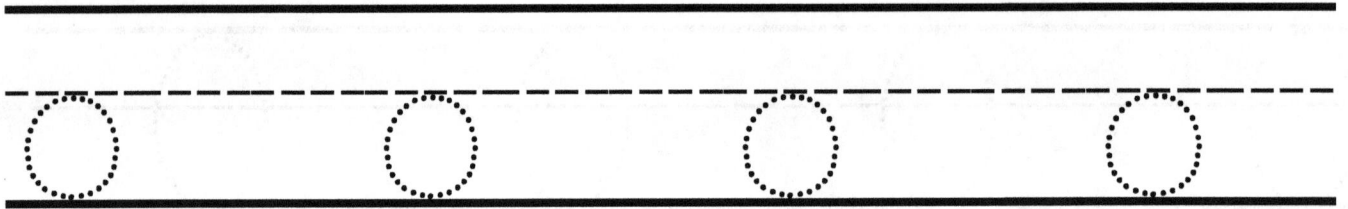

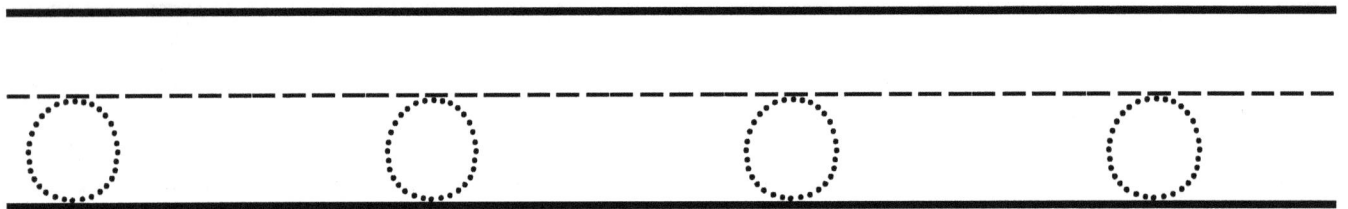

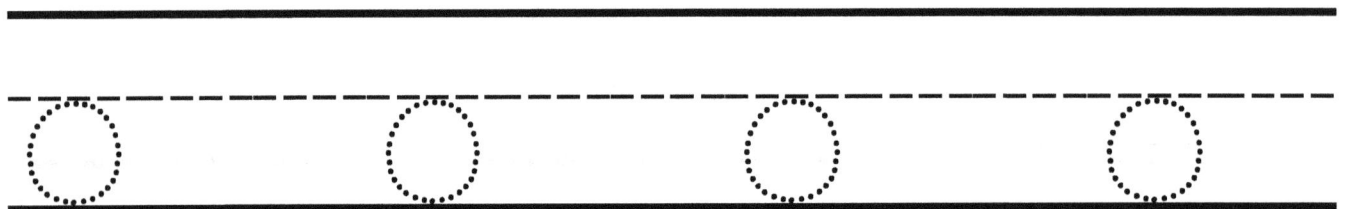

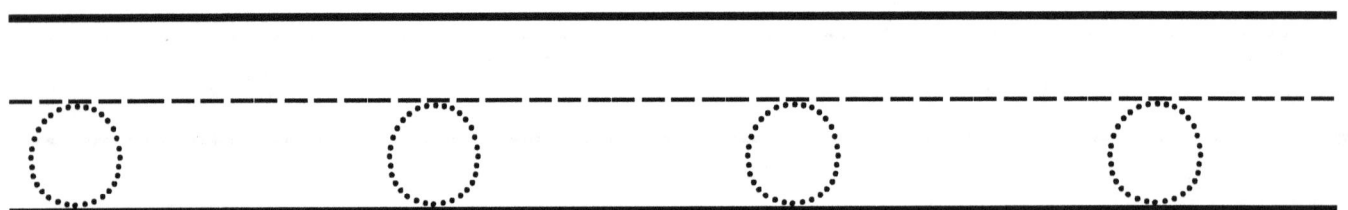

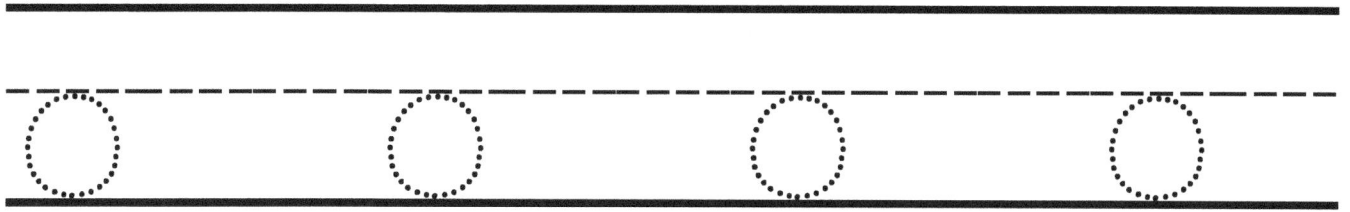

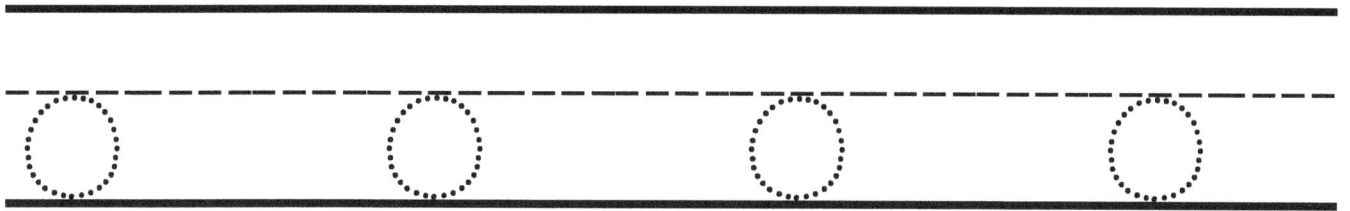

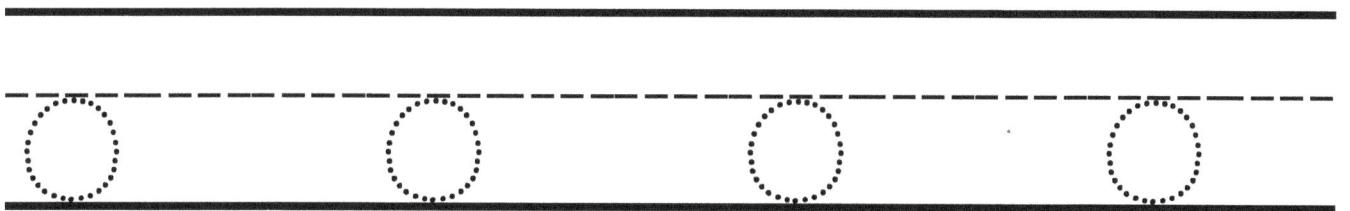

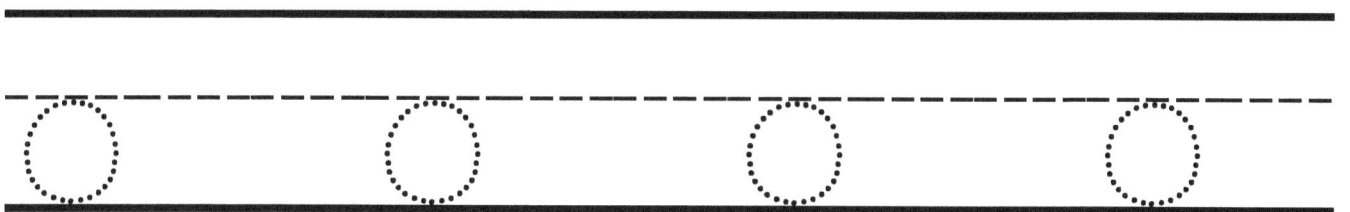

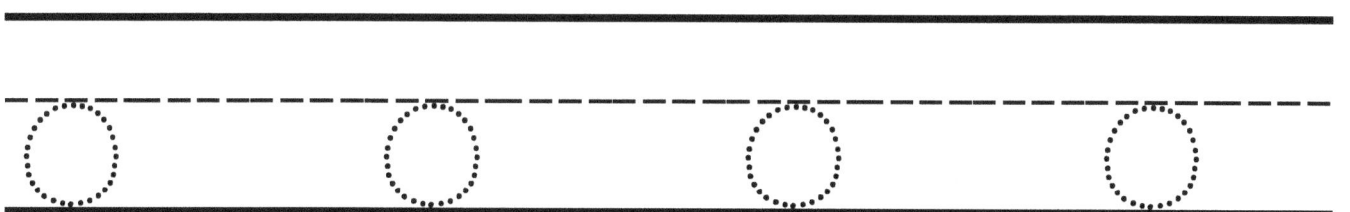

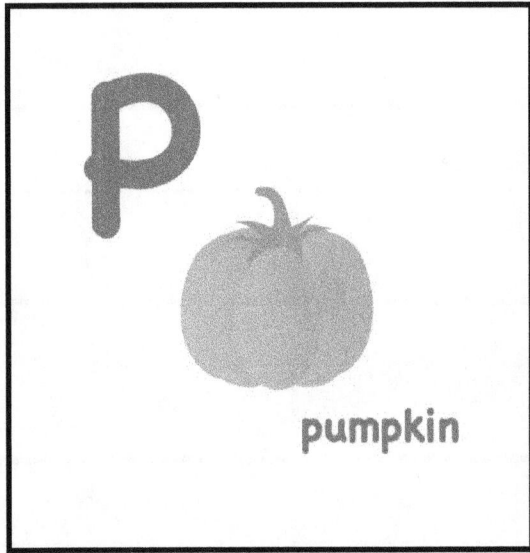

pumpkin

P for Pumpkin

P p

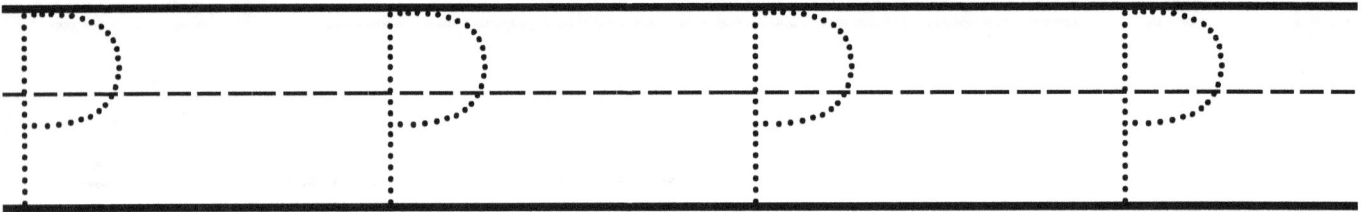

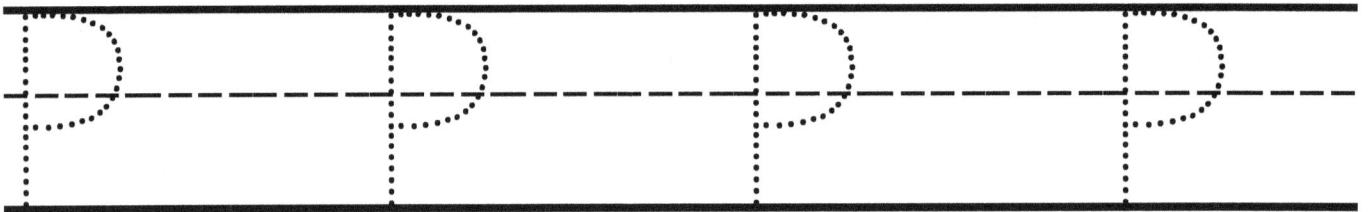

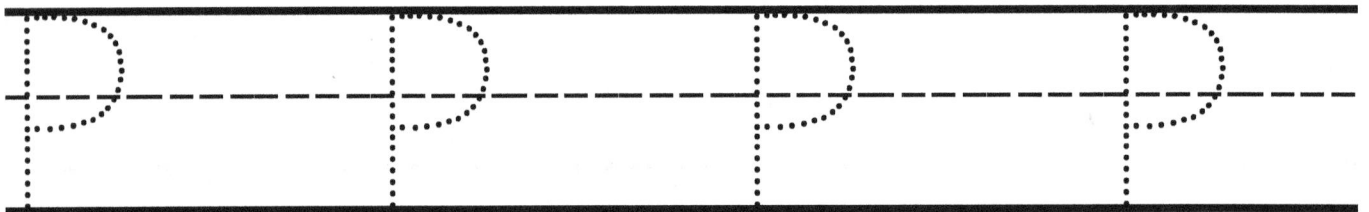

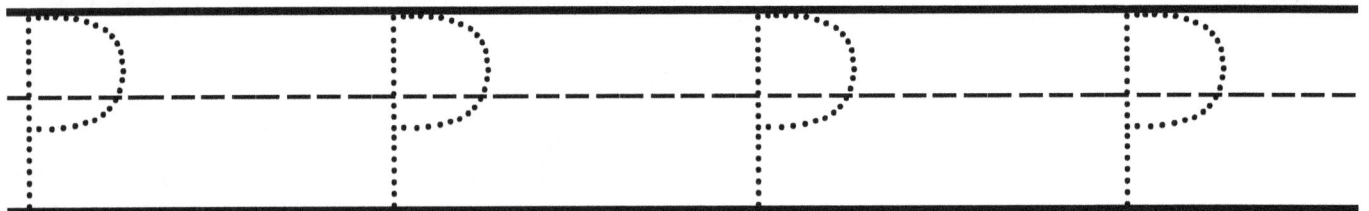

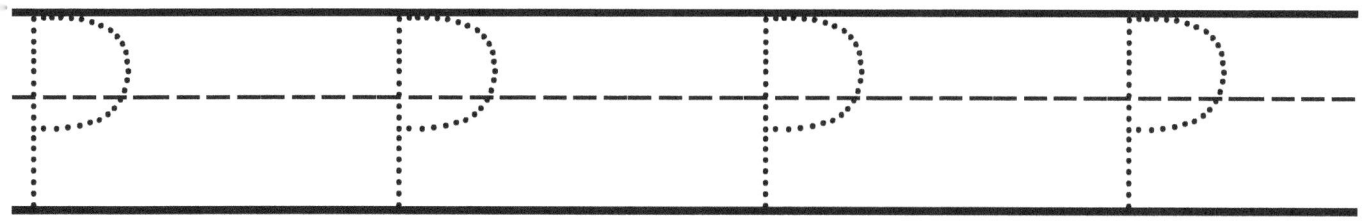

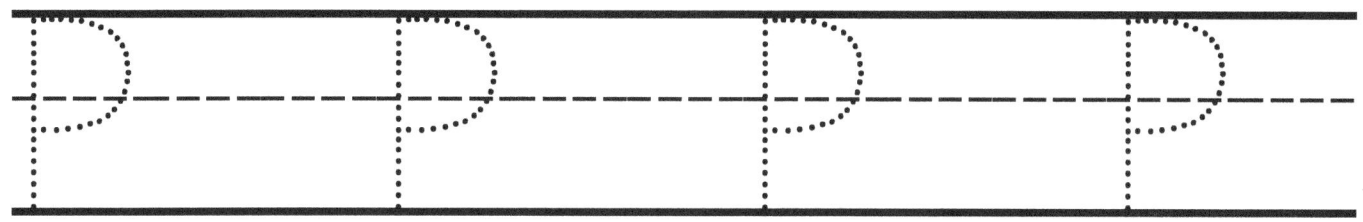

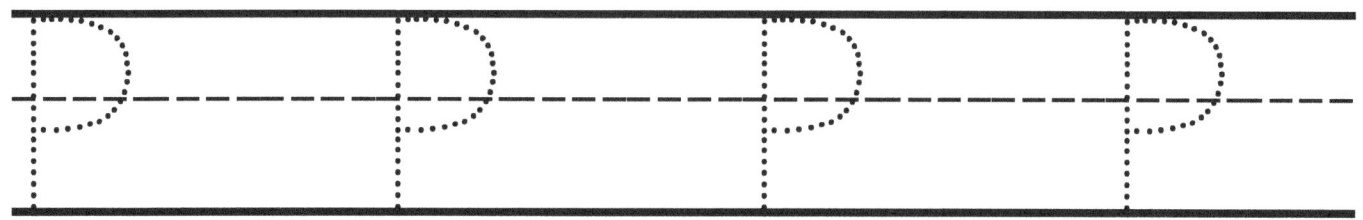

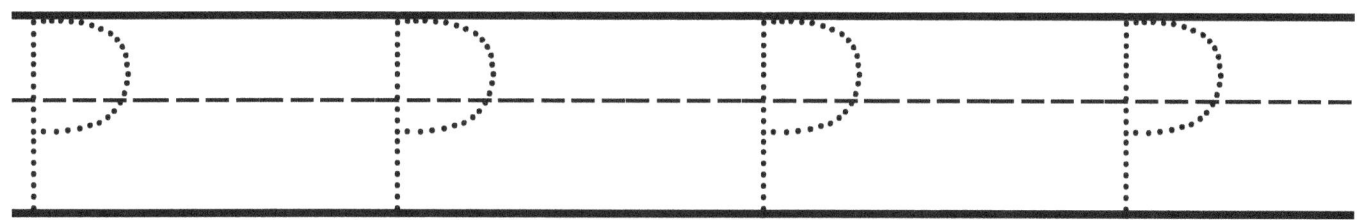

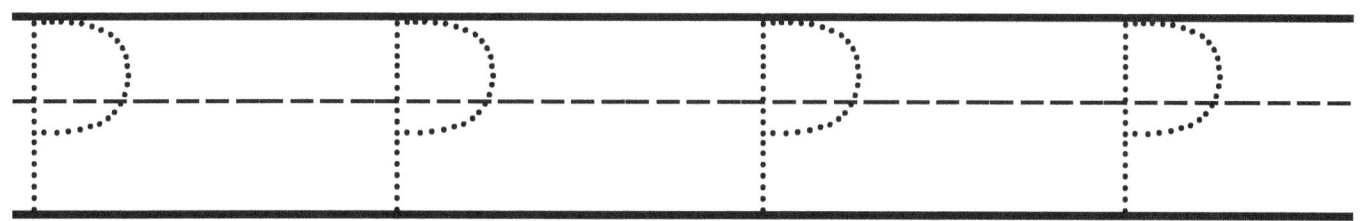

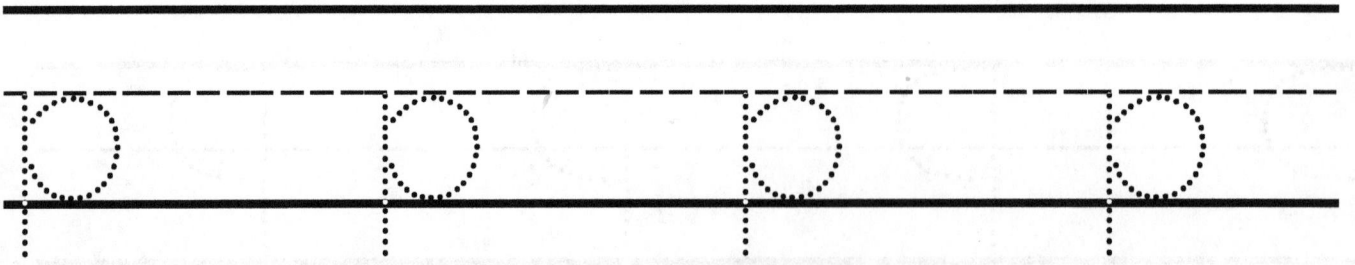

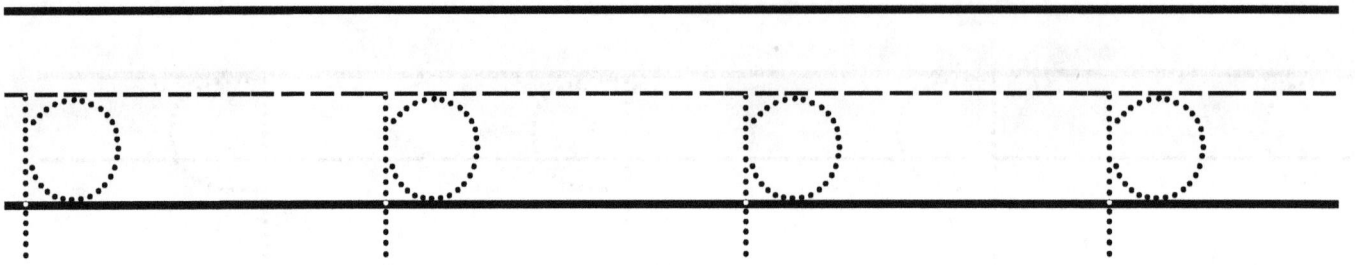

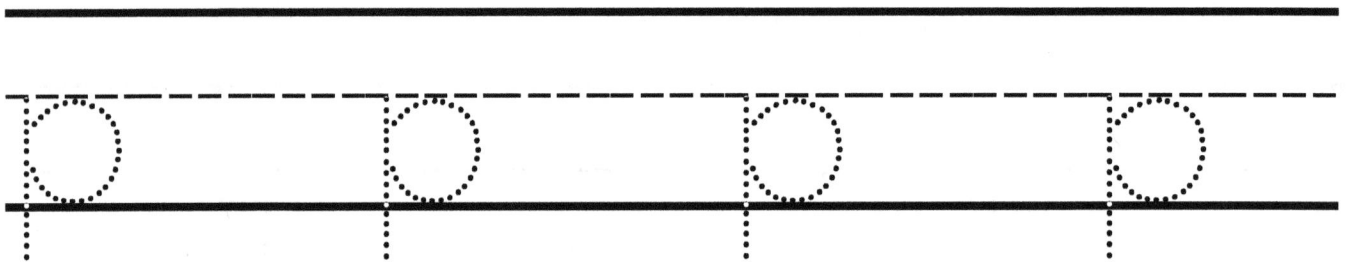

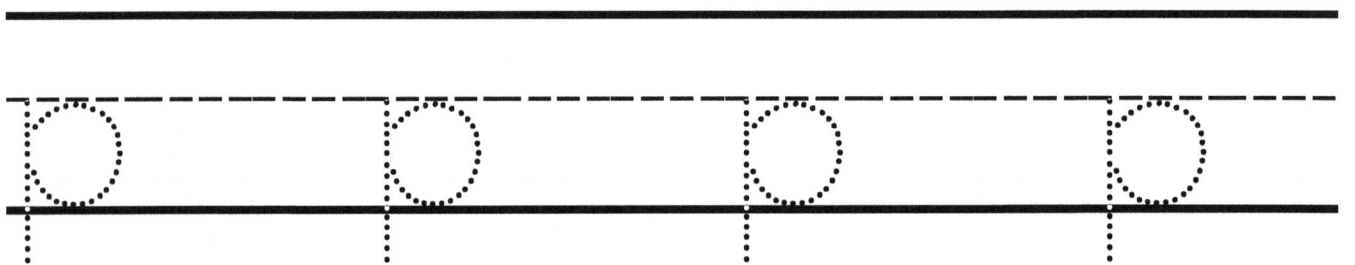

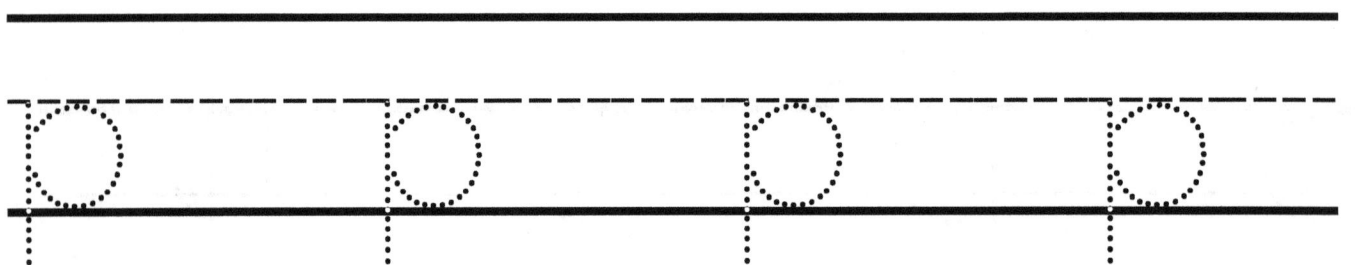

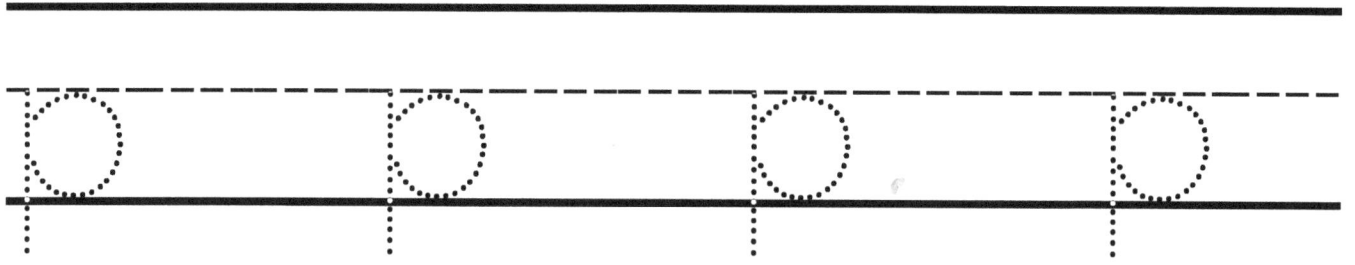

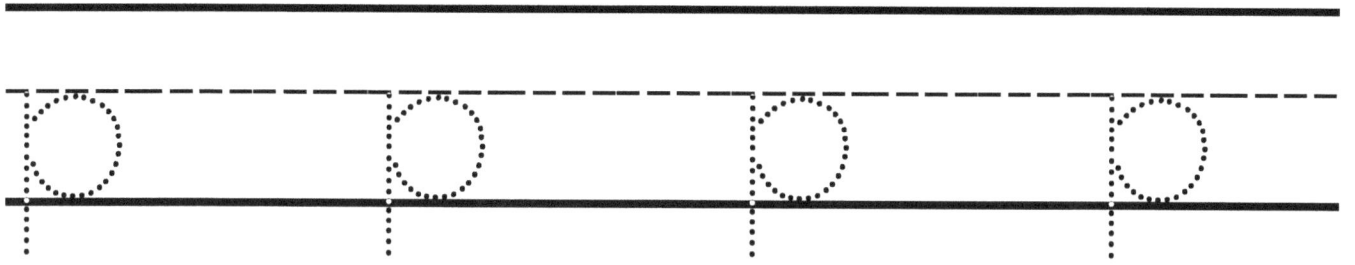

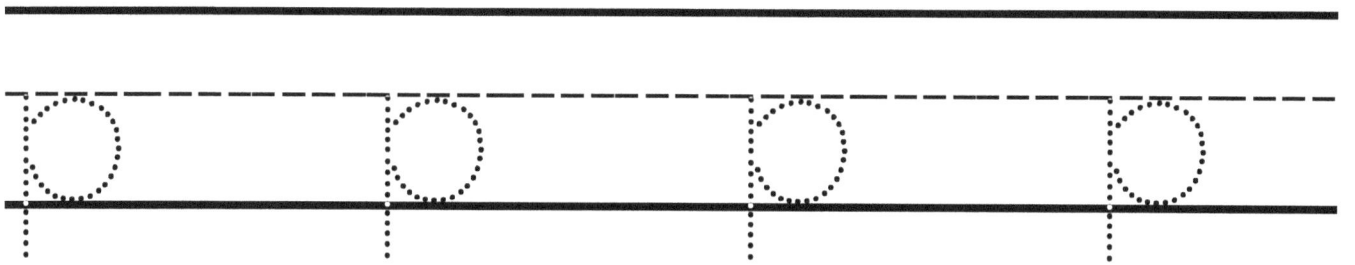

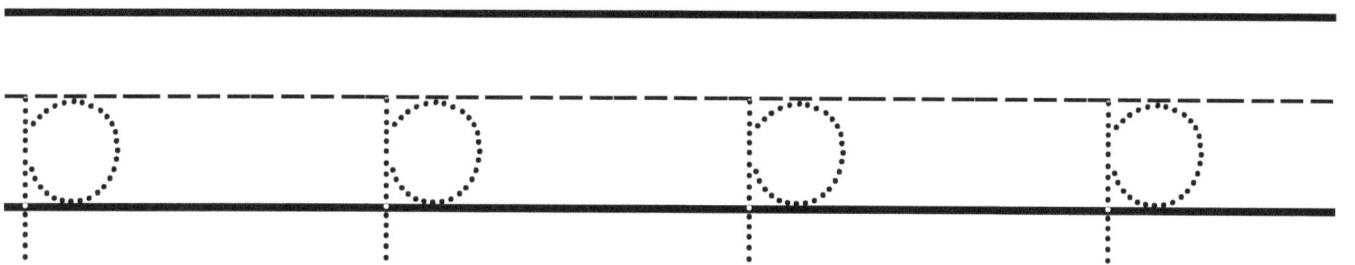

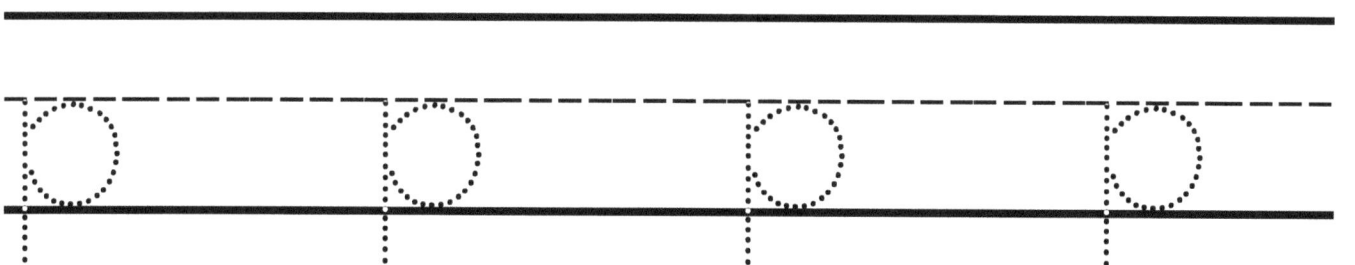

Q for Quince

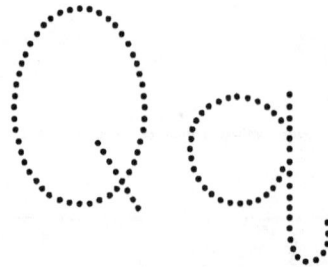

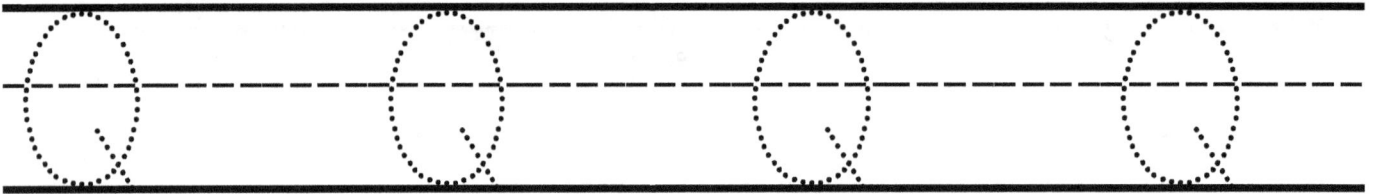

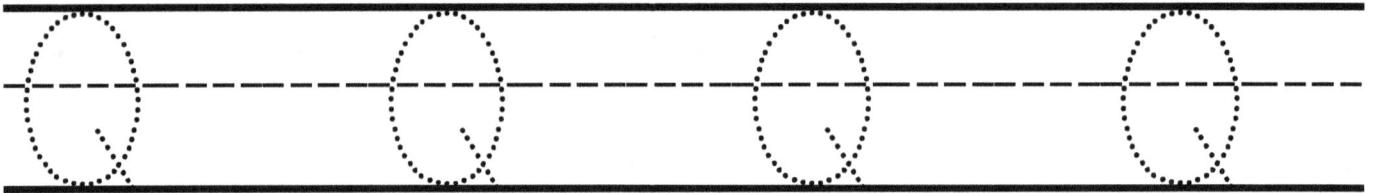

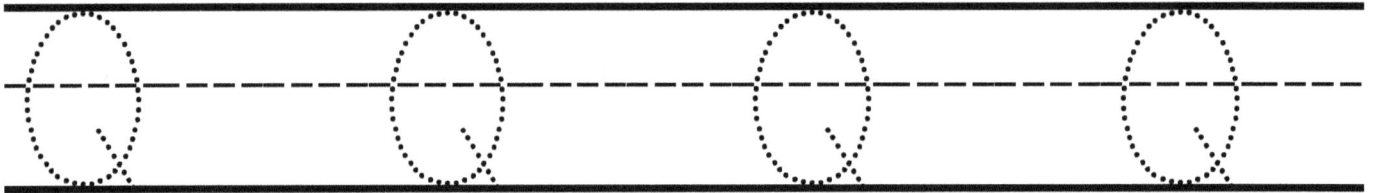

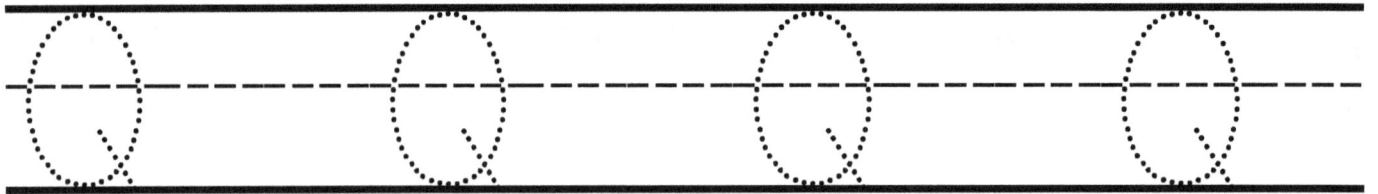

Q Q Q Q

Q Q Q Q

Q Q Q Q

Q Q Q Q

Q Q Q Q

q q q q

q q q q

q q q q

q q q q

q q q q

R for Radish

Rr

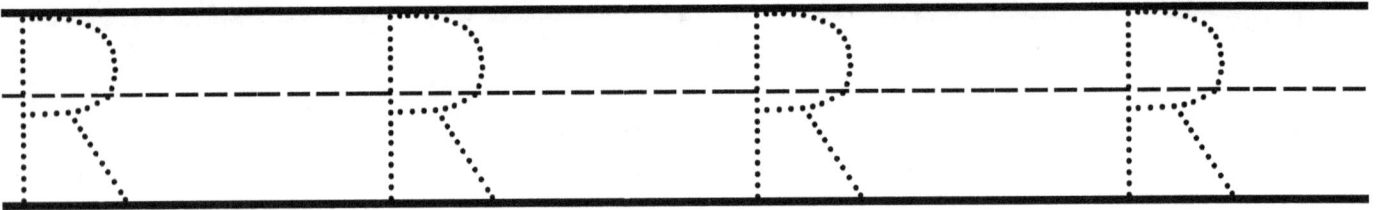

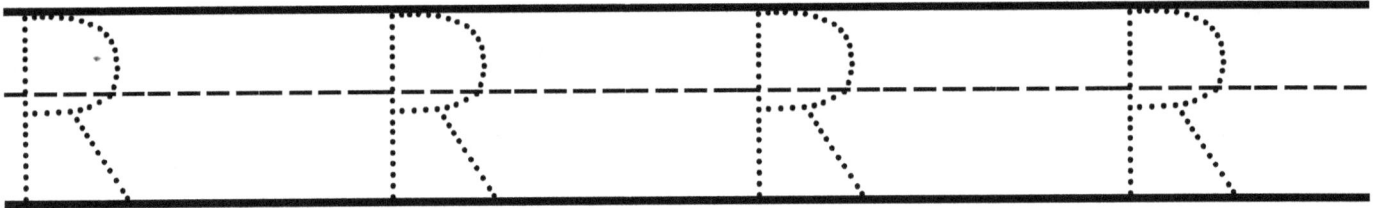

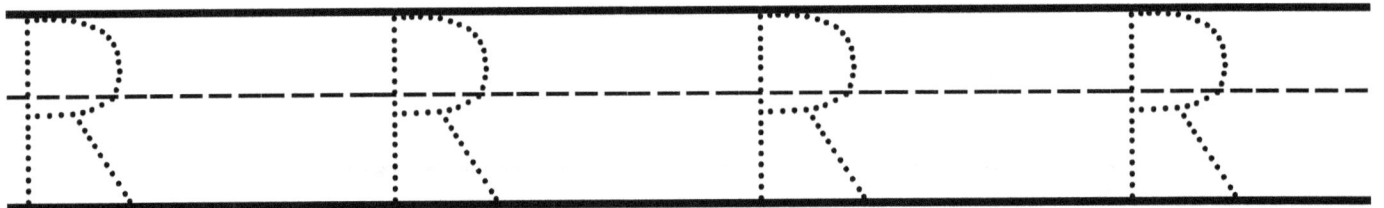

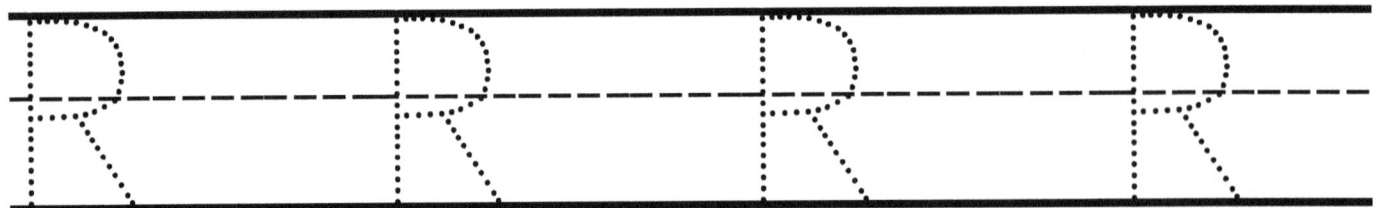

R R R R

R R R R

R R R R

R R R R

R R R R

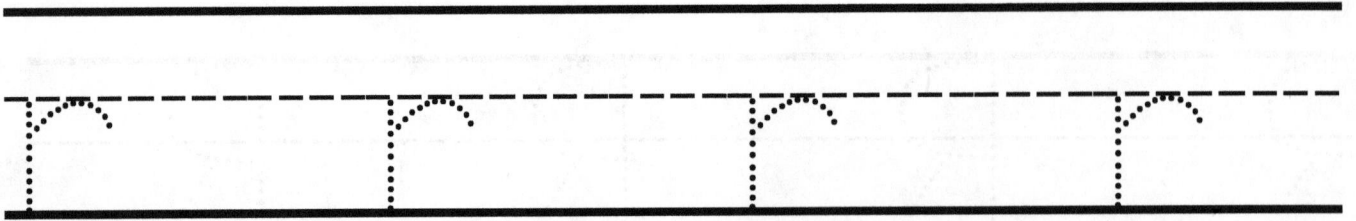

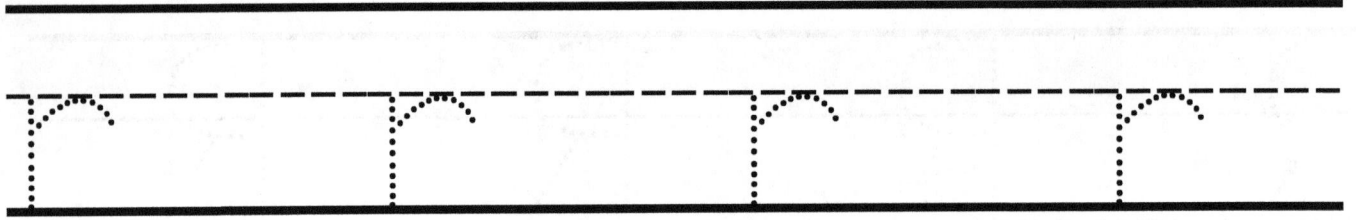

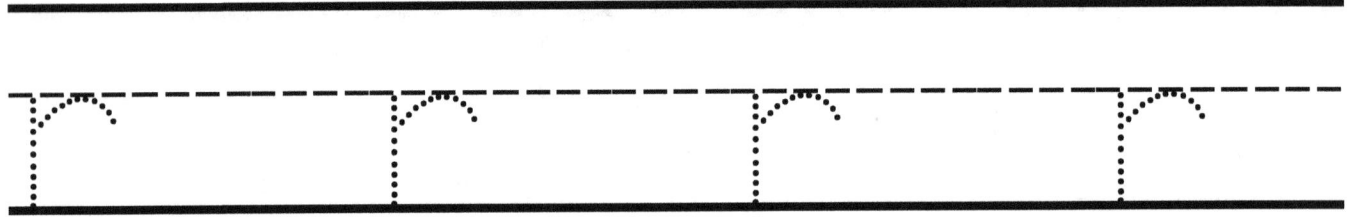

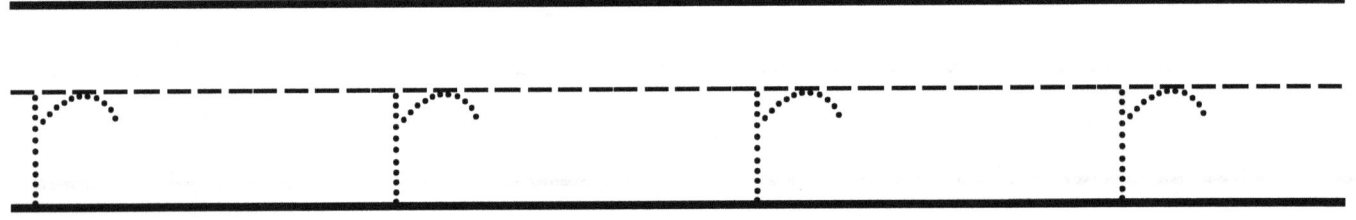

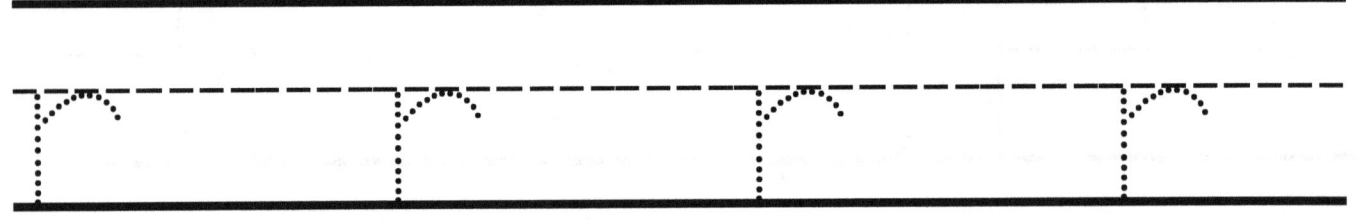

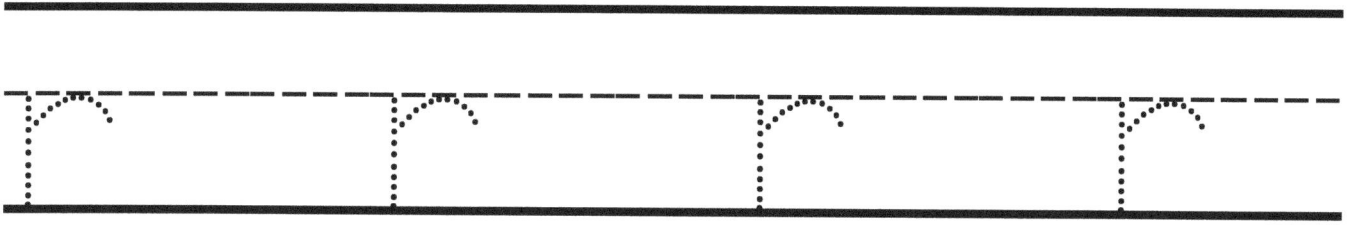

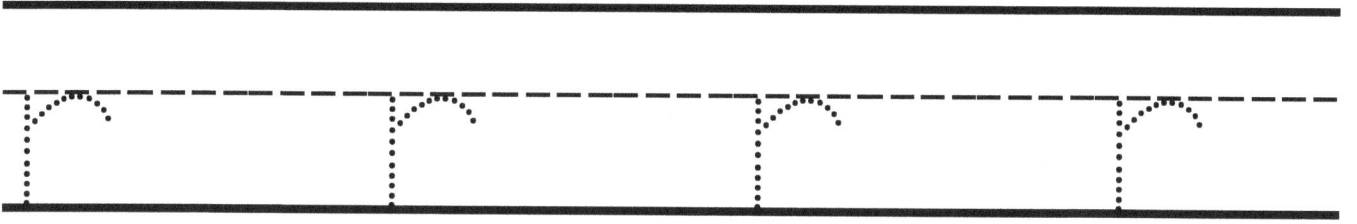

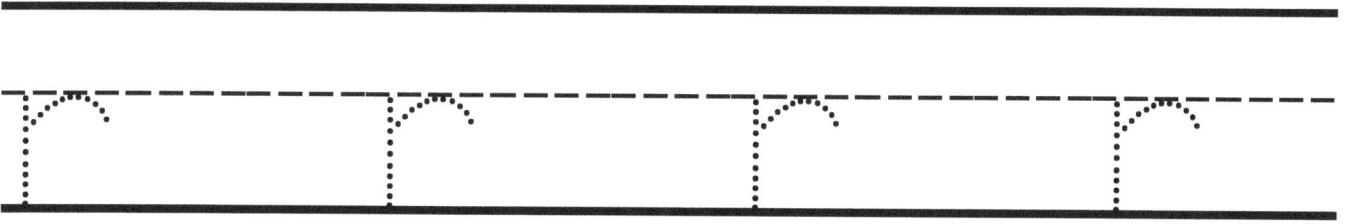

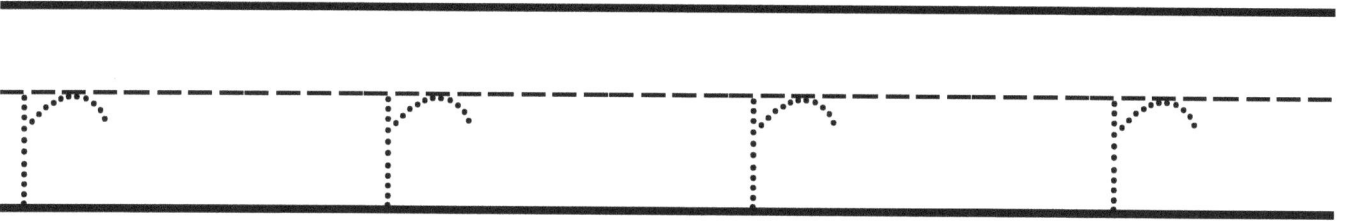

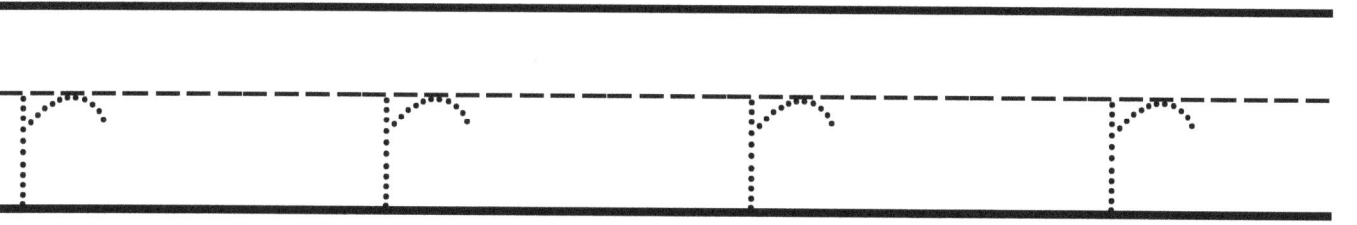

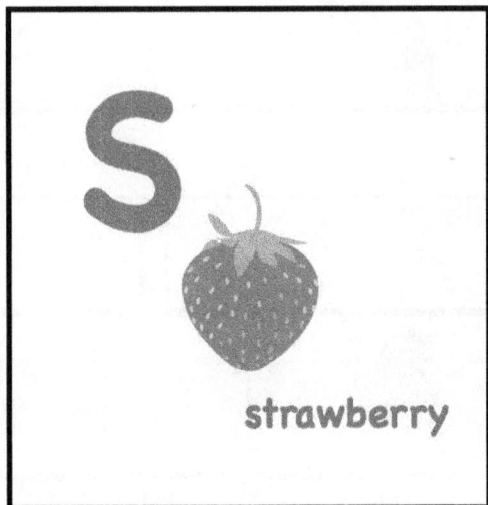

strawberry

S for Strawberry

S s

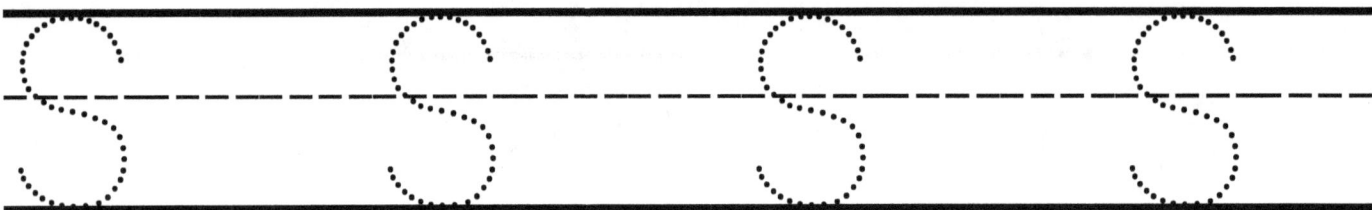

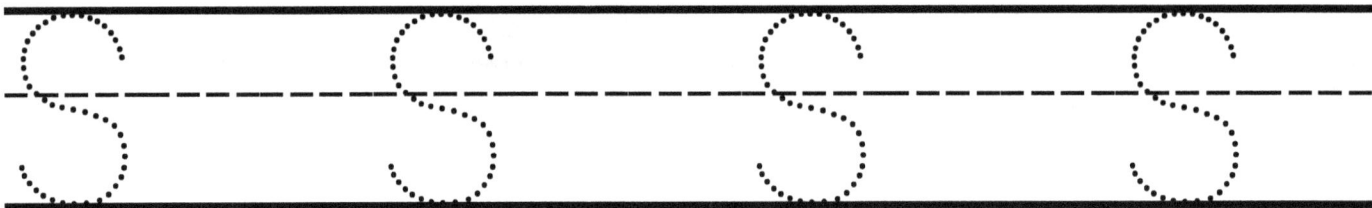

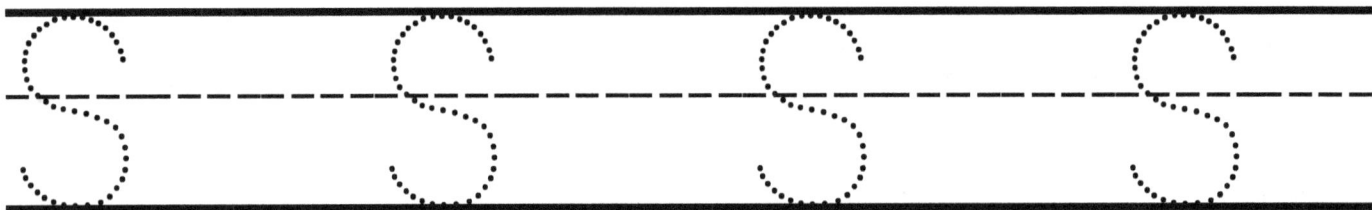

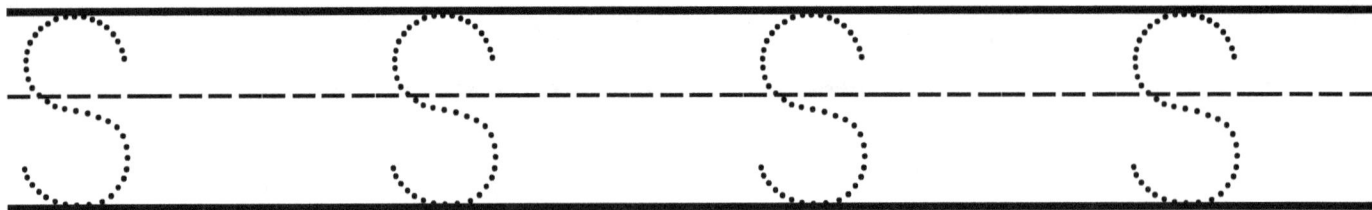

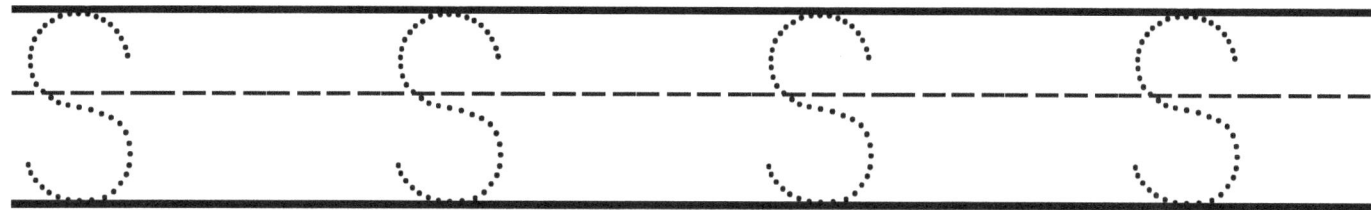

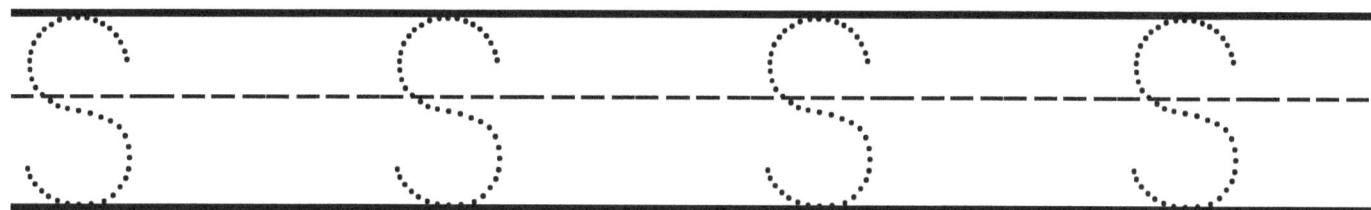

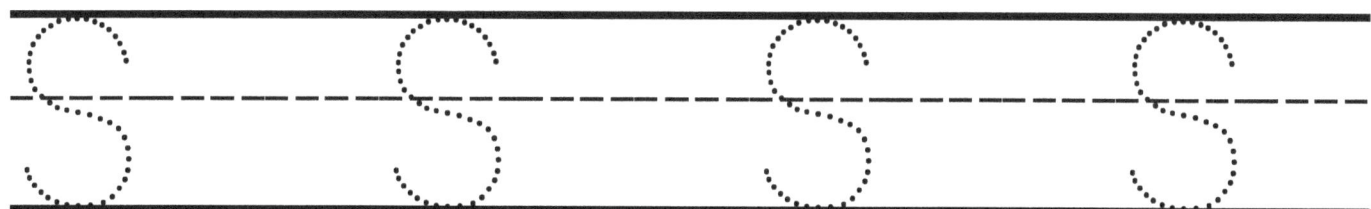

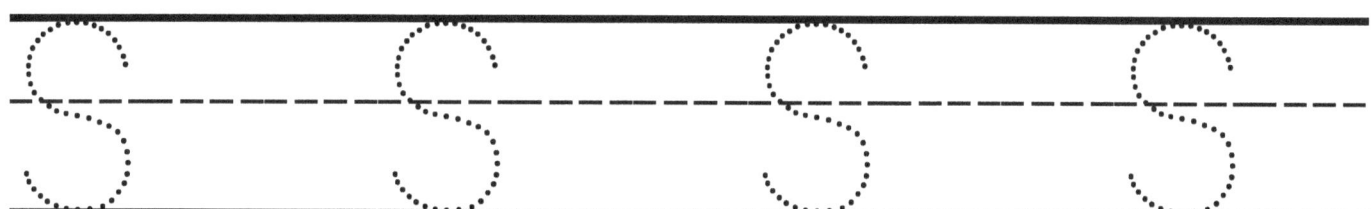

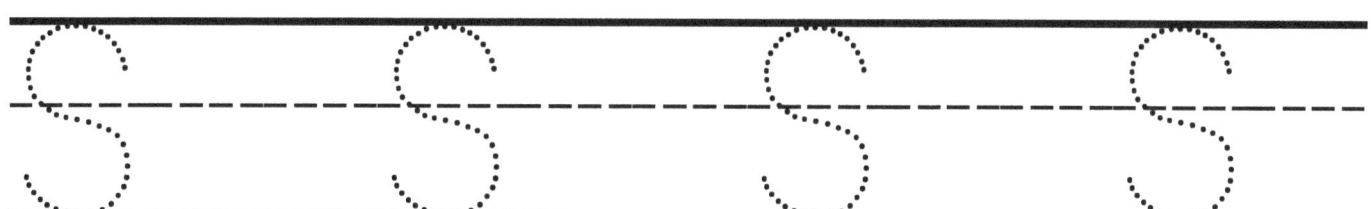

S   S   S   S

S   S   S   S

S   S   S   S

S   S   S   S

S   S   S   S

s　　s　　s　　s

s　　s　　s　　s

s　　s　　s　　s

s　　s　　s　　s

s　　s　　s　　s

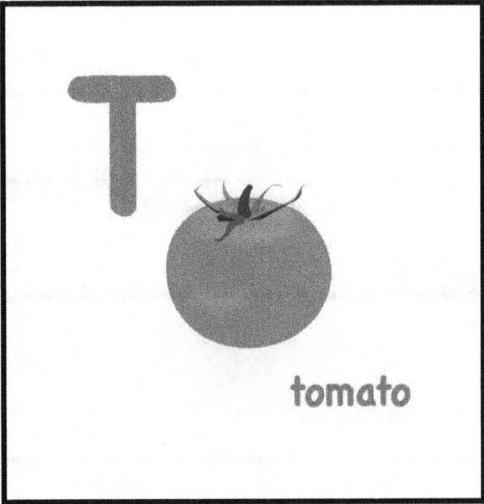

tomato

T for Tomato

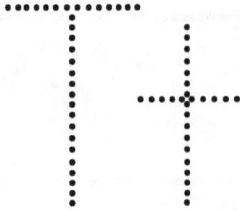

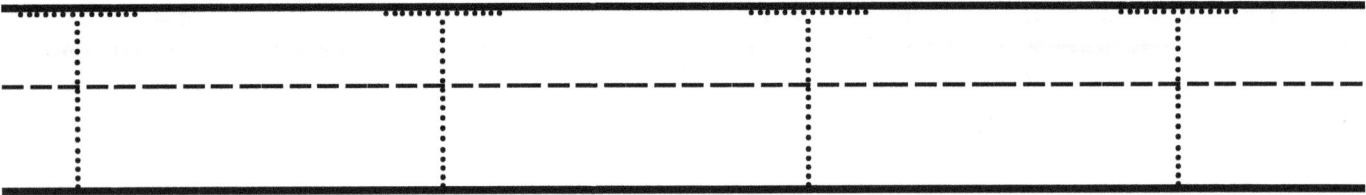

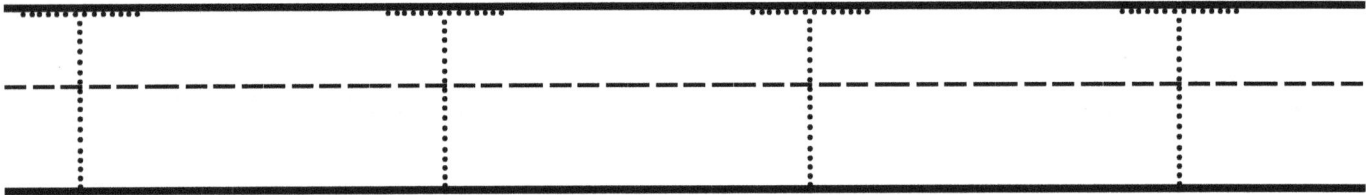

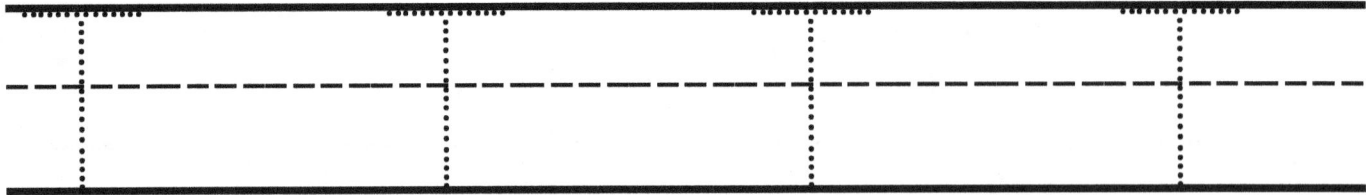

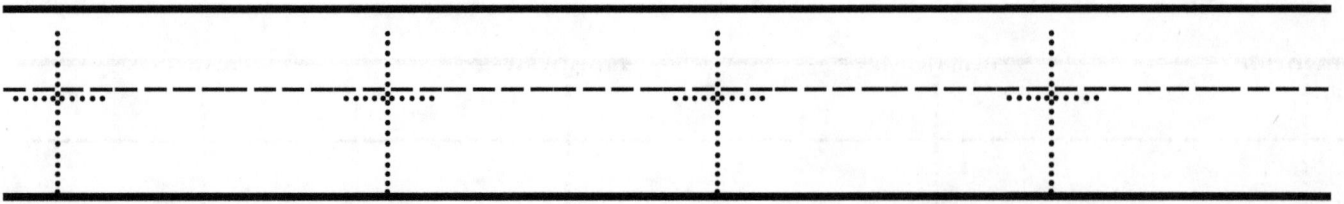

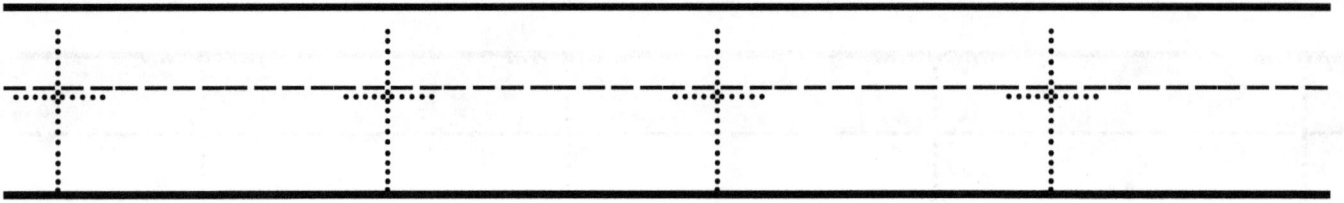

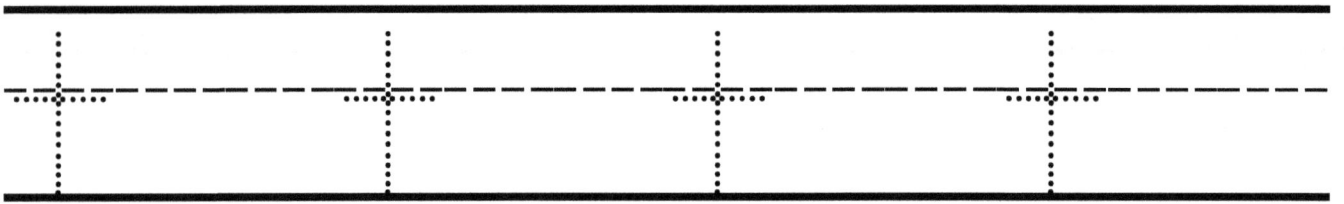

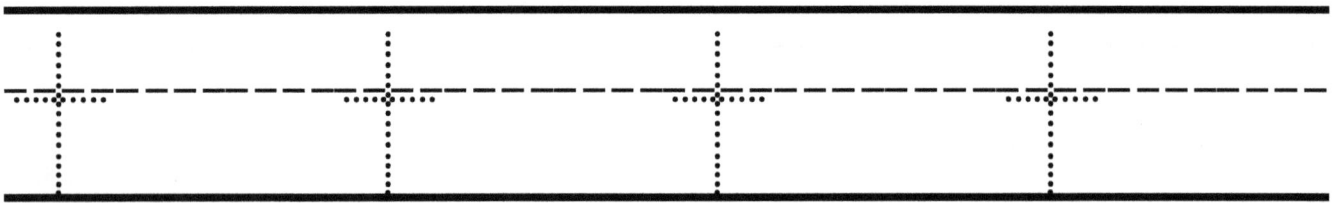

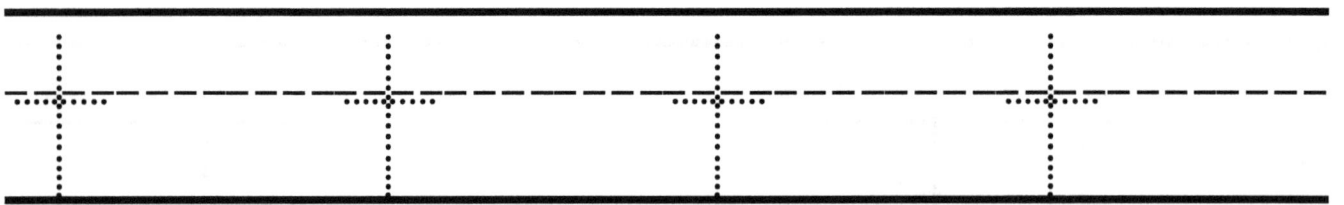

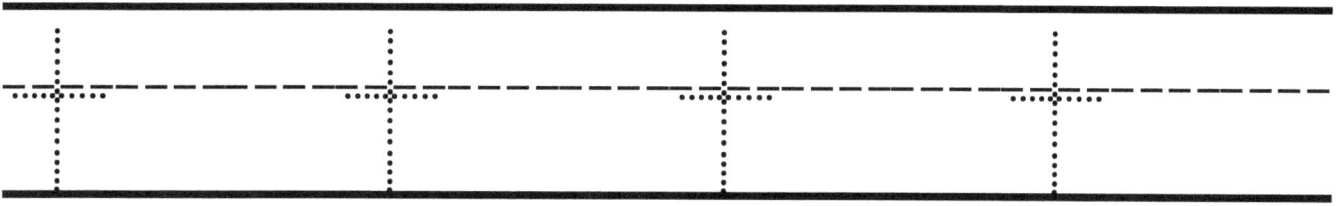

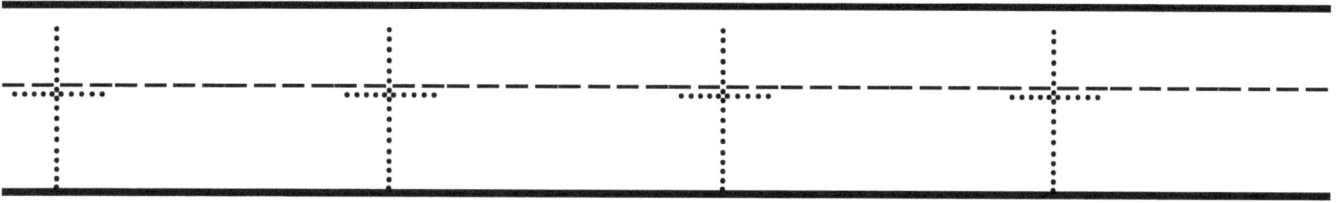

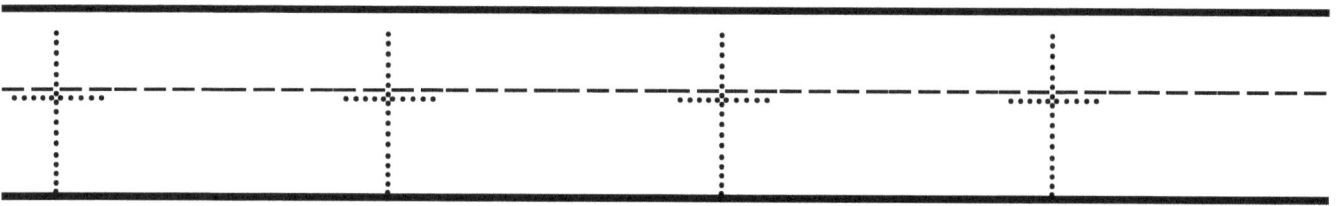

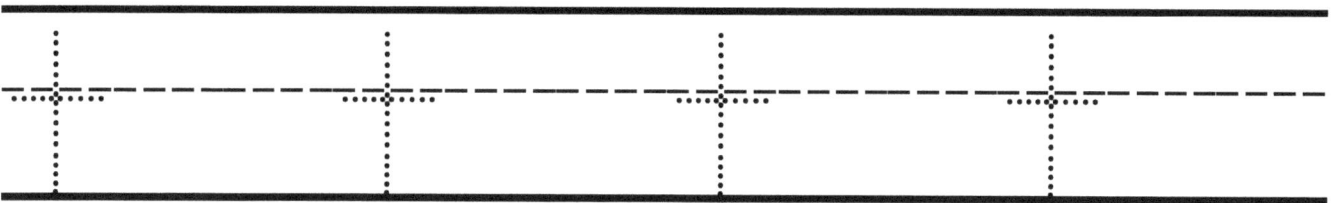

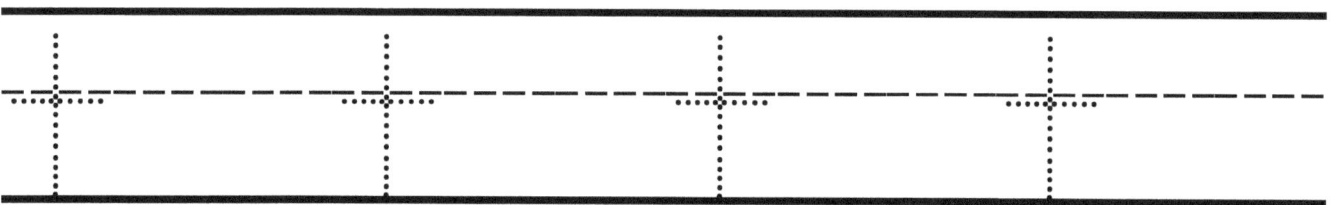

U for Ugli Fruit

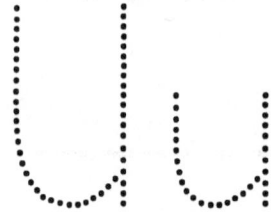

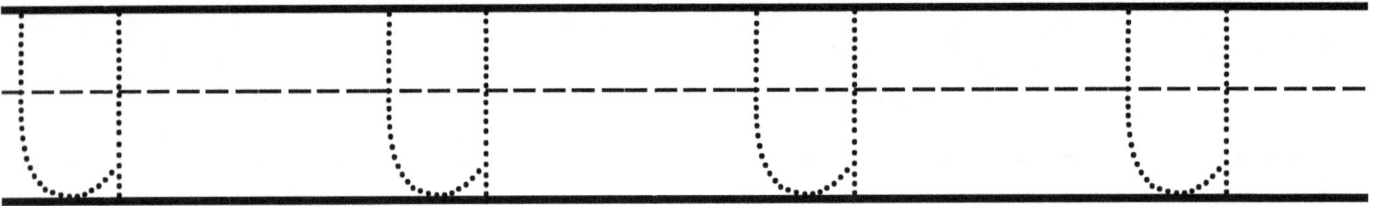

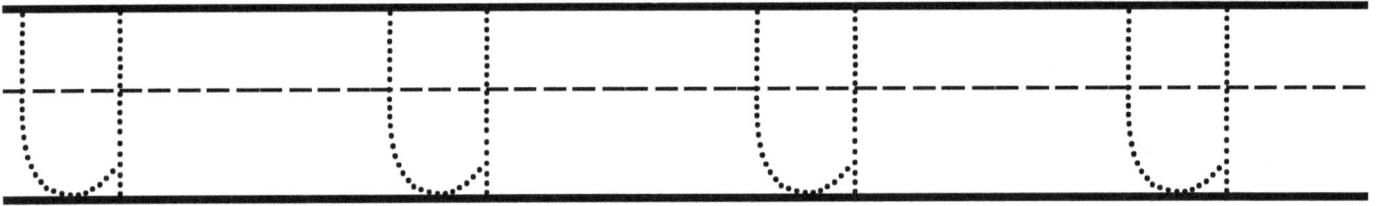

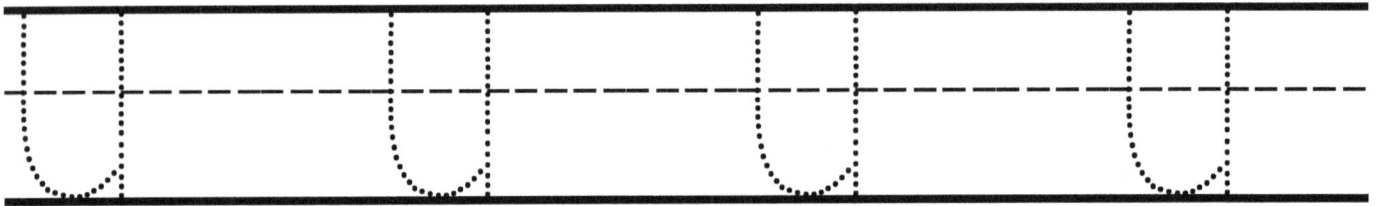

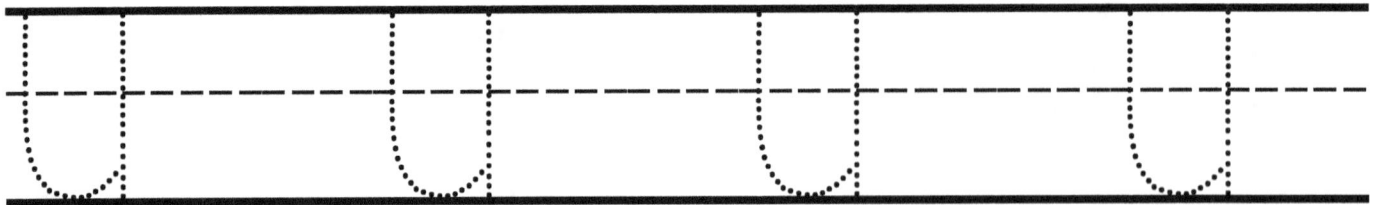

Ugli fruit

Uu

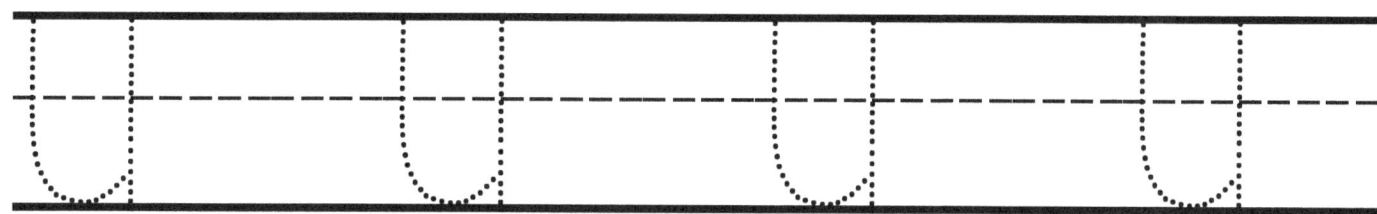

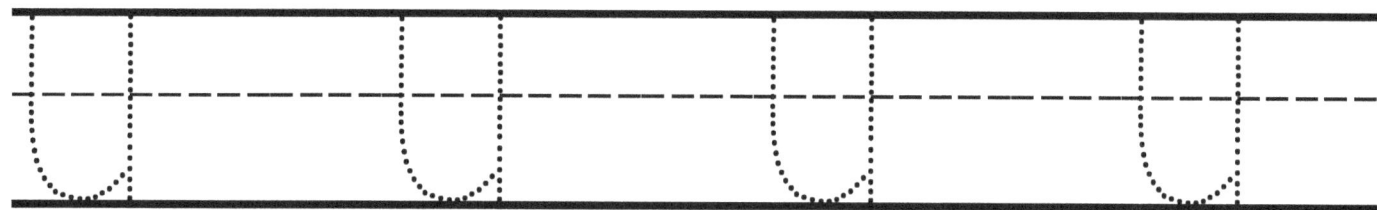

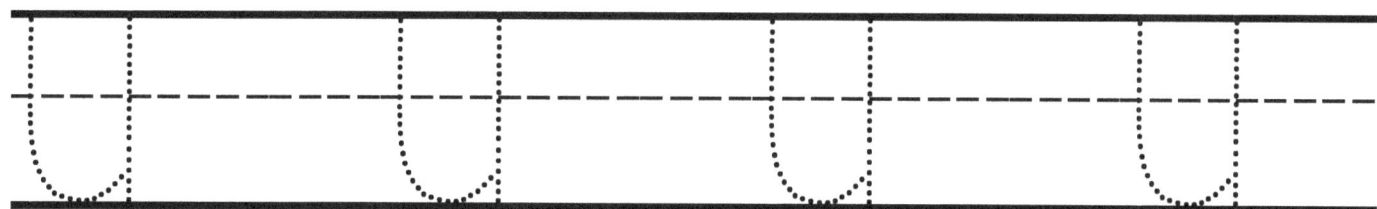

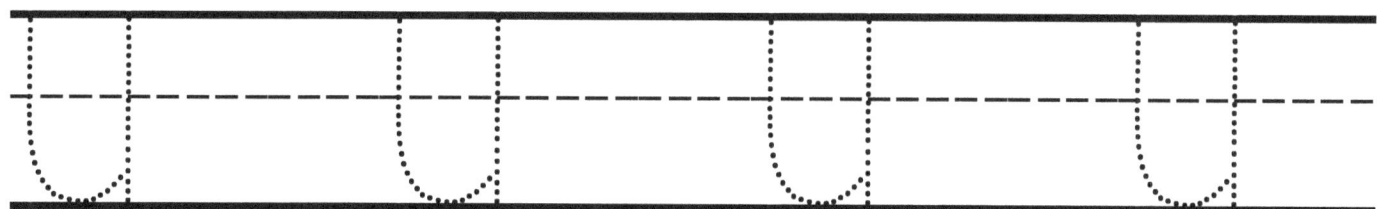

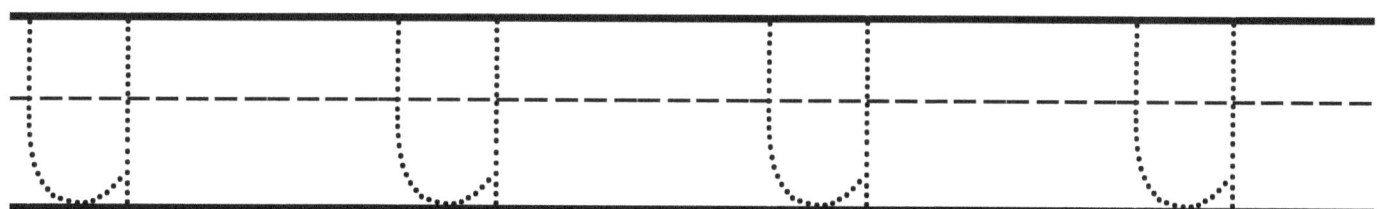

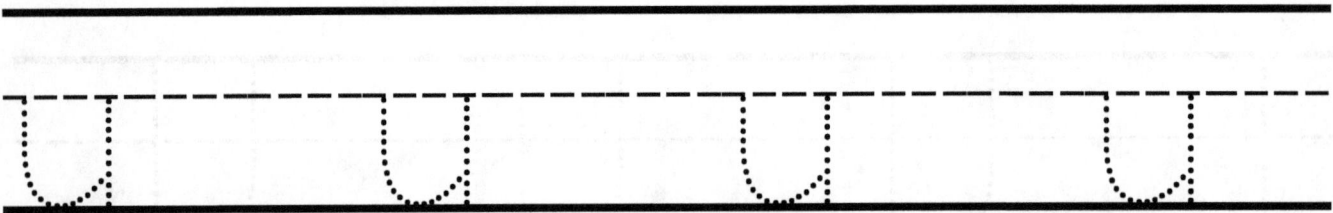

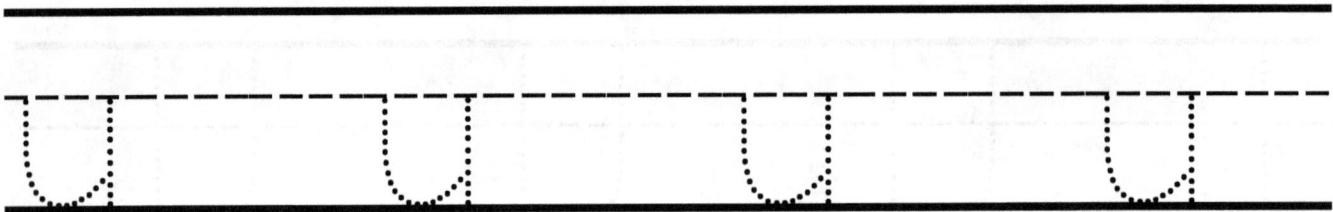

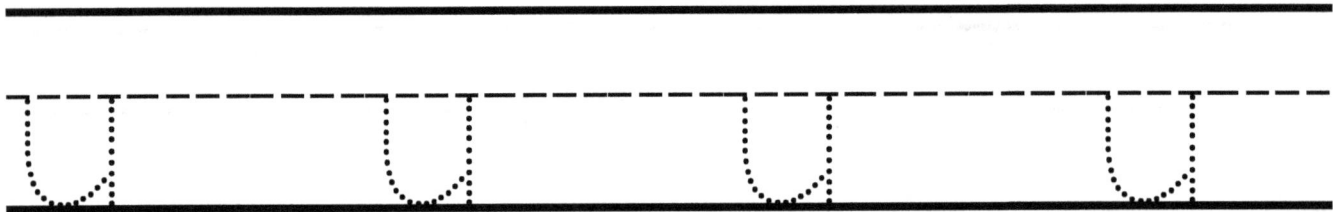

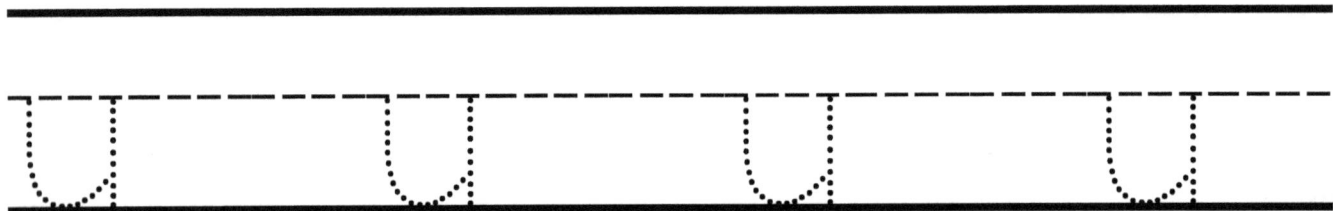

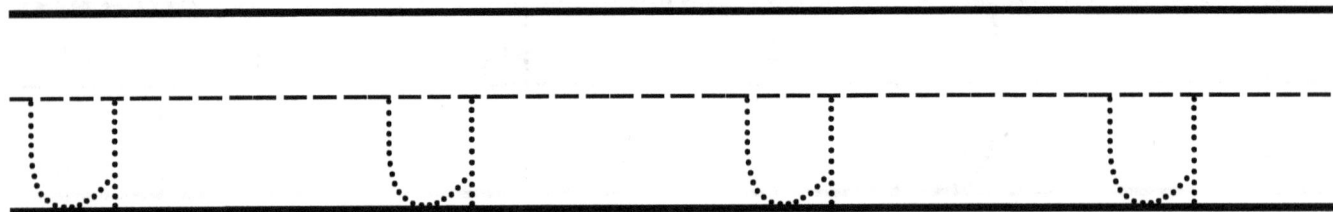

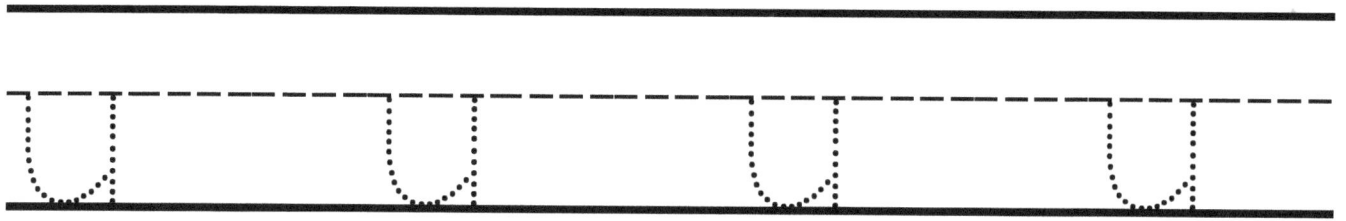

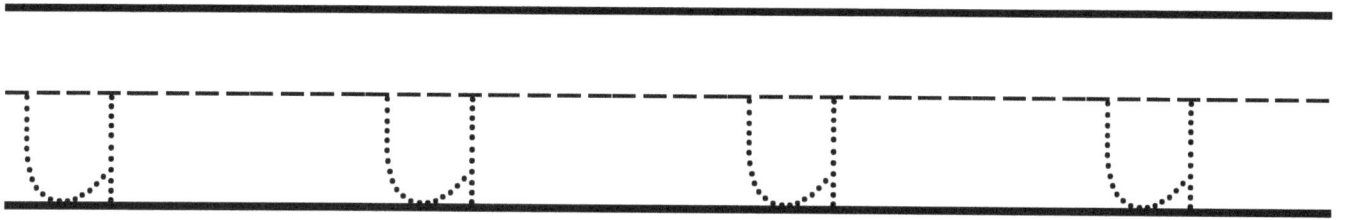

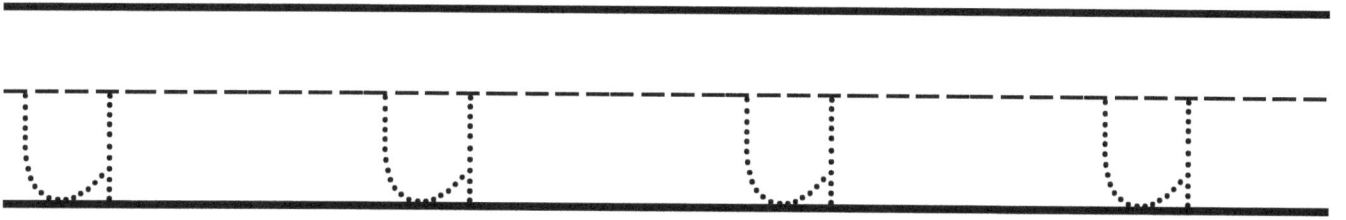

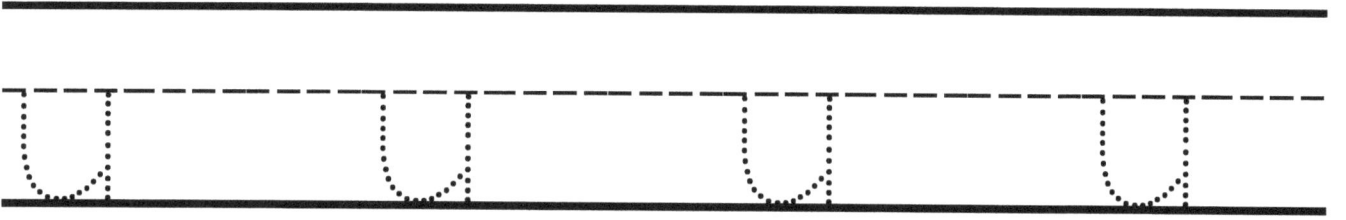

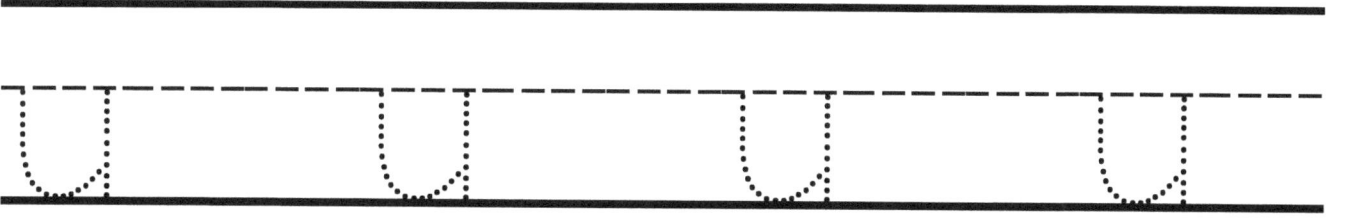

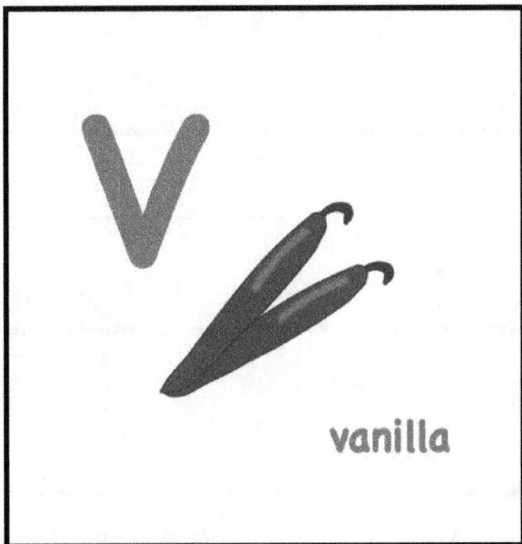

vanilla

V for Vanilla

Vv

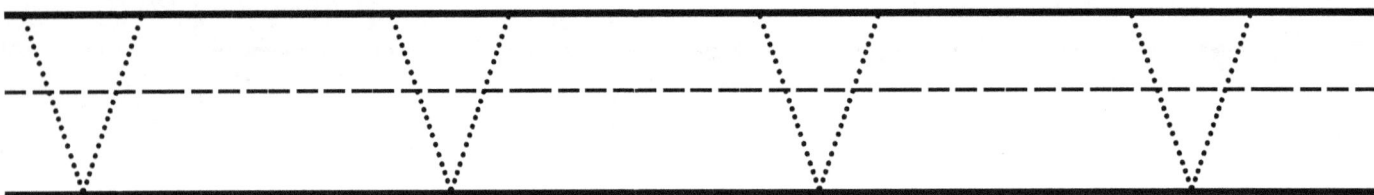

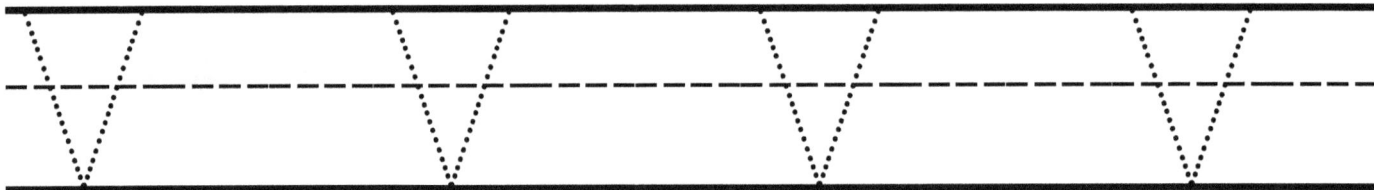

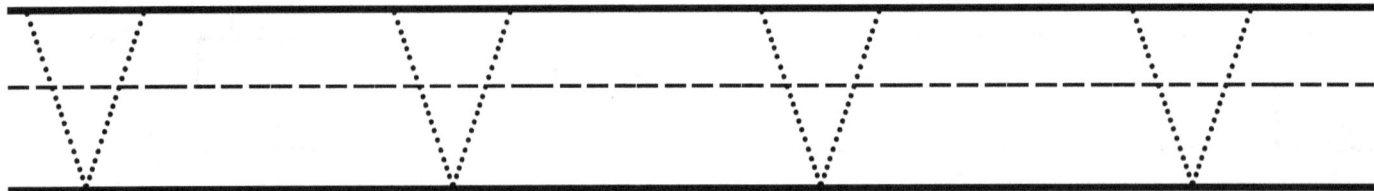

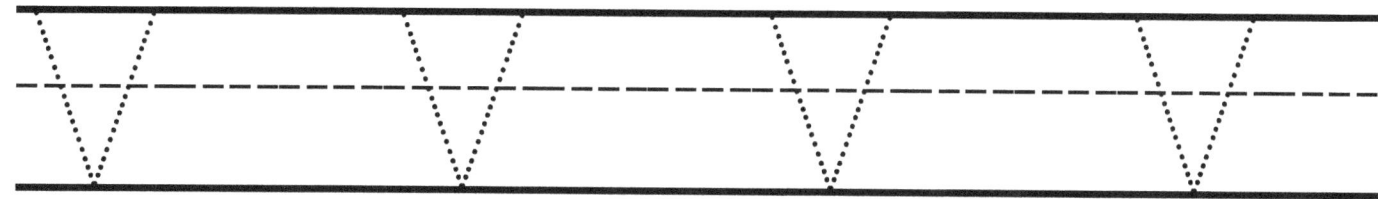

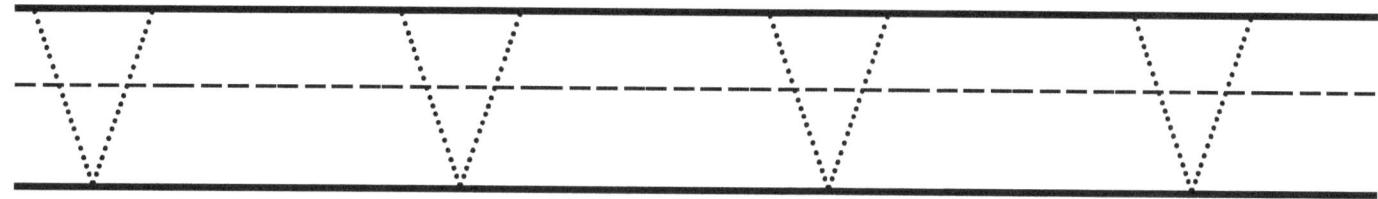

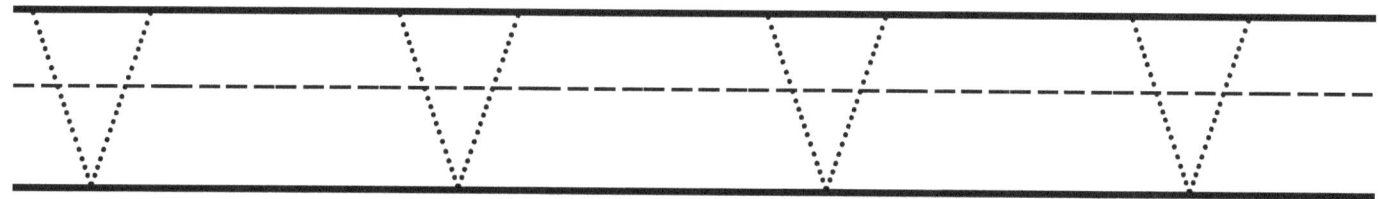

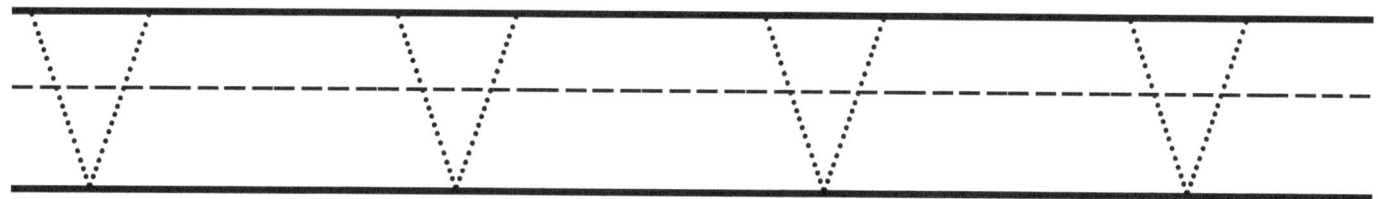

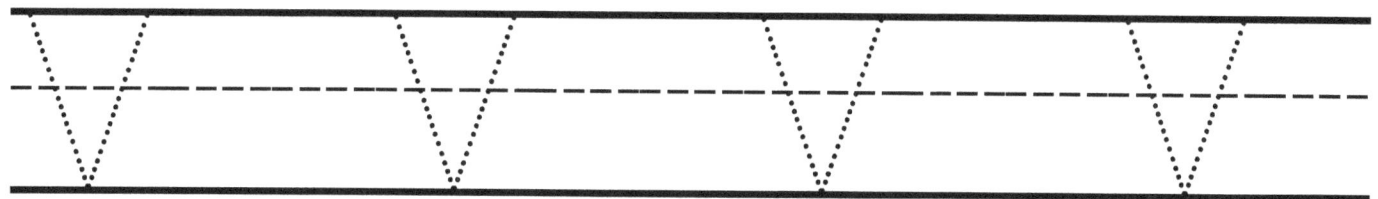

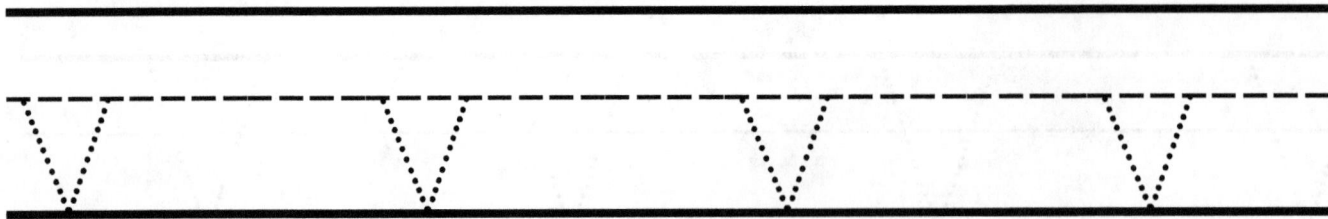

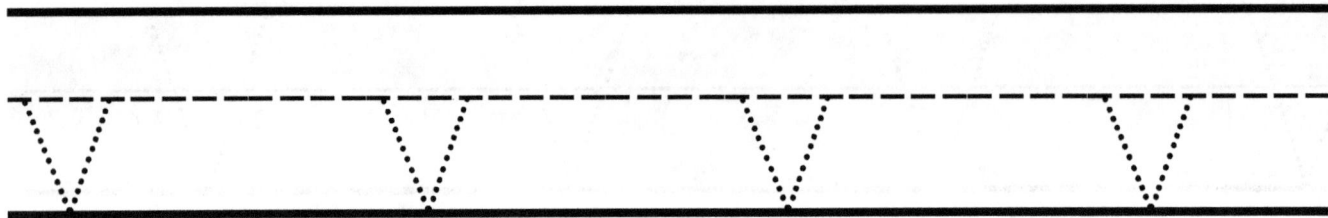

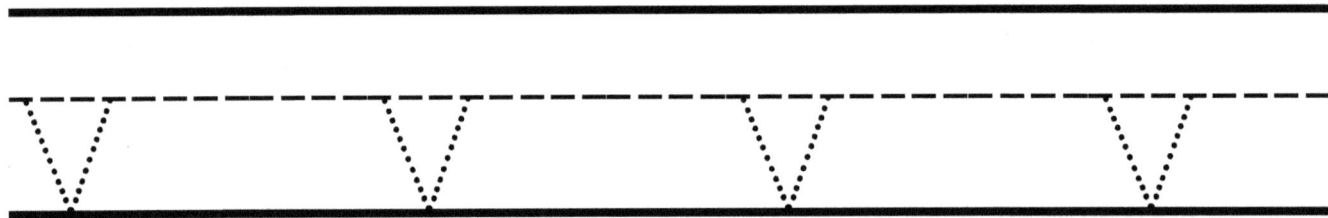

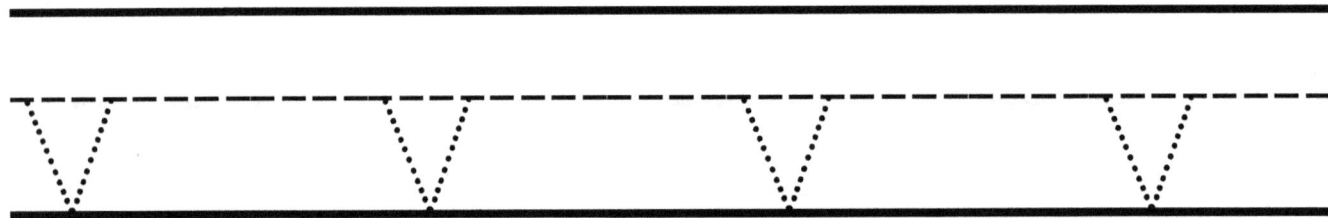

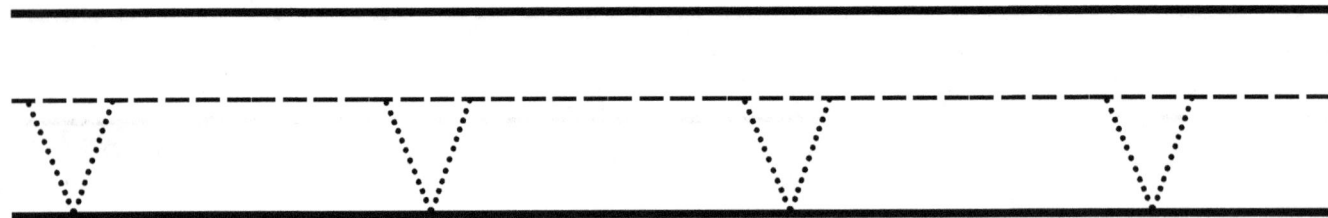

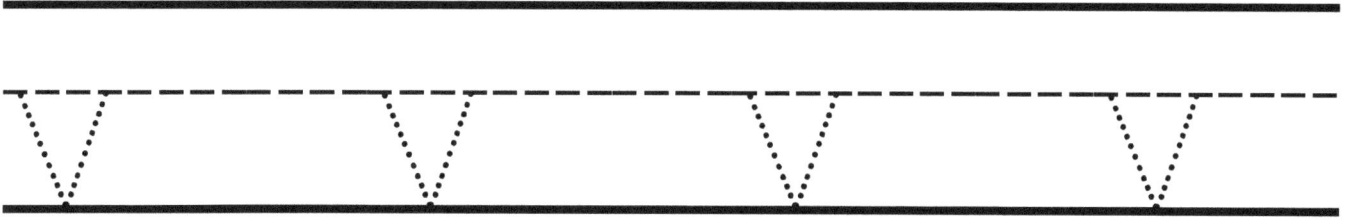
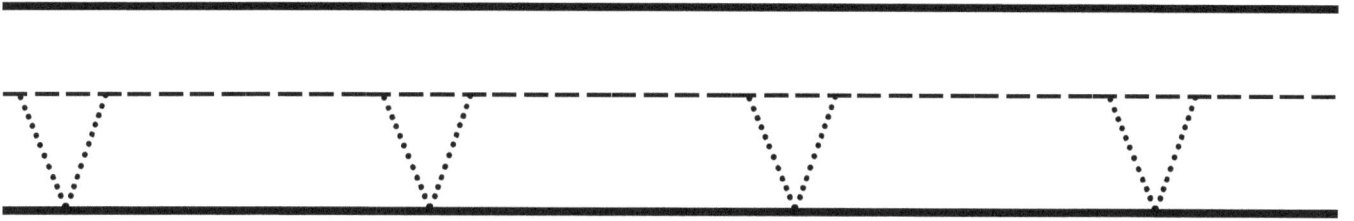
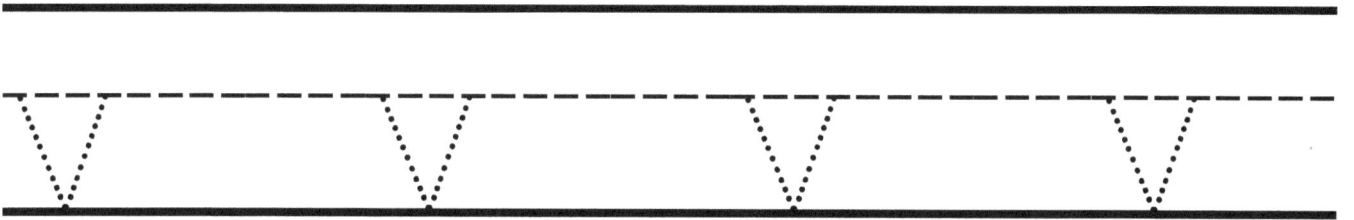
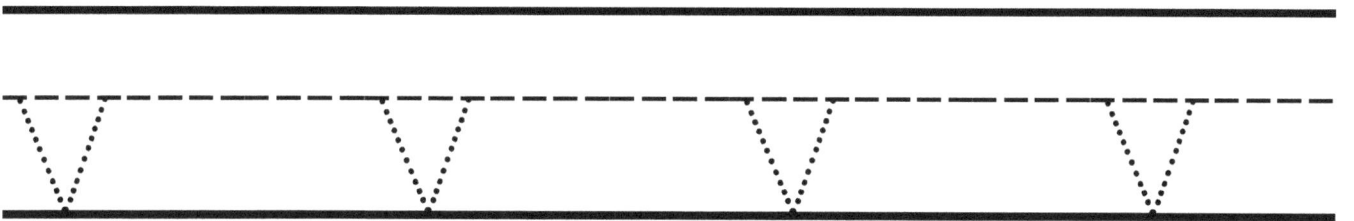
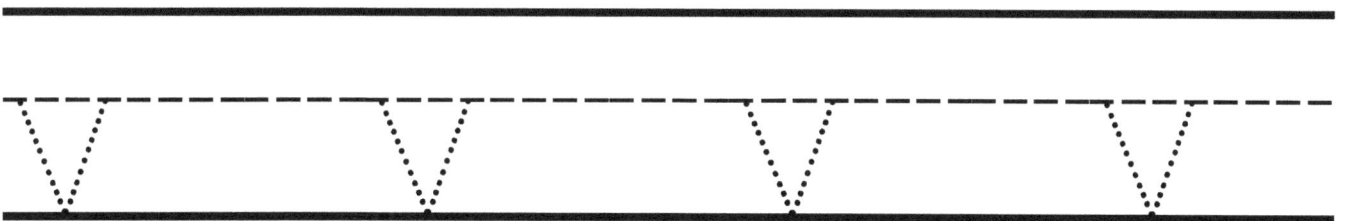

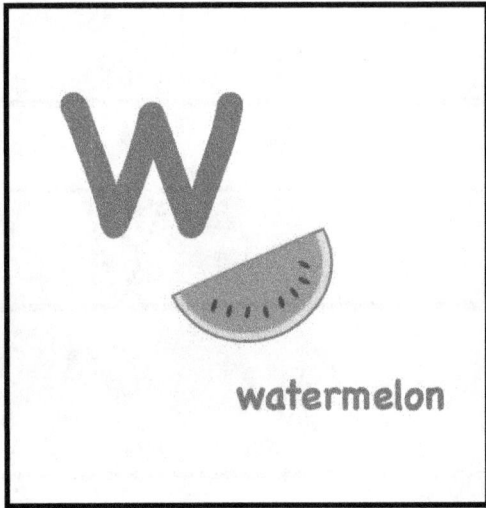

watermelon

W for Watermelon

Ww

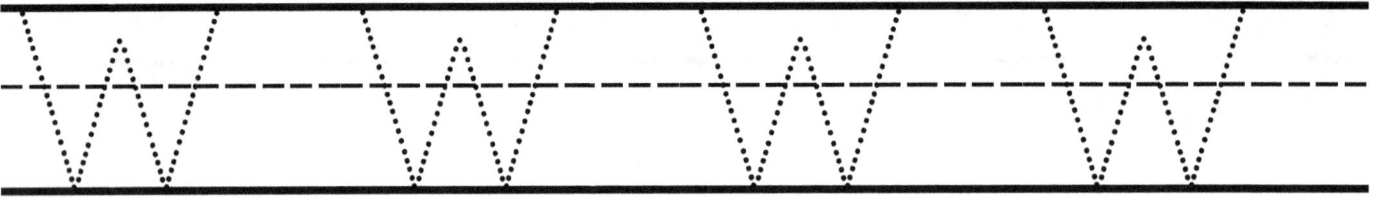

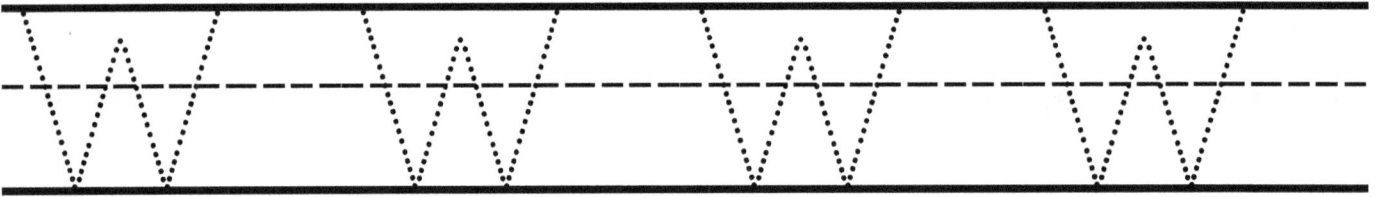

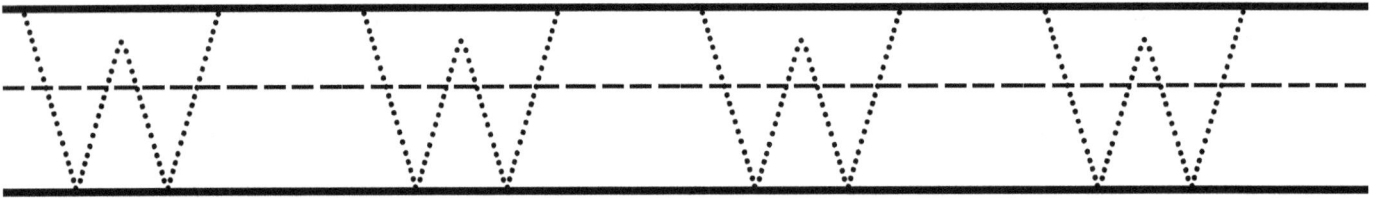

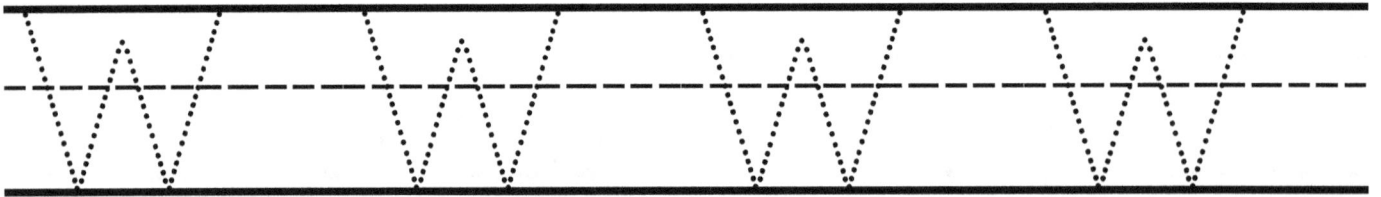

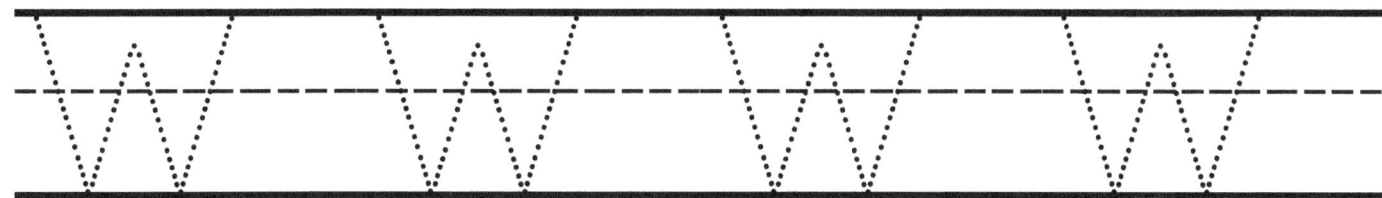

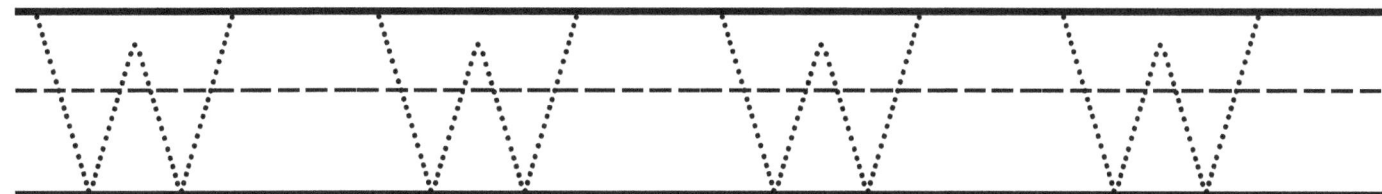

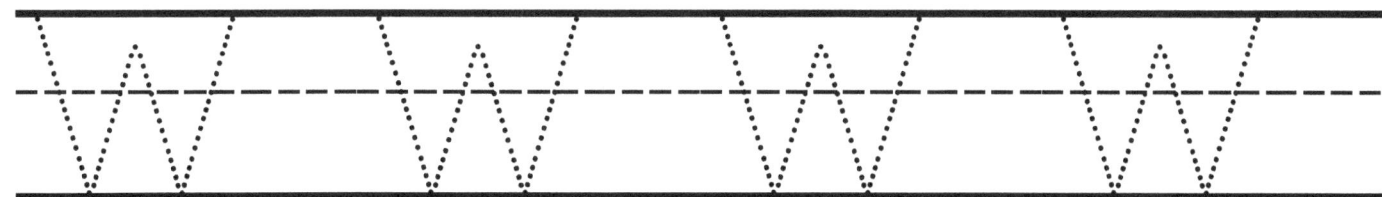

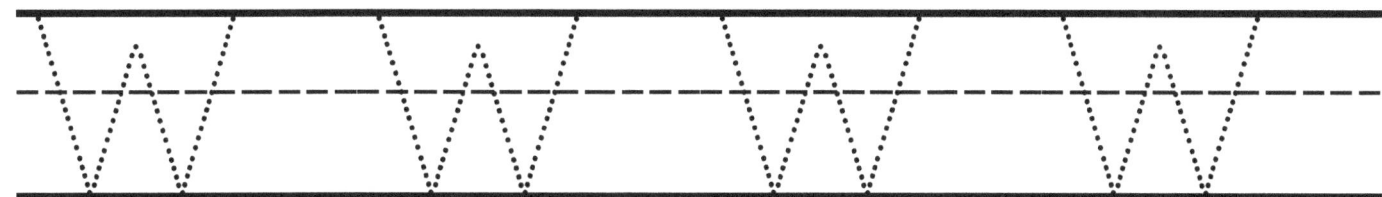

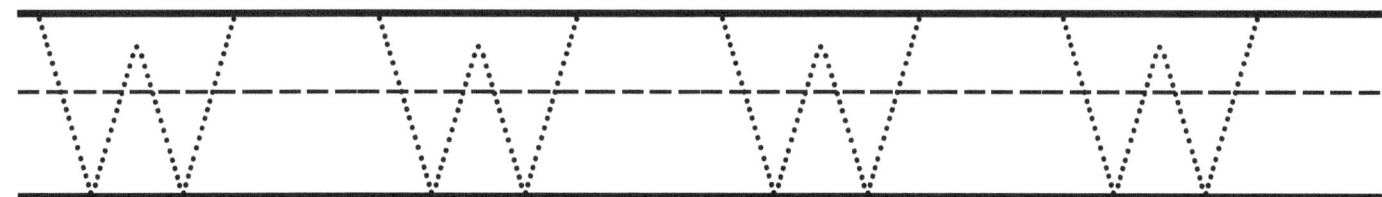

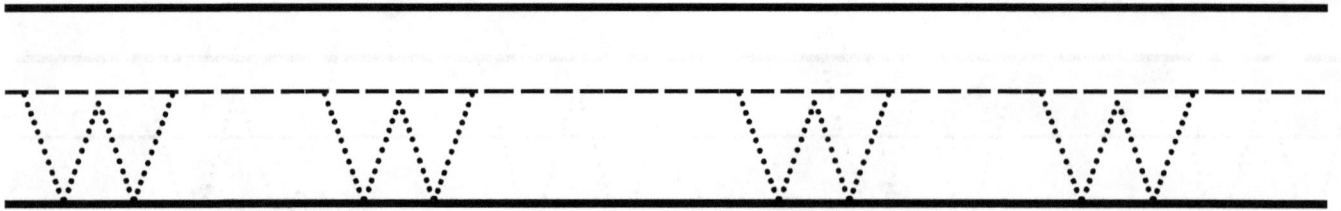

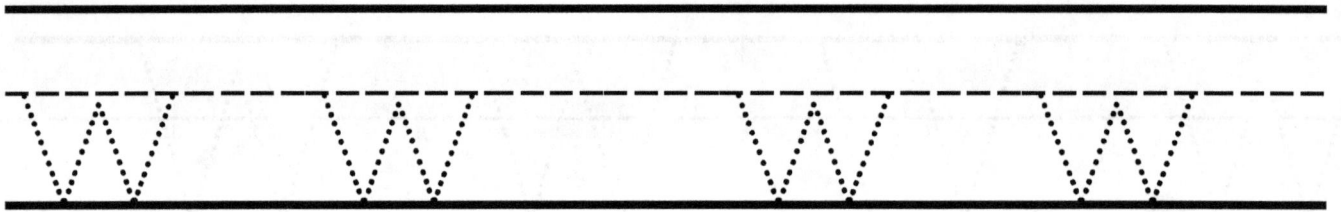

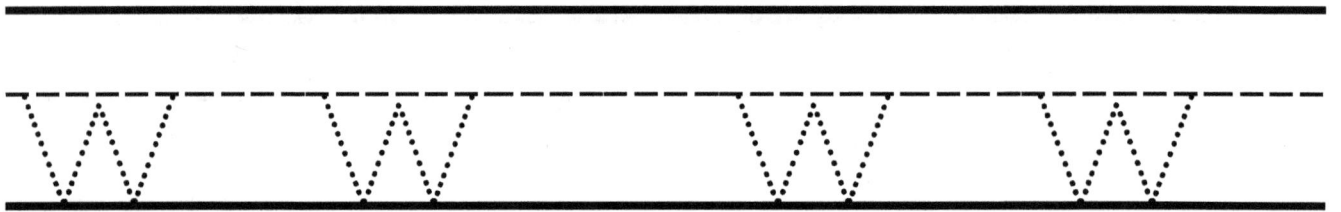

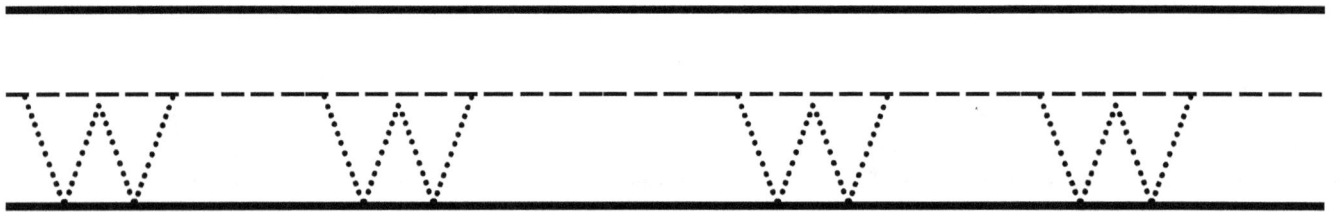

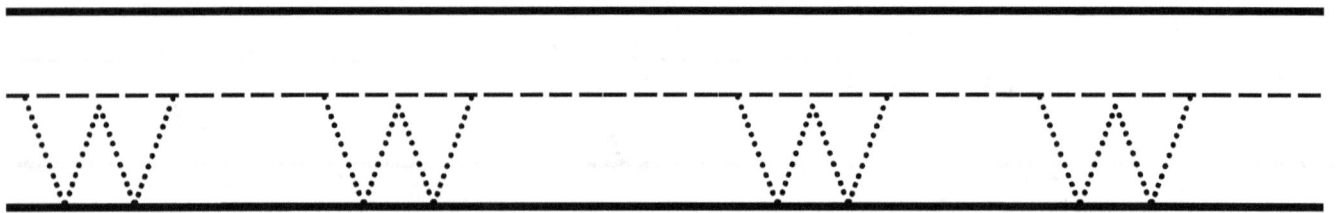

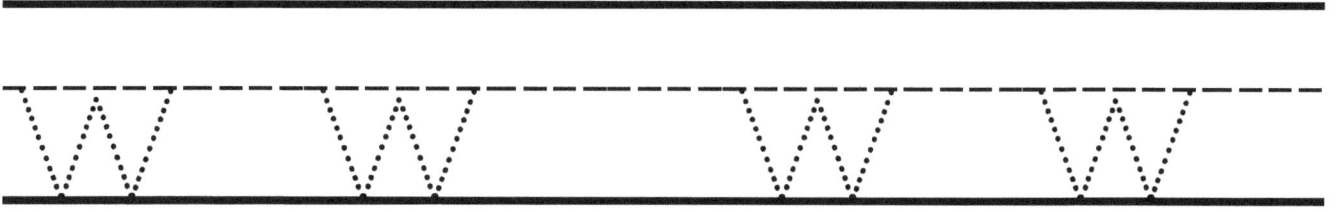

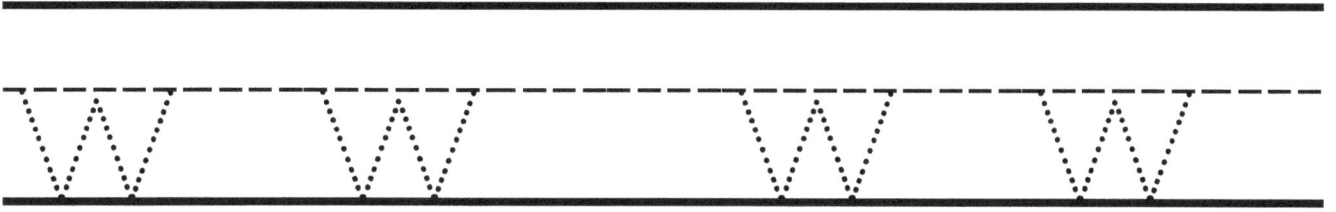

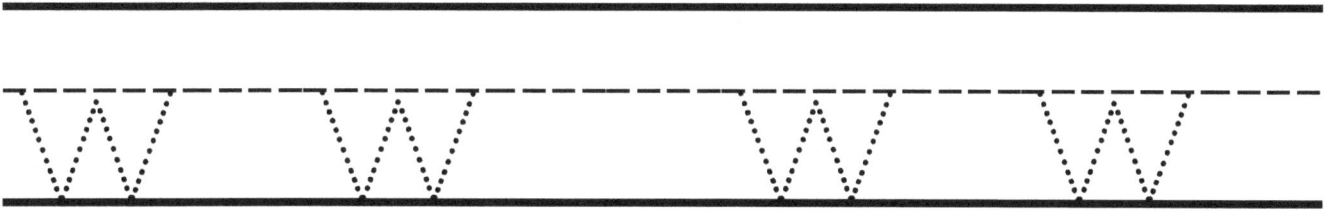

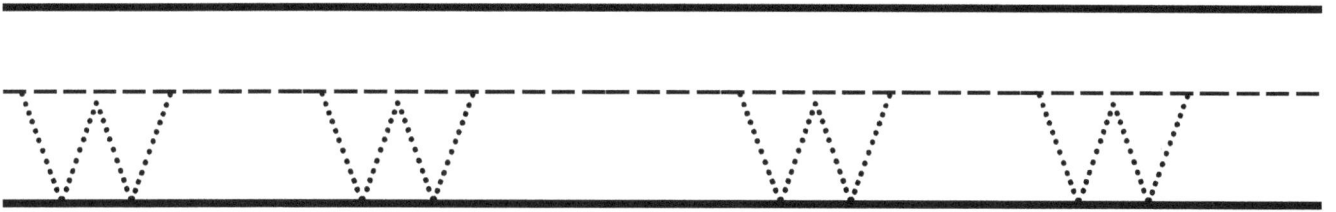

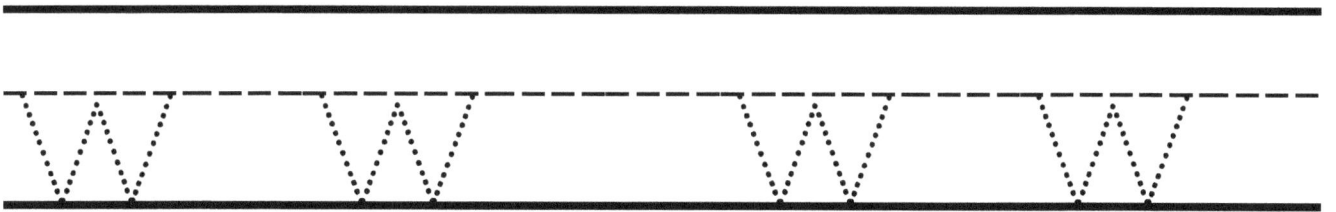

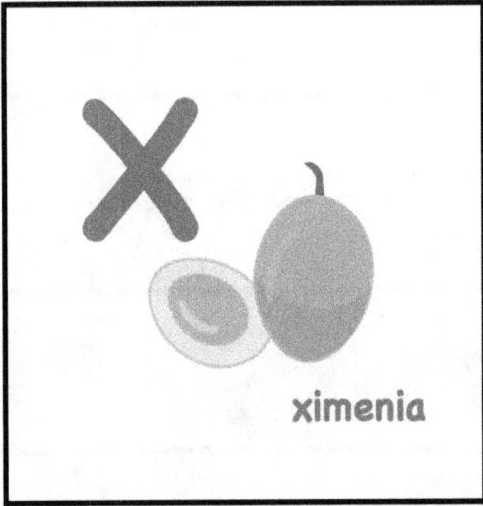

X for Ximenia

ximenia

X x

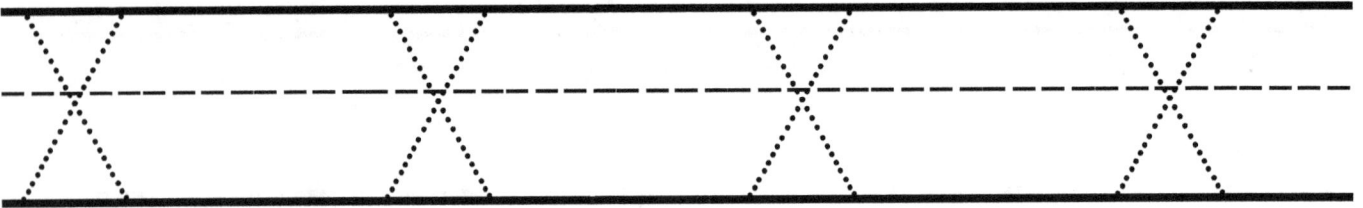

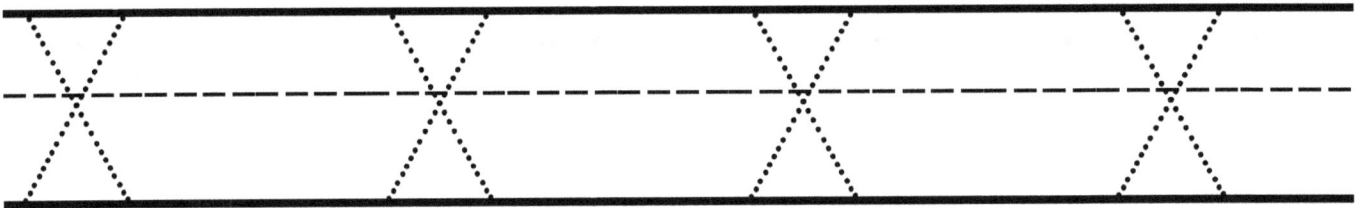

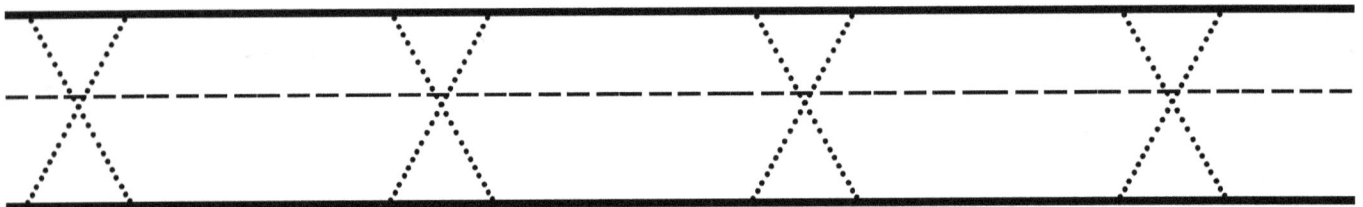

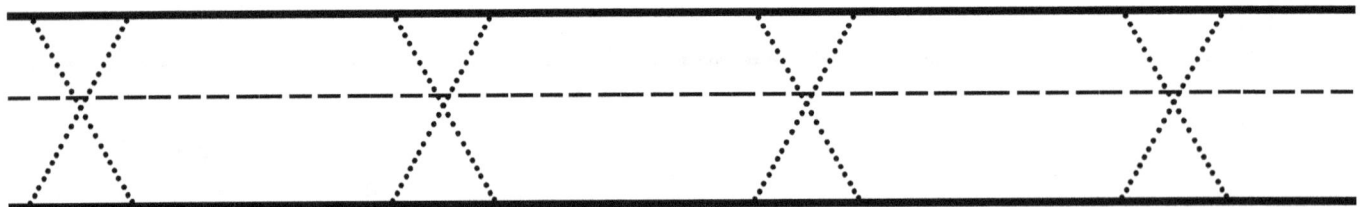

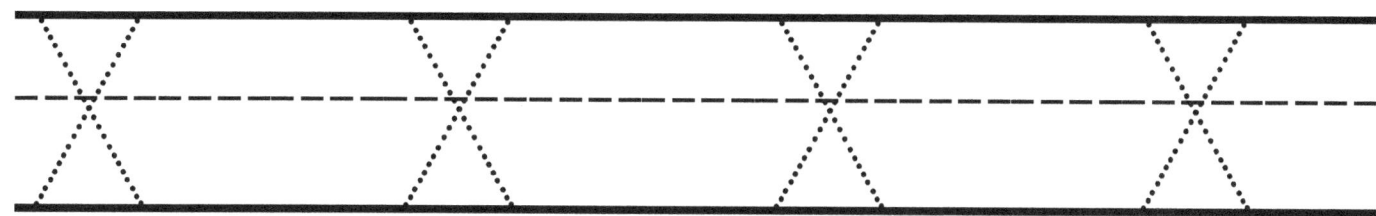

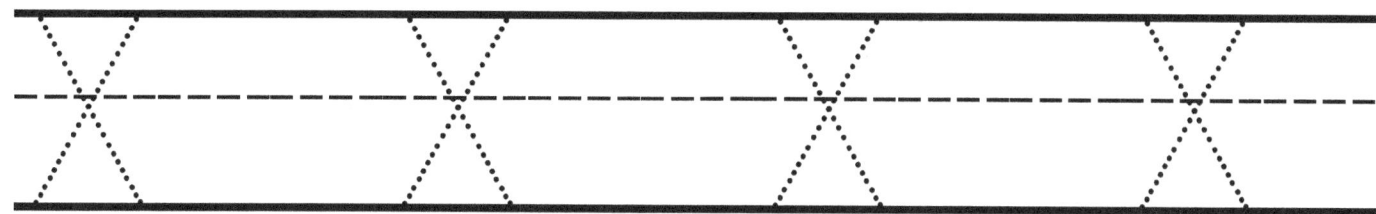

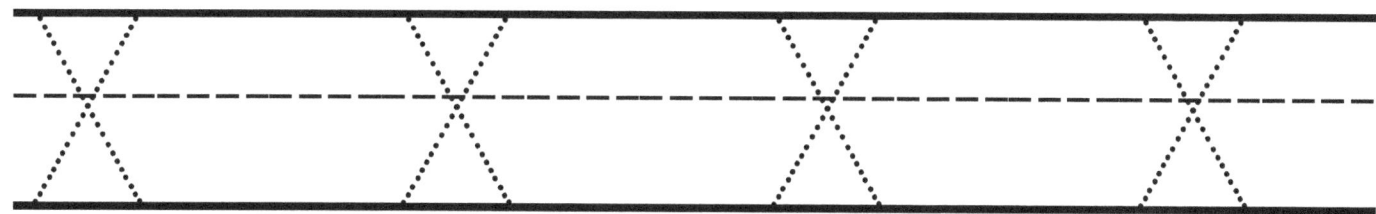

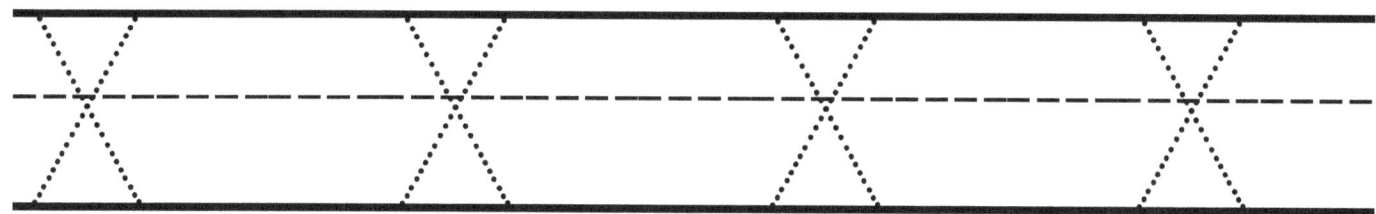

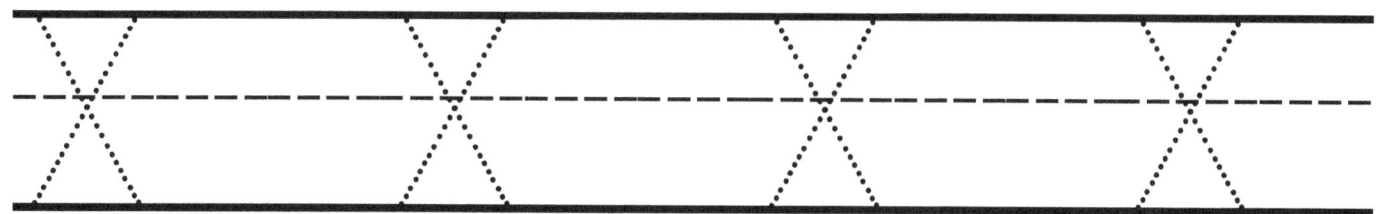

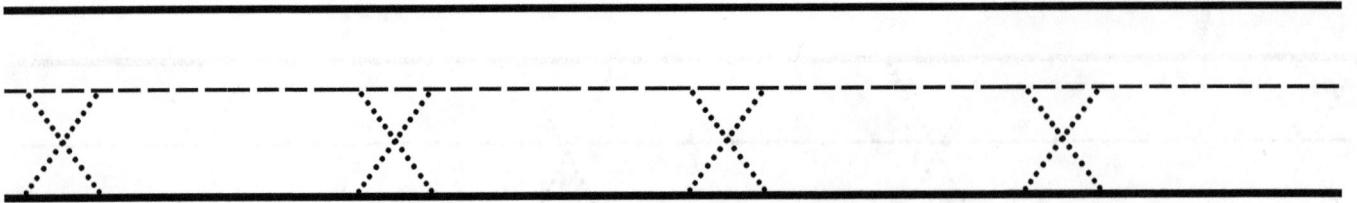

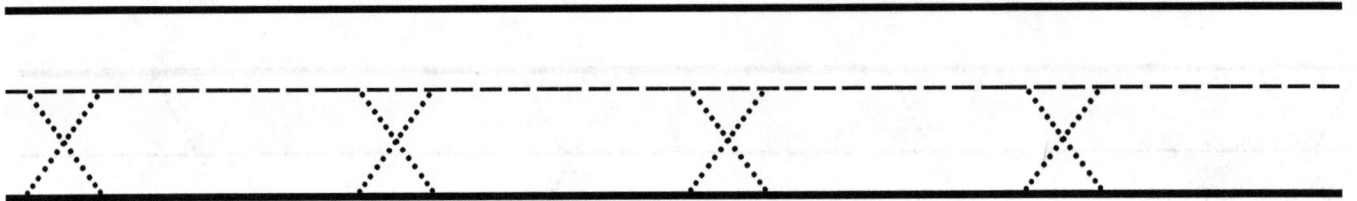

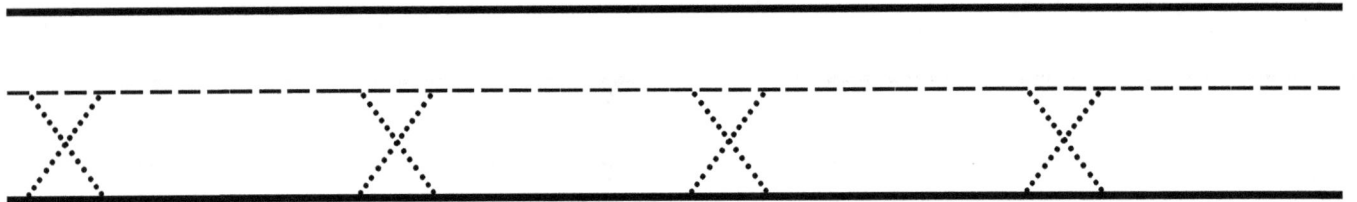

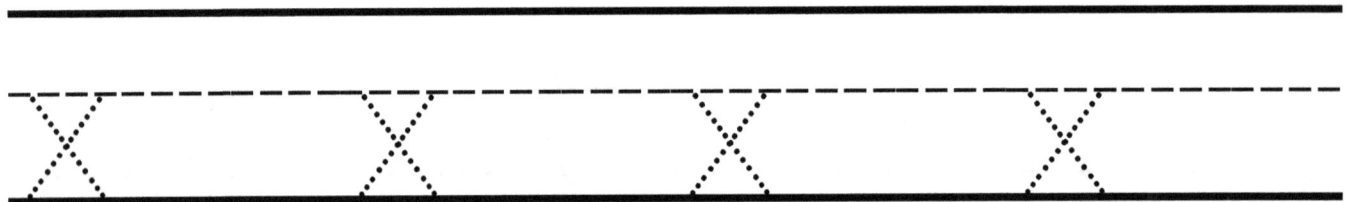

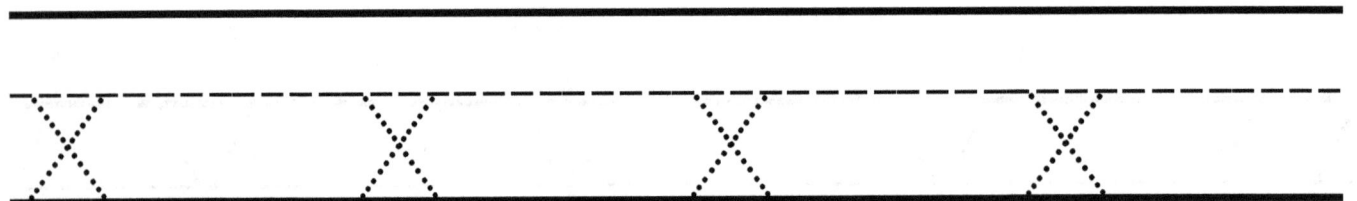

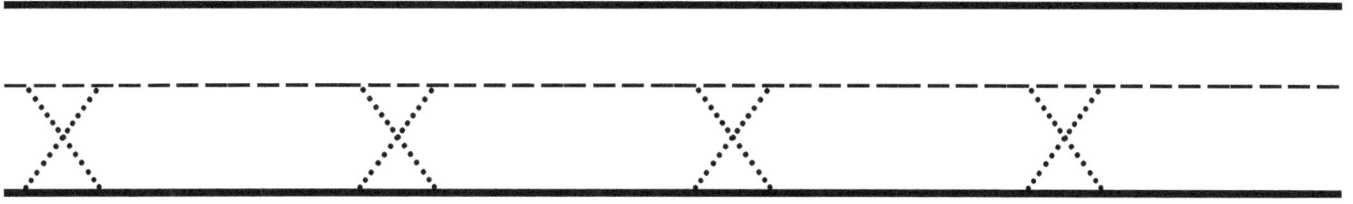

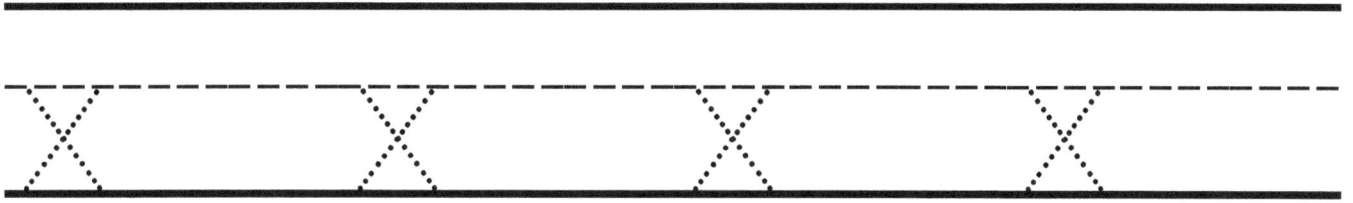

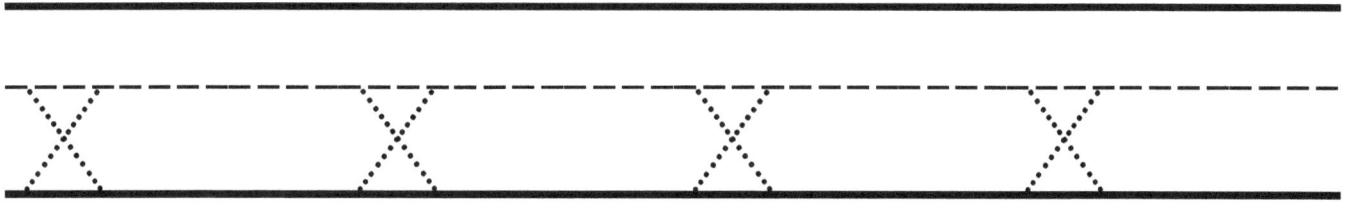

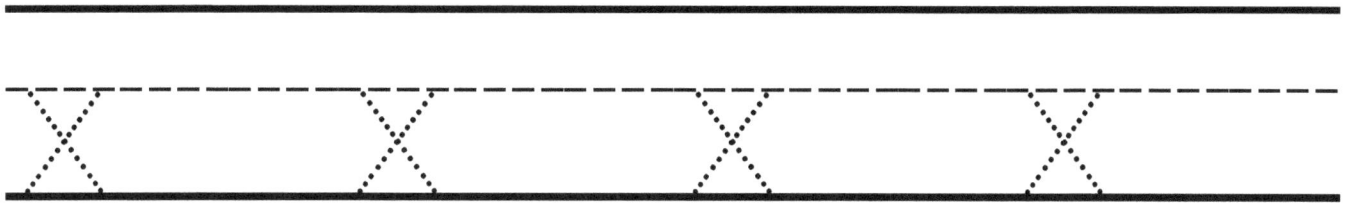

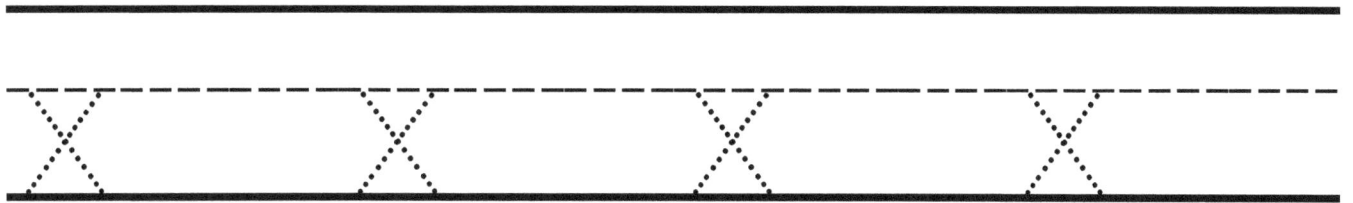

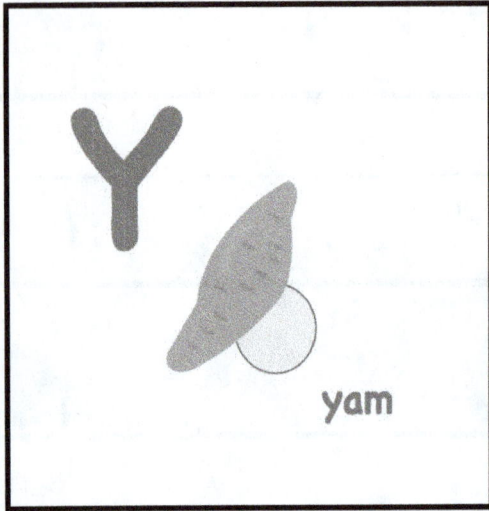

Y for Yam

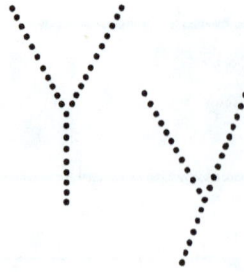

Yy

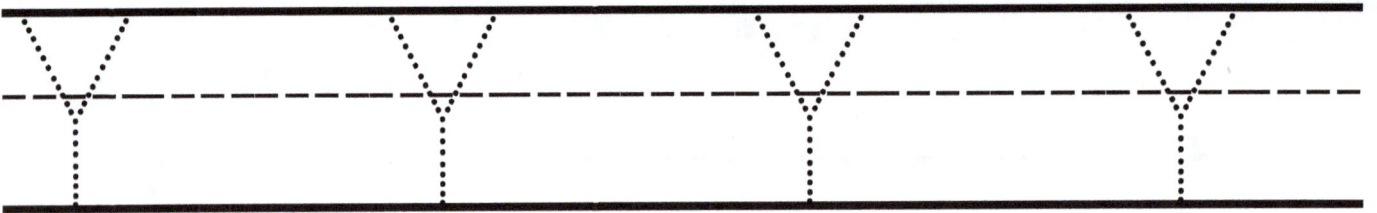

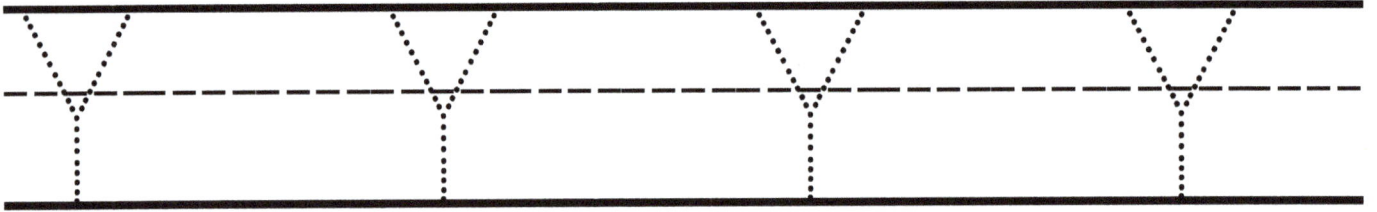

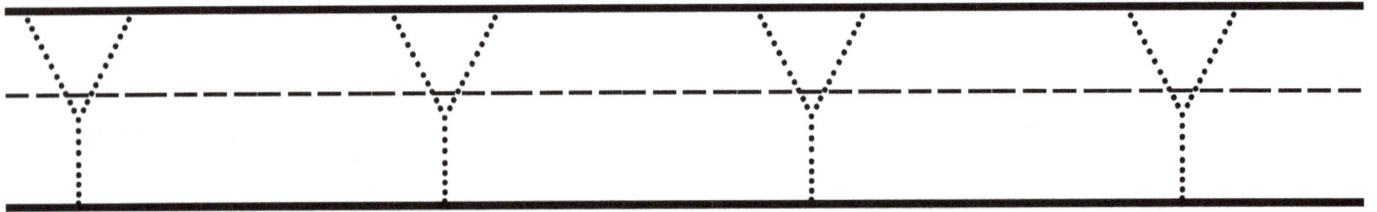

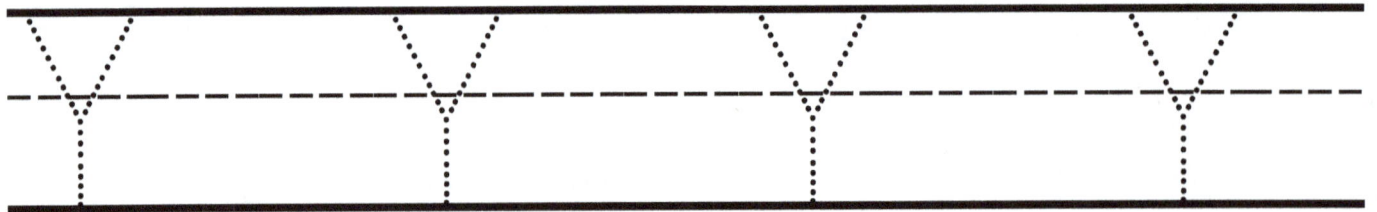

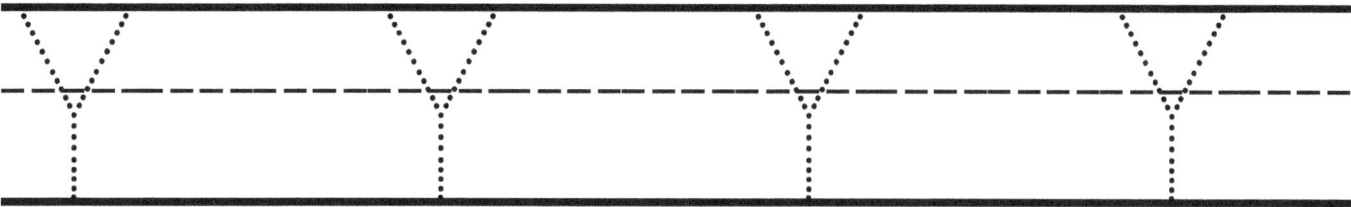

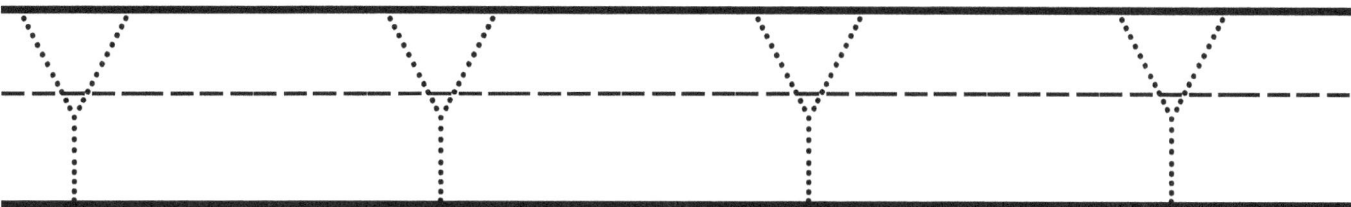

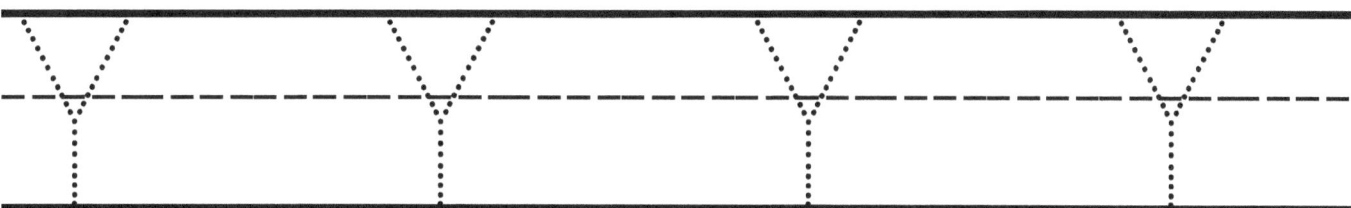

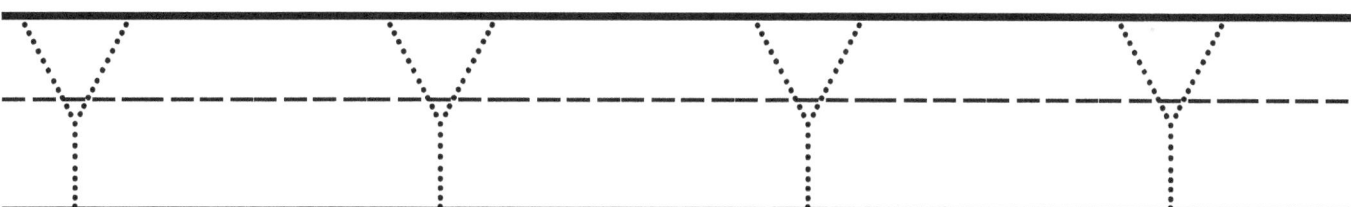

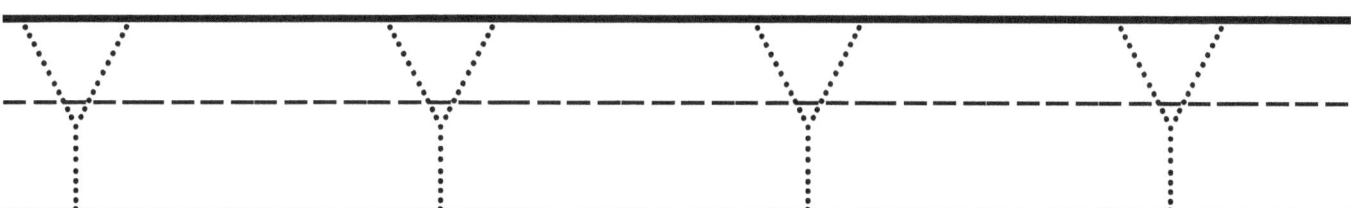

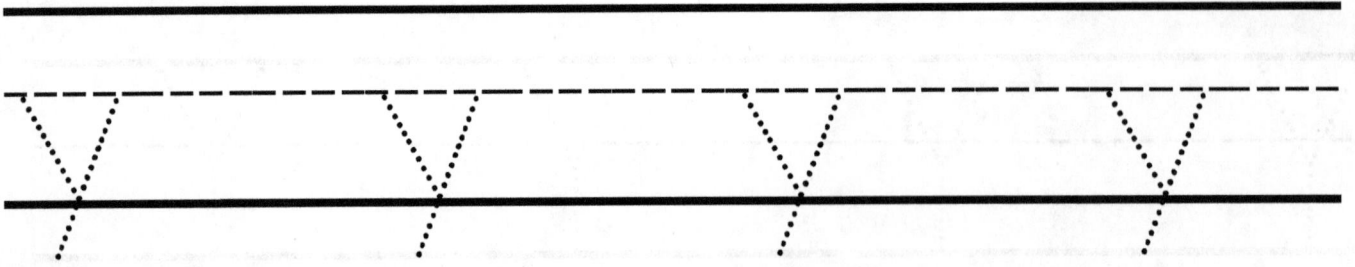

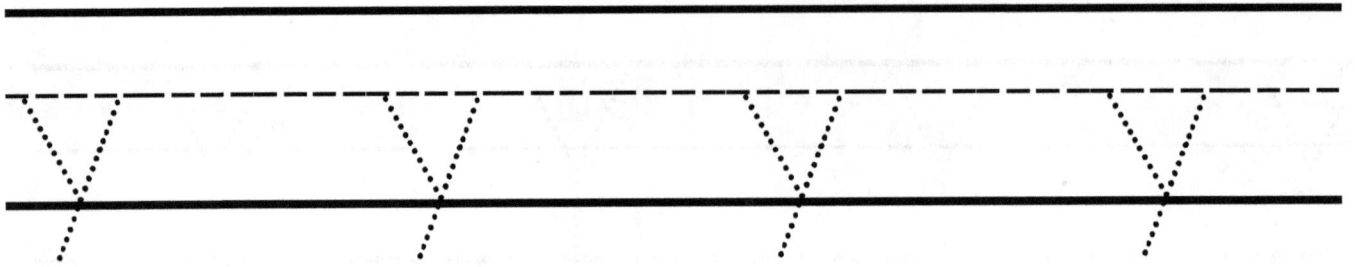

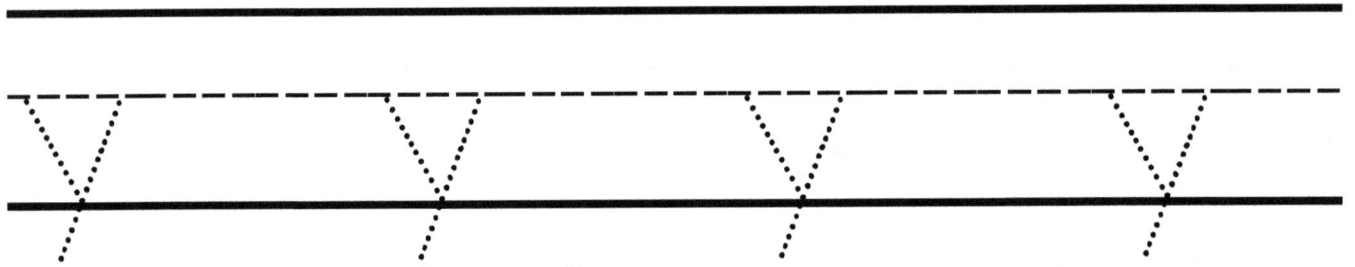

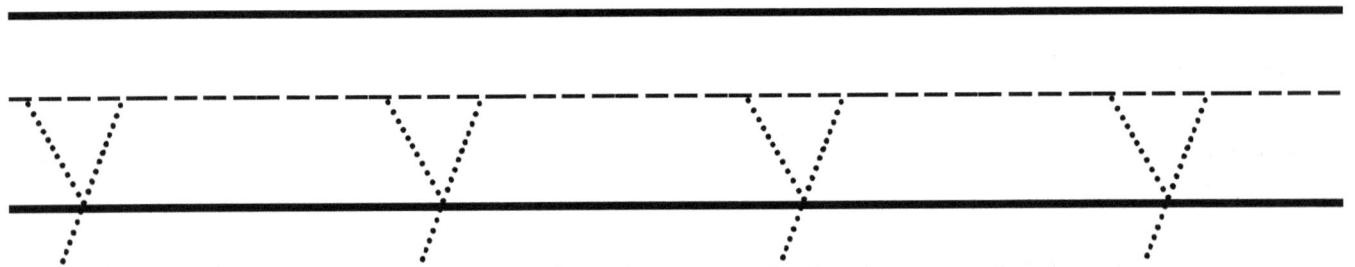

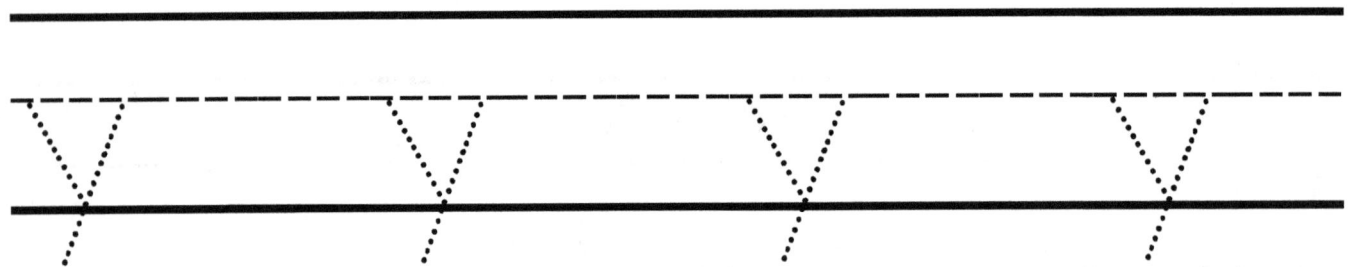

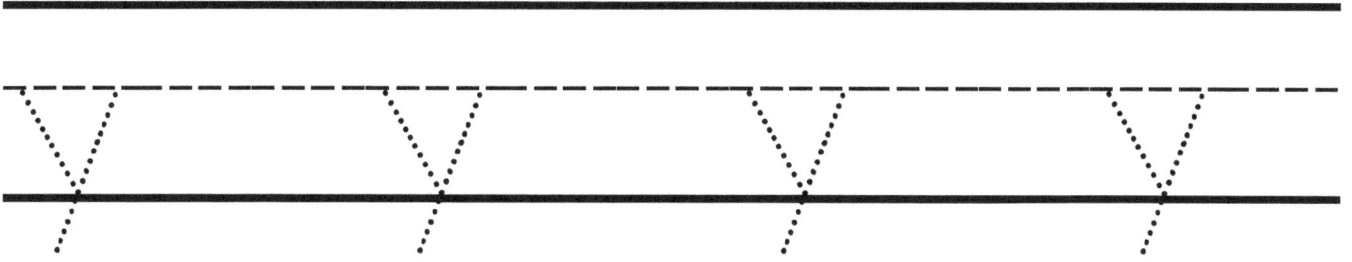

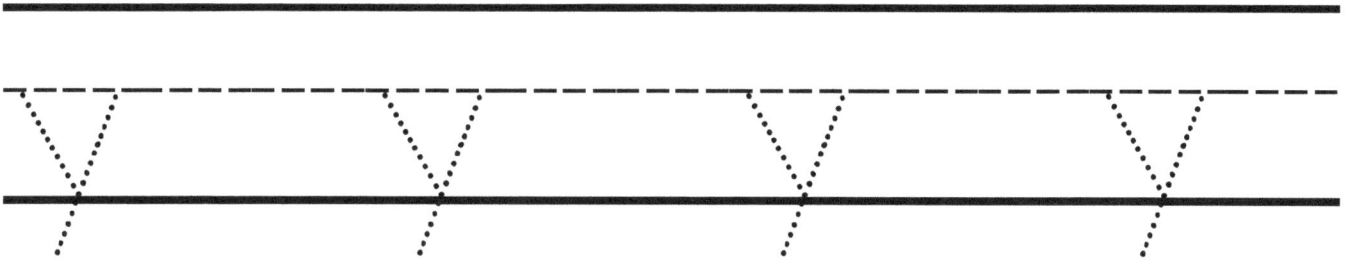

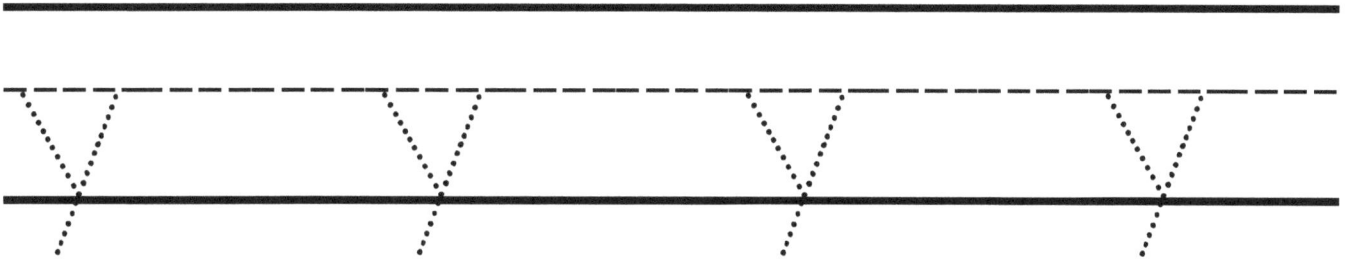

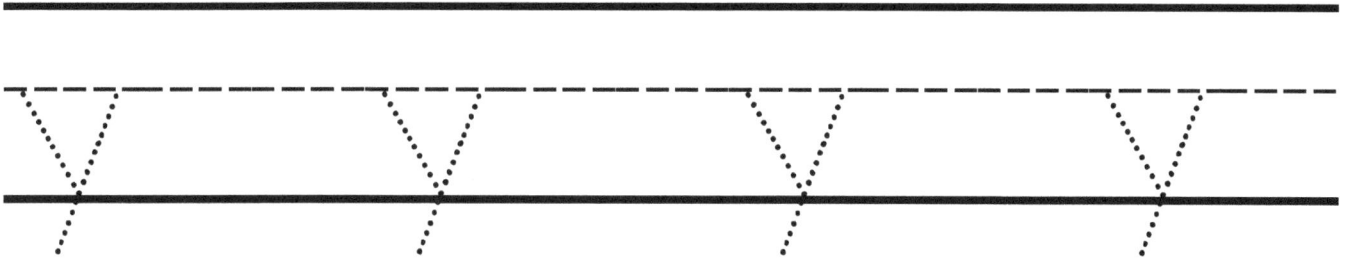

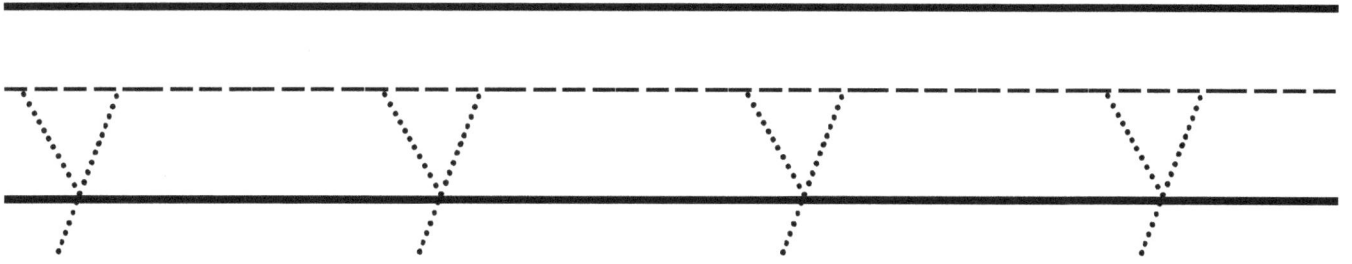

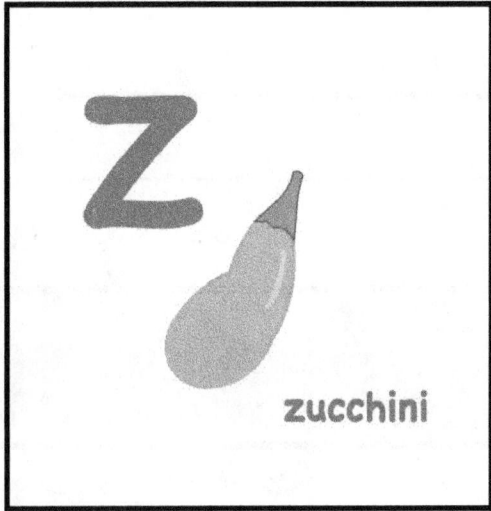

Z for Zucchini

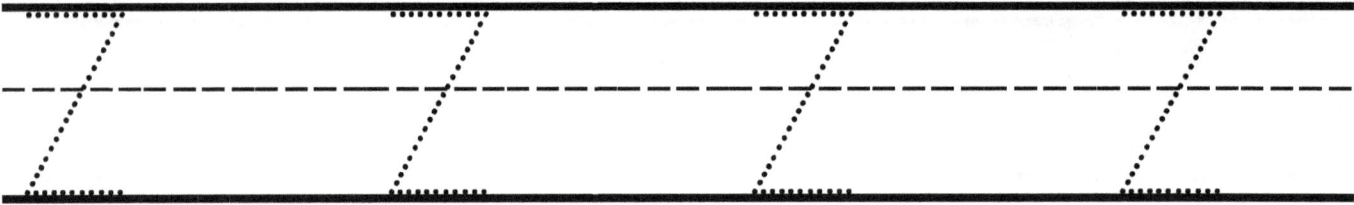

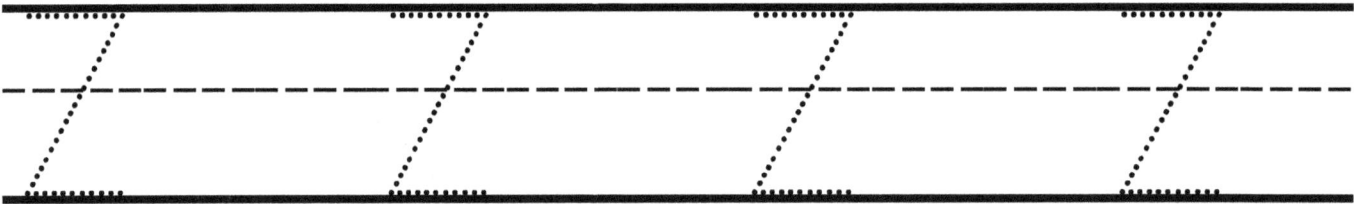

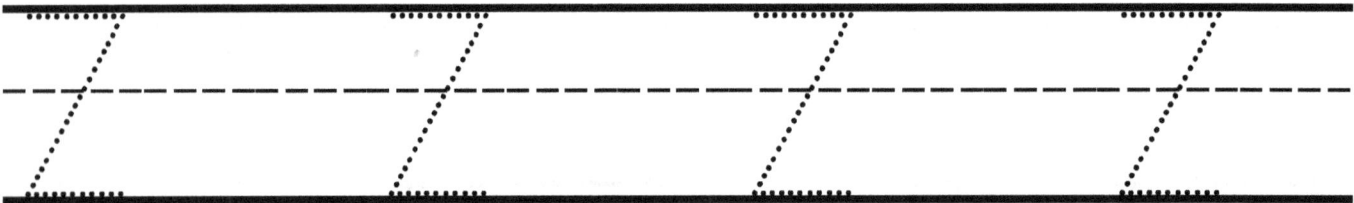

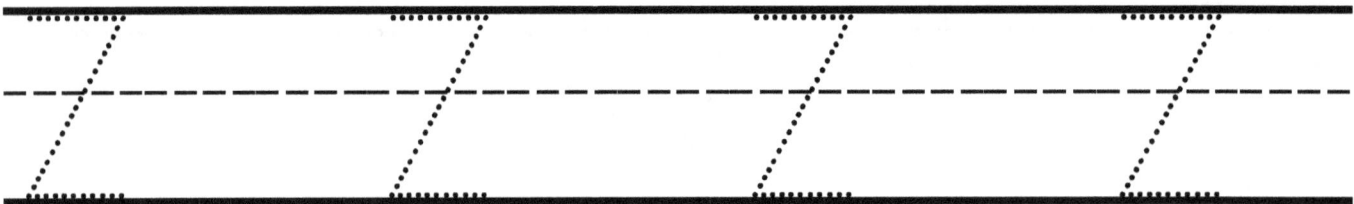

z

zucchini

Z z

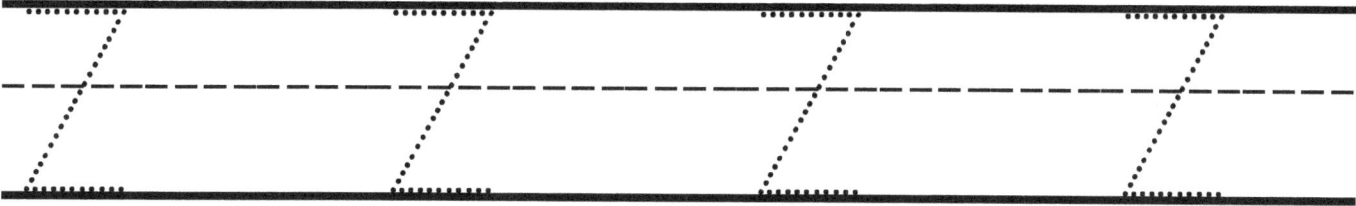

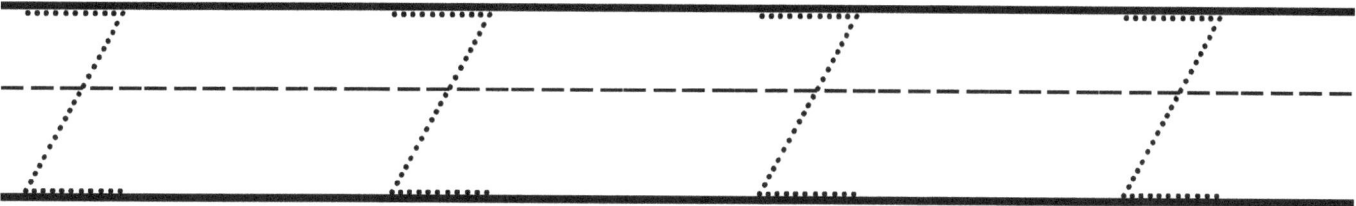

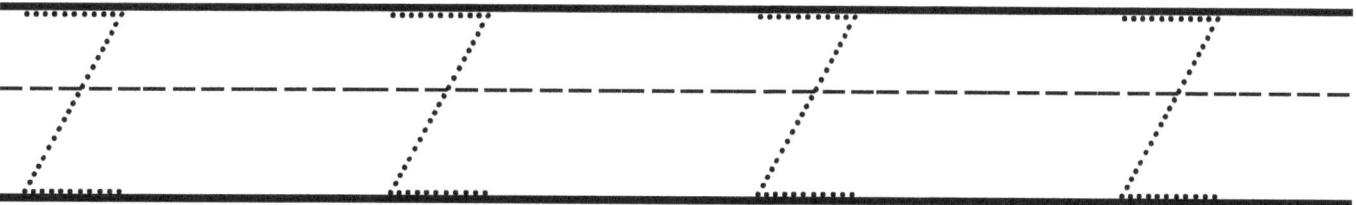

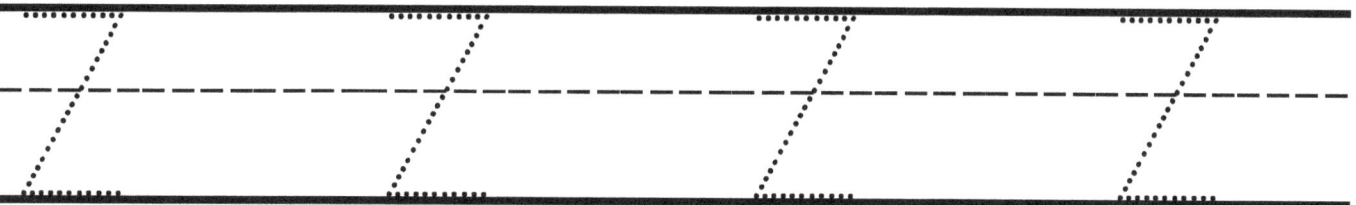

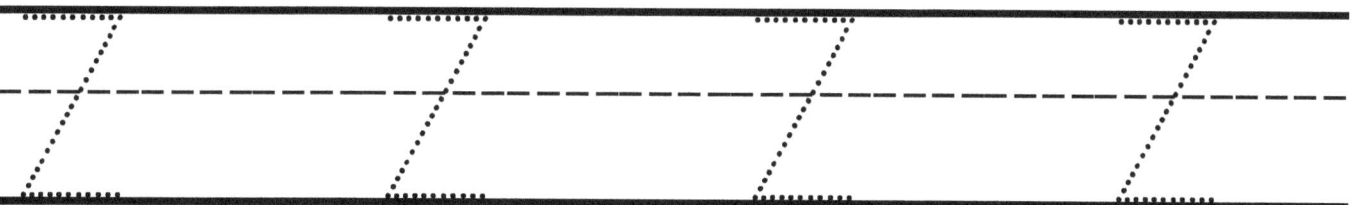

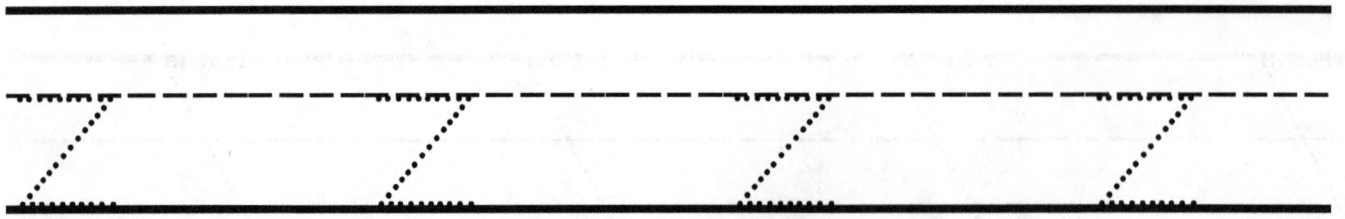

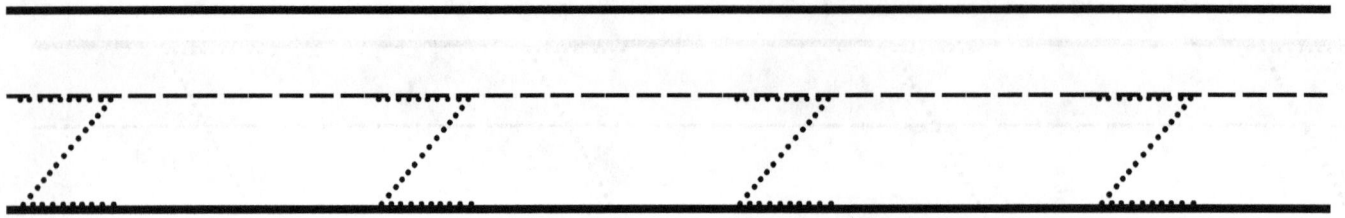

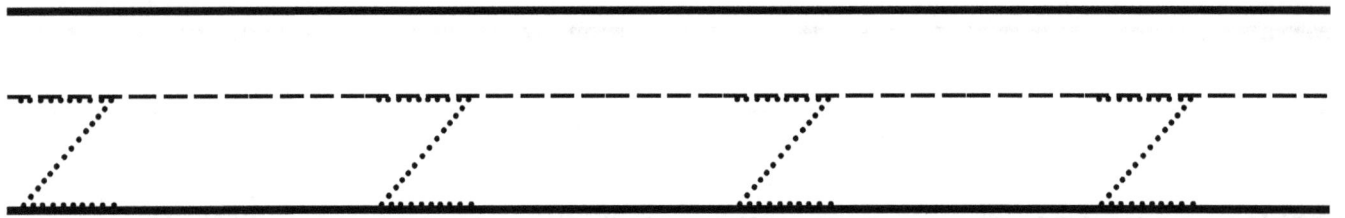

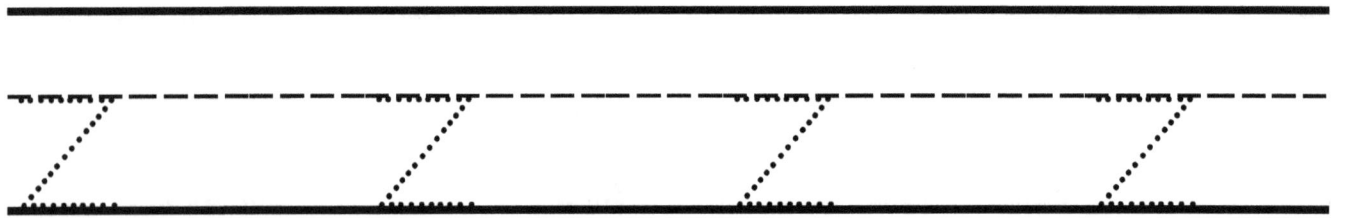

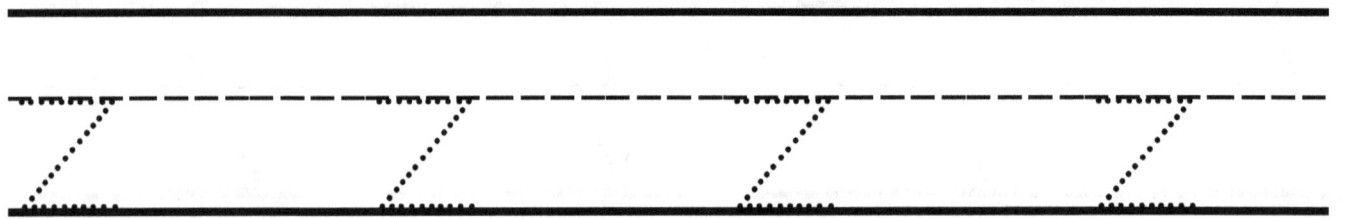

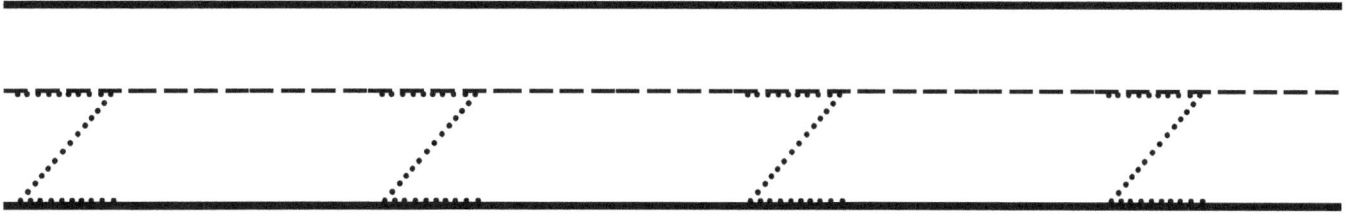

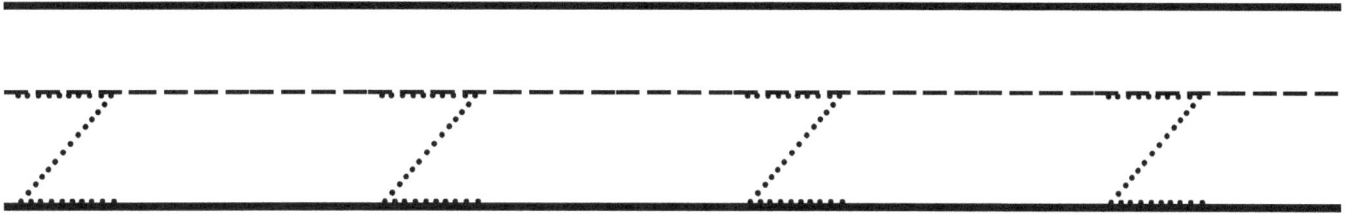

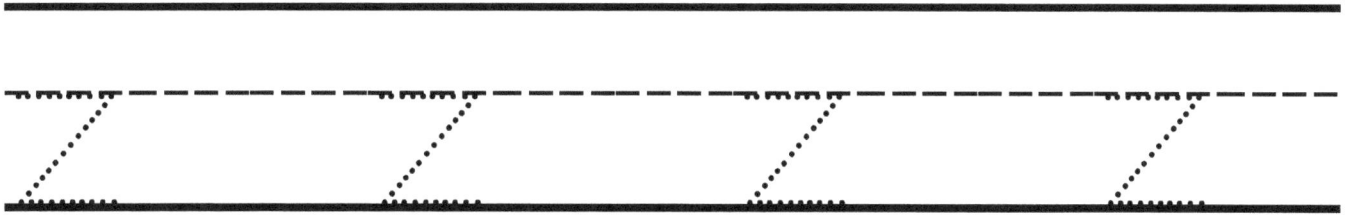

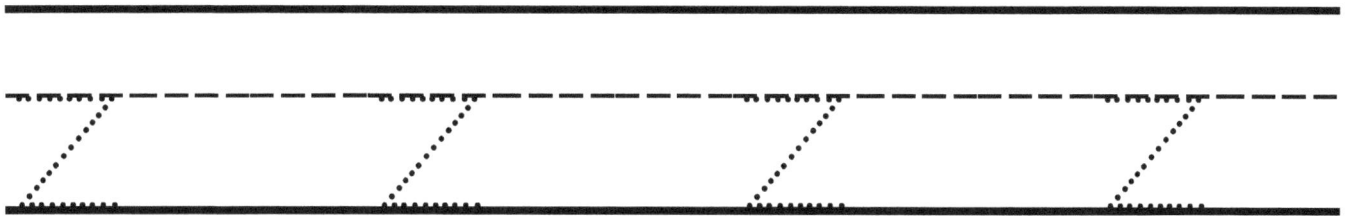

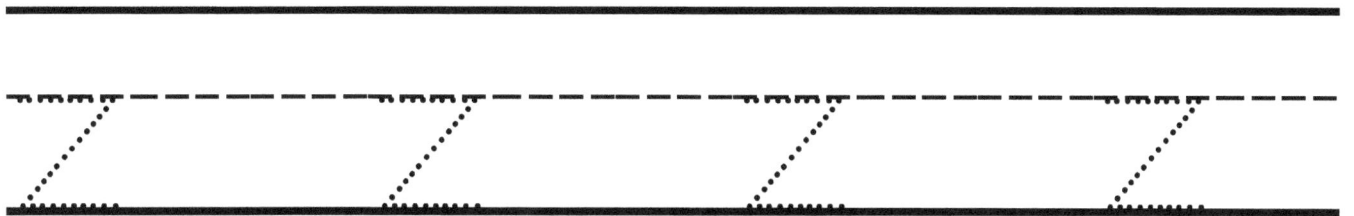

Thank You

Letter Tracing Workbook is brought you by **imlo** . We believe that inspiration should come early for every child, and that the future begins right now.

If you have any suggestions on how to improve to this book, please write to us at hello@inspiremylittleone.com

Please leave a review. Thank you for buying Letter Tracing Workbook

imlo
Inspire My Little One

www.ingramcontent.com/pod-product-compliance
Lightning Source LLC
Chambersburg PA
CBHW081215020426
42331CB00012B/3033

9781950579068